REVELATION

REVELATION

Through the Lens of Scripture

Rev. Harold G. Dailey Jr.

*Dear Del,
Blessings to you
and I pray you enjoy
the book.
Harold*

Copyright © Rev. Harold G. Dailey Jr.

All rights reserved.

No part of this work may be reproduced or transmitted in any form or by any means, electronic or mechanical, including photocopying and recording, or by any information storage or retrieval system, except as may be expressly permitted by the 1976 Copyright Act or in writing from the author. Requests for permission should be sent to Rev. Harold Dailey via email at pastor.harold.dailey@gmail.com.

Scripture taken from the NEW AMERICAN STANDARD BIBLE, © 1960, 1962, 1963, 1968, 1971, 1972, 1973, 1975, 1977, by The Lockman Foundation. Used by permission.

DEDICATION

This book is dedicated to our Lord Jesus Christ and may it glorify Him alone.

I would also like to express appreciation to my late wife, Carolyn Rene' for her witness and inspiration which made this book possible, and to my loving wife, Mary Kay for her help in proofing this work.

About This Book

Many books have been written about the book of Revelation from many different viewpoints. This book seeks to interpret Revelation through the lens of Scripture. It assumes that God is the same yesterday, today and forever. Therefore, in seeking to understand the mysterious images described in Revelation, we will look to where in scripture these images have been previously used to discern their meaning. The book of Revelation is perhaps the least understood book in the Bible, but it is the only book literally dictated by Jesus, and which we are told we will be blessed in our reading and hearing it read.

The content of this book originally comprised a set of twelve handouts created and used for small group Bible studies. Because it was not originally intended to be published in book form, no records were kept regarding the many sources consulted and studied in preparing the lessons and handouts. Outside sources were primarily used for deeper understanding of original Hebrew and Greek key words, their epistemology, and the historical and cultural context of the events contained within the Bible. Likewise, this book is intended to be a tool for study. It is my prayer that through reading it you will gain a deeper understanding of God's Word and His love for us all. May God alone be glorified as we journey together seeking His truth for our lives.

Table of Contents

The book of Revelation can be divided into specific sections to make it easier to study and understand. The Table of Contents follows an "outline" which is the best I have seen and comes from Volume 12 of "The Interpreter's Bible" published by Abingdon Press. Please note the significance of the number "seven" relating to the book's structure. According to Genesis the world was created in seven days and the number seven is often seen as a symbol of completeness and/or perfection. After an introduction and testifying vision, there are seven letters to seven churches, which possibly describes the history of the church (past, present and future). After another transitional introduction and two testifying visions we encounter the main body of the book, which is divided into seven groups of seven visions. The book concludes with a supplementary scene describing the New Jerusalem. This outline includes references to both chapters and verses from the book of Revelation, and corresponding page numbers in this book.

Contents

Preface 1

PART 1 5

Introduction and Cover Letter to the Churches 5

Introduction (1:1-11) 5

Testifying Vision (1:12-20) 10

PART 2 13

Letters to the Seven Churches 13

Letter to Ephesus (2:1-7) 15

Letter to Smyrna (2:8-11) 18

Letter to Pergamum (2:12-17) 19

Letter to Thyatira (2:18-29) 22

Letter to Sardis (3:1-6) 25

Letter to Philadelphia (3:7-13) 28

Letter to Laodicea (3:14-22) 32

PART 3 39

Introductory Visions 39

Vision of Adoration of God in Heaven (4:1-11) 40

Vision of Adoration of the Lamb of God (5:1-14) 45

PART 4 51

The Seven Seals 51

First Seal: The White Horse and Rider (6:1-2) 54

Second Seal: The Red Horse and Rider (6:3-4) 56

Third Seal: The Black Horse and Rider (6:5-6) 57

Fourth Seal: The Pale Horse and Rider (6:7-8) 58

Fifth Seal: Lament of the Martyrs (6:9-11) 60

Sixth Seal: Cosmic Woes (6:12-17) 61

    First Interlude (7:1-17) 62
    Sealing of the Martyrs (7:1-8) 63
    Glorified Multitude in Heaven (7:9-17) 65

PART 5 69

The Seventh Seal and the Seven Trumpets 69

Seventh Seal: Preparation for Trumpets (8:1-6) 70

First Trumpet: Hail and Fire (8:7) 72

Second Trumpet: Mountain falls into Sea (8:8-9) 73

Third Trumpet: Star falls into Sea (8:10-11) 73

Forth Trumpet: Darkening of Sun, Moon and Stars (8:12) 74

    The Eagle's Warning (8:13) 75

Fifth Trumpet: Plague of Demonic Locust (9:1-12) 76

Sixth Trumpet: Destroying Horseman (9:13-21) 79

    Second Interlude (10:1—11:14) 82
    John Eats the Scroll of Doom (10:1-11) 82
    Measuring of the Temple and the Two Witnesses (11:1-14) 87

Seventh Trumpet: Christ's Reign to Begin (11:15-19)   93

PART 6 95

Seven Visions of the Dragon's Kingdom 95

First Vision: Heavenly Mother and Birth of Messiah (12:1-6) 96

Second Vision: Michael's Victory Over the Dragon (12:7-9) 102

Third Vision: Song of Woe and Rejoicing (12:10-12) 104

Fourth Vision: The Woman and her Other Children (12:13-17) 106

Fifth Vision: The Beast from the Sea (13:1-4) 108

Sixth Vision: The Beast from the Sea Exercises His Authority 111

Seventh Vision: The Beast from the Earth (13:11-18) 115

PART 7 123

Seven Visions of Worshipers of the Lamb and Beast 123

First Vision: The Martyrs and the Lamb on Mount Zion (14:1-5) 124

Second Vision: Angelic Admonition to Worship God (14:6-7) 128

Third Vision: Angel Pronounces Doom of Babylon (14:8) 129

Fourth Vision: Condemnation of Worshipers of the Beast (14:9-11) ..130

Fifth Vision: Heavenly Benediction of the Martyrs (14:12-13) 132

Sixth Vision: The Son of Man and the Harvest of the Elect (14:17-20) 133

Seventh Vision: The Destruction of the Wicked (14:17-20) 135

PART 8 139

Seven Visions of the Bowls of God's Wrath...139

First Bowl: Plague of Ulcers (16:2) 144

Second Bowl: Sea Turned to Blood (16:3) 144

Third Bowl: Rivers and Springs Turned to Blood (16:4-7)..............................145

Fourth Bowl: Scorching Heat of the Sun (16:8-9)...................................146

Fifth Bowl: Darkening of the Beast's Kingdom (16:10-11).......................147

Sixth Bowl: Kings of East Assemble for Armageddon (16:12-16)............148

Seventh Bowl: Impending Destruction of Babylon (16:17-21)................152

PART 9 157

Seven Visions of the Fall of Babylon 157

First Vision: The Harlot, Babylon the Great (17:1-6a).........................158

Second Vision: Interpretation of Harlot and Beast (17:6b-18).............160

Third Vision: Angelic Proclamation of Babylon's Fall (18:1-3)...........169

Fourth Vision: Exultation and Mourning over Fall of Babylon (18:4-20)..171

Fifth Vision: Millstone into Sea and Final Dirge over City (18:21-24) 176

Sixth Vision: Hymn of Praise to God (19:1-5) 178

Seventh Vision: Marriage Hymn to the Lamb and His Bride (19:6-10).....180

PART 10 183

Seven Visions of End of Evil and Beginning of God's Righteous Age.......183

First Vision: The Conquering Christ (19:11-16) 184

Second Vision: Victory of Christ over Beast and Antichrist (19:17-21).....188

Third Vision: Satan Bound and Rule Suspended 1,000 Years (20:1-3)......192

Fourth Vision: The Reign of Christ and the Millennium (20:4-6)................193

Fifth Vision: Satan Released and Cast into Lake of Fire (20:7-10) 197

Sixth Vision: End of Heaven and Earth, and Judgment (20:11-15)...............201

Seventh Vision: The New Heaven and Earth (21:1-8) 204

PART 11 209

The New Jerusalem 209

External Appearance of the City (21:9-14)....................209

Measurement of the City (21:15-17) 212

Composition of the City (21:18-21) 213

Temple of the City (21:22-27)....................215

The River and the Tree of Life (22:1-5) 217

PART 12 223

Closing Message....................223

About the Author 233

Preface

Revelation is filled with symbolism and prophecies regarding the future. It is very difficult to understand and is subject to many interpretations. Everything in the book has been subject to controversy and continues to be debated by Biblical scholars. There has been disagreement regarding its authorship, its inclusion in the biblical Canon, and of course, it's meaning.

There have been four primary views of interpreting Revelation. The first, or "**preterist**" view, places the events and visions described as belonging to the past, particularly to the Roman Empire of the first century A.D. The believers of this view explain the highly symbolic character of the book as an endeavor by John to hide the real meaning of what he was saying from the general populace, but make it apparent to the believers who lived at that time. People holding to this view believe that the main purpose of this writing was to encourage the believers regarding God's ultimate intervention in the affairs of men. In my opinion it is very unlikely that this view is correct in light of the prophetic nature of the book. Some of the descriptions stated to be future events cannot be identified or correlated with any historical events.

The second view, or the "**historicist**" view, maintains that what we have in Revelation is a panoramic view of history from the first century to the Second Coming of Christ. This is the view of most of the Protestant Reformers. This view could be at least partially true, but historians have been unable to identify precise events in history which can be correlated to many of the visions symbolized. Of course, Christ has not yet returned, so some of the events would have to be "future" events.

The third view is the "**symbolic**" view which holds that Revelation portrays the continuing conflict between the forces of good and evil throughout the entire span of human history. According to this view the book is designed to give encouragement since at the end, the good will triumph. This view is also at least partially true, but I feel understates Revelation's truth and teaching.

The fourth view is the **"futuristic"** view which maintains that from chapter 4 on, Revelation deals with events at the end time. According to this view, Revelation is not concerning events of John's own day as much as later historical events, and particularly those happenings that will take place in connection with the Second Coming of the Lord. This view takes seriously the predictive element in the book (Rev. 1:19; 4:1). Very definitely, the final chapters of Revelation deal with the last days. But many of these "end time" events may have already taken place. Revelation does include future events, but is intended to teach all people of all time how to live now.

My approach in the study of the book of Revelation will be simple and straightforward. We will not view the book through the lens of history, attempting to make its content fit historic events. We will also not attempt to interpret its symbolism through human reasoning alone, which has proven to be limited and unreliable. We will instead attempt to allow the book to speak for itself, viewing and interpreting its meaning through the lens of Scripture. In other words, we will interpret Scripture using Scripture. To do this we will hold to two "truths" revealed in Scripture. The first truth is that all Scripture comes from God and can be trusted. Peter wrote: *"But know this first of all, that no prophecy of Scripture is a matter of one's own interpretation, for no prophecy was ever made by an act of human will, but men moved by the Holy Spirit spoke from God"* (2 Peter 1:20-21). Second, we will assume that God is "consistent" in the truth He has revealed through Scripture, as Hebrews 13:8 states: *"Jesus Christ is the same yesterday and today and forever."* When Scripture is interpreted out of context or without being compared to all that God has revealed, its interpretation becomes subject to the distortions of time, culture, personal experience and even our own selfish desires. While all of these may lend themselves to the process of interpretation, we must remember that God is consistent and does not contradict His Word. Therefore, Scripture will become our authority to understanding what God is revealing in the book of Revelation.

In our scientific culture today we believe there is an explanation for everything and that every question can be answered through investigation and reasoning. It is important that we remind ourselves that we are finite but God is infinite. We must concede that we can only understand what God is willing and ready to reveal through the presence of His Holy Spirit. It is OK if we do not fully understand all that is written in Revelation and that some things may remain a mystery. This does not mean we are ignorant, incapable or unworthy. What is important is that we learn all that we can learn from all God will reveal to us, and apply it to the living of our lives. Our intent must not be to gain special knowledge but to grow closer to God and prepare ourselves for the end of time and judgment we will all face, either at the point that our physical life ends, or our Lord and Savior returns. May God grant us ears to hear, minds to comprehend, and hearts to cherish the precious truth He will reveal to us in this study.

Why do pastors avoid preaching and/or teaching the Book of Revelation?

Pride is probably the largest reason on the list. Pastors tend to fear teaching what they themselves don't completely understand, and often avoid the controversial. Pastors feel that they are supposed to be an authority on Scripture, but in reality we are on the same journey of learning and understanding as those we attempt to teach. None of us have arrived or know all the answers, and that is sometimes hard to admit. Second, many fear the Book of Revelation itself because of the unique warning it contains: ***"I testify to everyone who hears the words of the prophecy of this book: if anyone adds to them, God shall add to him the plagues which are written in this book; and if anyone takes away from the words of the book of this prophecy, God shall take away his part from the tree of life and from the holy city, which are written in this book"*** (Revelation 22:18-19). Any pastor who believes in the authority of Scripture is given pause by this warning. You will note as I attempt to lead this study of Revelation that I will be very careful not to talk in absolutes—presenting my opinions and interpretations as the only or absolute truth. As has been said, there have been many interpretations of Revelation and everyone is encouraged to share their own understandings and opinions.

Why do we risk preaching and teaching the Book of Revelation?

We must teach Revelation because Christ our Lord has instructed us to do so. Jesus instructed John, saying: ***"Write in a book what you see, and send it to the seven churches..."*** (Revelation 1:11a). In Revelation 19:9 the Lord commands, ***"Write, "Blessed are those who are invited to the marriage supper of the Lamb.'" And He said to me, "These are true words of God.""*** John is repeatedly commanded to write what he sees and hears because God intends the message to be shared and to be taught. Revelation is the only book in the Bible literally dictated by the Lord. Revelation is also the only book in the Bible which states that those who read and hear its words will be blessed. Revelation 1:3 states: ***"Blessed is he who reads and those who hear the words of the prophecy, and heed the things which are written in it; for the time is near."*** The Book of Revelation must be preached and must be taught as God has instructed.

PART 1

Introduction and Cover Letter to the Churches

Chapter-1 has four distinct divisions: introduction (vv. 1-3); salutation (vv. 4-8); Christ in His glory (vv. 9-18); and the instruction to write (vv. 19-20). In the Gospels, Christ is presented as the Lamb sacrificed for our sins. Here He is presented as the Roaring Lion. It is interesting that in John 1:29, 36, Jesus is presented as the *amnos*, the "Lamb of sacrifice," while throughout Revelation He is never presented as the *amnos* but as *arnion*, the "Lamb which lives and is not marked for sacrifice."

Introduction (1:1-11)

<u>Verse-1</u>: The first five words of the book are ***"The Revelation of Jesus Christ."*** The word "Revelation" comes from the Greek word *Apokalupsis* which means "an unveiling or uncovering." The word appears in the singular and not the plural therefore this is not the uncovering of many different things but of one. Revelation is not the unfolding of a story by John or a series of prophetic truths, but the message of the "appearing of Christ."

Next, most English translations of the Greek use the words "shortly" or "soon" regarding the things that the book reveals will take place. It is wrong to interpret this to mean the events will take place in the "near future" because that is not the meaning of the Greek. A more accurate translation would be that the events will take place "with speed, swiftness, or quickness." The original meaning of the Greek could best be translated as "rapidity of action once there is a beginning." In other words, the future events depicted in Revelation will not necessarily take place soon, as in the near future, but when they do begin to take place they will occur rapidly in a relatively short time period. This is consistent all through Scripture. A good example might be found in Matthew 24:34 when Jesus is talking about the signs that will immediately precede His return, and says: ***"Truly I say to you, this generation will not pass away until all these things take place."*** Jesus clearly seems to be saying that the same generation that sees the signs preceding His return will see His return, i.e., it will all take place within one generation. God allows man to have his day, but God is also going to have His day in which He will intervene suddenly and speedily.

Verse-2: John is a ***"witness to the word of God and to the testimony of Jesus Christ."*** Scripture makes clear that John is not the source of the message but a witness testifying to the message revealed to him by Jesus Christ, who is the true source of the message.

Verse-3: This verse reveals both a blessing and a warning associated with what is about to be revealed. Regarding the blessing, we are told: ***"Blessed is he who reads and those who hear the words of the prophecy, and heed the things which are written in it;"*** (v. 3a). It is important to note that one must both "hear" and "heed" the message in order to be blessed. Regarding the warning, we are told: ***"for the time is near"*** (v. 3b). As in verse 1 the word translated as "near" does not necessarily mean within a short time from the present. Many English translations use the phrase "at hand" or the word "imminent" rather than "near." Both are better translations of the Greek. The intended meaning is that these events could happen at any time so we need to be ready. This interpretation is consistent with Jesus' words in Matthew 24:42, where He states: ***"Therefore be on the alert, for you do not know which day your Lord is coming."*** 1 Peter 4:7 states: ***"The end of all things is at hand; therefore, be of sound judgment and sober spirit for the purpose of prayer."*** The warning is that the future events depicted in Revelation are ready to happen or "at hand" so we need to heed the message and be ready.

Verses 4-6: John now commends on behalf of the Father, Son and Spirit of God, a salutation of grace and peace to the "seven churches that are in Asia." The seven churches to which John writes all existed in what today is western Turkey. We know that there were far more churches in existence at that time and it is widely believed that these churches are representative of the entire Christian Church. As I have stated, the message clearly seems to be from God the Father, Son and

Spirit. God the Father is likely represented in verse 4 as *"from Him who is and who was and who is to come."* The Holy Spirit may be seen in the portion which reads: *"and from the seven Spirits who are before His throne."* The number seven often depicts perfection and/or completeness. Jesus says in John 14:26: *"But the Helper, the Holy Spirit, whom the Father will send in My name, He will teach you all things, and bring to your remembrance all that I said to you."* Revelation 1:20 and 4:5 indicate that the "seven Spirits" dwell with the "seven lamp stands," which are the "seven churches," indicating that the seven-fold Spirit of God dwells in and shines through the Church. Revelation 5:6 also indicates an integral connection between the Spirit and the Christ, saying, *"...a Lamb standing, as if slain, having seven horns and seven eyes, which are the seven Spirits of God, sent out into all the earth."* Scripture often depicts "horns" as a symbol of "power" and "eyes" for vision. Jesus says in Matthew 6:22: *"The lamp of the body is the eye; if therefore your eye is clear, your whole body will be full of light."* And finally, the Son is clearly represented in verse 5, which begins with *"and from Jesus Christ, the faithful witness, the first-born of the dead, and the ruler of the kings of the earth."*

Furthermore, in **verses 5 and 6**, and of great importance, we hear three glorious statements concerning Christ's work on our behalf. In verse 5, Christ is said to be *"Him who loves us"* and as the One who has *"released us from our sins by His blood."* Then in verse 6, we are told that Christ *"has made us to be a kingdom, priests to His God and Father."* We are being told that Christ loves us, saved us, and has made us into a kingdom of priests for the Father. This indeed is not a description limited to any one or group of churches, but the Church Universal.

Verse 7: The author, Jesus Christ, has been established. The instrument to be used to communicate the message, John, has been made known. And the recipient of the message, the seven churches or the Church, has been made known. Now in verse 7 we hear the primary and central message of the Book of Revelation: that the Lord Jesus Christ will return. *"Behold, He is coming with the clouds, and every eye will see Him, even those who pierced Him; and all the tribes of the earth will mourn over Him. Even so. Amen"* (v. 7). This message is consistent with Jesus' words to His disciples when telling them about

His return. In Matthew 24:30, Jesus said to them, *"and then the sign of the Son of Man will appear in the sky, and then all the tribes of the earth will mourn, and they will see the Son of Man coming on the clouds of the sky with power and great glory."* Everyone who has ever lived will see His coming, including those who crucified Him. The earth will mourn over Him because He comes to pass judgment on the whole world. Frequently, Jesus spoke to His disciples about the "day of judgment." For example, in Matthew 12:36, Jesus said, *"And I say to you, that every careless word that men shall speak, they shall render account for it in the day of judgment."* The day of judgment is reserved for the end of time when God will punish the earth by fire, but punishment is reserved for the guilty and not those who have put on the righteousness of Christ. Peter states: *"But the present heavens and earth by His word are being reserved for fire, kept for the day of judgment and destruction of ungodly men"* (2 Peter 3:7). The "day of judgment" is also frequently referenced throughout the Bible as the "day of the Lord." Peter helps us see this by repeating shortly after verve 7 above, *"But the day of the Lord will come like a thief, in which the heavens will pass away with a roar and the elements will be destroyed with intense heat, and the earth and its works will be burned up"* (2 Peter 3:10). Here Peter also reinforces the quickness in how it will come. This truth has been long known, as the prophet Isaiah declared: *"Behold, the day of the Lord is coming, cruel, with fury and burning anger, to make the land a desolation, and He will exterminate its sinners from it"* (Isaiah 13:9). Joel 3:14 also associates the "day of the Lord" with the judgment, stating, *"Multitudes, multitudes in the valley of decision! For the day of the Lord is near in the valley of decision."*

Revelation 1:7 ends with two Greek words translated as, *"Even so. Amen"* in the (NASB), or *"So shall it be! Amen."* in the (NIV). These Greek words can also be translated as "yes indeed, amen" or "certainly so, truly indeed." What is interesting is that what we often translate as "Amen" has the same meaning in the Old Testament Hebrew and the New Testament Greek. Essentially, what we are hearing is a double amen, or "Amen and Amen!" This is a double affirmation of the truth just spoken, placing great emphasis on the revelation that Christ will return to pass judgment.

Verse 8: Now we hear the Lord speaking to us directly to add His emphasis and authority to what we have and are about to hear in His Revelation. *"I am the Alpha, and the Omega," says the Lord God, "who is and who was and who is to come, the Almighty."* The alpha and omega, are respectively, the first and last words in the Greek alphabet so the Lord is saying that He is the beginning and the end of everything. This is reinforced with the statement that the Lord is He *"who is and who was and who is to come."* The Lord is Lord over all things for all time and we should listen to His words.

Verse 9: John now seeks to identify with the Christians to whom He writes, not speaking of his own authority but with humility calling himself their brother. He identifies with them as one who also suffers because of his testimony in proclaiming the Word of God and Jesus as Lord, and one who perseveres in Jesus and through His grace. One can almost hear the echo of Jesus' words from the "Sermon on the Mount" when He said: *"Blessed are those who have been persecuted for the sake of righteousness, for theirs is the kingdom of heaven. Blessed are you when men cast insults at you, and persecute you, and say all kinds of evil against you falsely, on account of Me"* (Matthew 5:10-11).

Verses 10-11: Now John introduces us to the vision he has received at Patmos and his instruction to write an account of it for the seven churches. We are told that at the time of the vision John was in the Spirit on the Lord's day. To be in the Spirit is to be in the Presence of the Spirit of God, perhaps in prayer or meditation. John's reference to the "Lord's day" is generally interpreted as meaning that the vision occurred on a Sunday, which had become known as the Lord's day because it was the day of the Resurrection. Some believe John is speaking of being transported into the future to the "Day of the Lord" and the descriptions which follow are of the events of that final time. Either or both could be true, but the distinction does not affect the message itself.

John continues saying that he hears a loud voice behind him *"like the sound of a trumpet."* Often in Scripture the sound of a trumpet is equated with the voice of God. For example, when God descended upon the mountain of God to meet with Moses, we are told: *"So it came about on the third day, when it was morning, that there were thunder and lightning flashes and a thick cloud upon the mountain and a very loud trumpet sound, so that all the people who were in the camp trembled... When the sound of the trumpet grew louder and louder, Moses spoke and God answered him with thunder"* (Exodus 19:16, 19). And in Psalm 47:5 it is written: *"God has ascended with a shout, the Lord, with the sound of a trumpet."*

Finally, in verse 11, we hear the Lord's instruction to John, saying, *"Write in a book what you see, and send it to the seven churches..."* As previously stated, the message is from the Lord, John will be the instrument of transmission, and the Church will be the recipient.

Testifying Vision (1:12-20)

<u>**Verses 12-20**</u>: Verses 12-16 describe the first scene that John is shown. The vision contains four things which include; (1) seven lamp stands; (2) a being who looks like a man wearing a robe that reaches to His feet; (3) seven stars being held in the being's hand; and, (4) a two-edged sword coming from the being's mouth. Verses 17 and 18, make it clear that the brilliantly illuminated being is the glorified Son of God, our Lord Jesus Christ who is the one speaking to John and the source of Revelation. Verse 20 reveals that the seven lamp stands represent the seven churches, and that the seven stars represent the seven angels of the seven churches. An explanation of the meaning behind Christ's attire and the sword are not offered.

Regarding the seven churches being represented as seven lamp stands, this symbolism may tie back to Jesus' words in Matthew when He says to His disciples: *"You are the light of the world"* (Matthew 5:14a), and He instructs them saying, *"Let your light shine before men in such a way that they may see your good works, and glorify your Father who is in heaven"* (Matthew 5:16). The churches (Church Universal) are called to be Christ's light, a lamp or lamps in a dark world.

Regarding the attire described to be worn by Christ in the vision, I could find no direct correlation or meaning in Scripture, but some scholars attribute it to being similar to that worn by priests. Hebrews 9:11-12 describes Christ as our "high priest" stating: *"But when Christ appeared as a high priest of the good things to come, He entered through the greater and more perfect tabernacle, not made with hands, that is to say, not of this creation; and not through the blood of goats and calves, but through His own blood, He entered the holy place once for all, having obtained eternal redemption."* It is also similar to the being described in Daniel 4:9 and 10:5-6.

Regarding the appearance of Christ described in verse 14, the image is very similar to that described of the "Ancient of Days" in Daniel 4:9, which reads: *"I kept looking until thrones were set up, and the Ancient of Days took His seat; His vesture was like white snow, and the hair of His head like pure wool..."* The image is even more similar to the being that appeared to Daniel in Daniel 10:5-6, which states: *"I lifted my eyes and looked, and behold, there was a certain man dressed in linen, whose waist was girded with a belt of pure gold of Uphaz. His body also was like beryle, his face had the appearance of lightning, his eyes were like flaming torches, his arms and feet like the gleam of polished bronze, and the sound of his words like the sound of a tumult."* The images found in the book of Daniel in the Old Testament closely correspond to many of the images found in Revelation as we will see as we continue our study. The book of Daniel will be but one source helping us interpret Revelation.

Regarding the churches each having an angel, Psalm 91:11 states, *"For He will give His angels charge concerning you, to guard you in all your ways."* Indeed, there is evidence in Scripture that God has assigned angels to watch over individuals, churches and even nations. For example, in the book of Daniel we learn that the angel Michael stands guard over Israel. Speaking of the end of time Daniel 12:1 reads: *"Now at that time Michael, the great prince who stands guard over the sons of your people, will arise. And there will be a time of distress such as never occurred since there was a nation until that time; and at that time your people, everyone who is found written in the book, will be rescued."* We may also understand John's vision to be saying that what is happening on earth is connected with events taking place in heaven. In Revelation 12:4, we hear of a red dragon (presumably Satan) who's *"tail swept away a third of the stars of heaven, and threw them to the earth."* Many believe this symbolism describes a rebellion in heaven when a third of the angels sided with Satan and were cast to the earth to become "fallen angels" or demons.

Finally, regarding the two-edged sword, it most likely represents the Word of God as illustrated in Hebrews 4:12, which reads: ***"For the word of God is living and active and sharper than any two-edged sword, and piercing as far as the division of soul and spirit, of both joints and marrow, and able to judge the thoughts and intentions of the heart."*** The two-edged sword cuts "both ways" separating good from evil, the righteous from the unrighteous. The sword may be another symbol of the judgment that corresponds with the return of Christ.

Many argue that John did not see the literal images that he described but that they are only representative of the message he is attempting to convey. There is no doubt that the images represent truth being revealed by the Lord, but there is no reason to believe that John is not describing literally what he saw. We do not need to convert the images into something more familiar to our finite and logical world in order to understand their meanings or believe the truth they represent. It has been my experience that God often uses unworldly symbols in communicating His divine message. In a way, perhaps the symbols are like the parables Jesus used for teaching. The symbols and parables relay a message of truth that only the faithful can understand guided by God's Holy Spirit. To everyone else they are meaningless and foolishness. In Matthew 13:10-13 it is written: "And the disciples came and said to Him, *"Why do You speak to them in parables?"* Jesus answered them, ***"To you it has been granted to know the mysteries of the kingdom of heaven, but to them it has not been granted. For whoever has, to him more shall be given, and he will have an abundance; but whoever does not have, even what he has shall be taken away from him. Therefore I speak to them in parables; because while seeing they do not see, and while hearing they do not hear, nor do they understand."*** Using parables and symbols is an act of mercy from God. Only those who believe and seek with faith will find answers revealed by God's Holy Spirit. Those who do not believe will not see because if they truly understood, and continued to be disobedient due to their lack of faith, their condemnation would be much more severe.

PART 2

Letters to the Seven Churches

Chapters 2 and 3 contain seven distinct letters written to seven churches that actually existed at the time of Christ's Revelation to John. The letters were not only written to particular churches but perhaps even to particular individuals within these churches because in each case Christ commands John to write the letter and send it *"to the angel of the church."* In all cases the word angel could be interpreted as the messenger who is the presiding bishop or elder of the church in that community.

At the end of the previous chapter, Christ orders John to *"Write therefore the things which you have seen, and things which are, and the things which shall take place after these things"* (Revelation 1:19). The implication is that John is being told to write about things that he has already been shown, things that are happening in the present time and things that will take place in the future. This would seem to effectively kill the argument of many scholars that John is strictly writing about things which have already happened. What is clearly implied is that Christ is speaking about things that were currently taking place within these particular churches and/or would take place in their future. Historically, we know that the things which are described regarding each church actually took place. The question that must be raised is why did Christ pick only these seven churches to address when there were certainly many more churches in existence at that time, and many of these other churches were of even greater prominence. Many believe that these churches were selected because each of them portrays the "Church" at various stages of its history, and/or various aspects of the Church throughout history. An examination of Church history from the time Revelation was written through today reinforces this view because these churches and the Church have gone through various stages that seem to strongly correlate with the characteristics of the seven churches to which John has been instructed to write. But churches continue to struggle with all these same challenges even today, making the message timeless.

Consistent in most of the letters, after first crediting them for what they have done right, Christ then clearly states their failures and calls them into repentance and reward. Christ is telling them what they are doing wrong and the punishments that wait if they fail to repent. He then tells them what they must do to correct their error, and what will result if and when they do. Applying these letters to the greater Church, Christ is appealing to the Church in all ages, pronouncing judgment, calling them to repentance, and providing reassurance of the blessings which accompany repentance and obedience to the Lord. Viewing these seven letters through the lens of the entire book of Revelation, reinforced by what God has consistently revealed throughout the Scriptures contained in the Bible, it seems clear that the Lord is writing about the <u>church throughout all of history</u>. Therefore, by learning from the mistakes and experiences of these churches we can examine ourselves to determine if we are making these same errors. If we are willing to recognize and repent of our errors, we also can receive the blessings and reassurances that Christ provides to the seven churches.

Map shows locations of churches in what today is Turkey.

Letter to Ephesus (2:1-7)

In each letter Christ is portrayed by a symbol which was shown to John in Revelation chapter one or by an attribute unmistakably identified with Christ. To the church in Ephesus the letter is said to be from *"The One who holds the seven stars in His right hand, the One who walks among the seven golden lamp stands"* (2:1). It was revealed in the previous verse (1:20) that *"the seven stars are the angels of the seven churches"* and that the *"seven lamp stands are the seven churches."* Therefore, Christ is saying that He is the One who holds the churches in the palm of His hand and walks in their midst. Christ is not separate but present with the Church.

Also, following the greeting in most letters, Christ praises the church for the good things it has done. To Ephesus, Christ says: *"I know your deeds and your toil and perseverance, and that you cannot endure evil men, and you put to the test those who call themselves apostles, and they are not, and you found them to be false; and you have perseverance and have endured for My name's sake, and have not grown weary"* (2:2-3). The church in Ephesus began in all purity, as can be confirmed by a study of Acts. Paul had visited Ephesus during his second missionary journey (Acts:18-21) and left Aquila and Priscilla there to help them. Paul spent three years in Ephesus on his third tour (Acts 19). The major theme of Paul's letter to the Ephesians is: (1) that the Church is the mystical body of Christ; (2) that God's great master plan is to bring everything together (Eph. 1:10) under Christ as head (Eph. 1:22, 23); and, (3) that we, as the body of Christ on earth, have a part in this plan and the Holy Spirit is the guarantee of God's promise (Eph. 1:13, 14). Perhaps the best expression of Paul's emphasis on the unity of the Church in Christ comes in Ephesians 4:4-6, which states: *"There is one body and one Spirit, just as also you were called in one hope of your calling; one Lord, one faith, one baptism, one God and Father of all who is over all and through all and in all."* In other words, in Ephesus we see a shining example and a struggle over what the Church is supposed to be.

Following the praise is a warning of judgment with Christ stating that the church has left its first love, or in other words, it has stopped being what it was in the beginning. It has lost its passion, its purpose, and its discipline for doing what is right. In verse 2:2 above, Christ has praised the church at Ephesus for not tolerating *"evil men,"* and putting *"to the test those who call themselves apostles, and they are not."* It may be presumed that when Christ says, *"you have left your first love"* (2:4), that the church has become tolerant of other influences and allowed them to dwell in its midst. Referring back to Acts 20:29-31 we can hear Paul's prophetic warning that this would come upon them. Paul writes: *"I know that after my departure savage wolves will come in among you, not sparing the flock; and from among your own selves men will arise, speaking perverse things, to draw away the disciples after them. Therefore be on the alert, remembering that night and day for a period of three years I did not cease to admonish each one with tears."* This understanding of a struggle between maintaining the true faith against intrusive and corrupting influences is reinforced by Christ's words found in Revelation 2:6, which read: *"Yet this you do have, that you hate the deeds of the Nicolaitans, which I also hate."* The Nicolaitans (also mentioned in Revelation 2:15) were advocates to a return to pagan worship. Early Church fathers alleged that the Nicolaitans were founded by Nicolas of Antioch mentioned in Acts 6:5. In Ephesus was the great temple, dedicated to the goddess Artemis, or "Diana" as the Romans called her. Pagan rituals were well established within society and many Christians wanted to hold on to their pagan rituals. The accepting of these rituals as harmless to Christians was a mistake and hated by God. A good example today would be the celebration of Halloween, a pagan holiday filled with pagan ritual, but accepted by most Christians as harmless.

What makes all of this so profound is what will happen later and that we now view as history. Ephesus will become the center of a Church controversy between the orthodox doctrine that the Incarnate Christ was a single Person, at once God and man and, "Nestoriansim"—the doctrine that there were two separate Persons in the Incarnate Christ, the one Divine and the other Human. This may seem to be a minor distinction but in essence it espouses a separation of "God from man." Nestorius, for which it gets its name, was condemned by Rome in 430 AD but the controversy persisted. Finally, the Council of Ephesus was called in 431 AD which upheld Christ as "Theotokos" (God-bearer). After the Council of Ephesus the Bishops who refused to accept the Formula gradually constituted themselves a separate Nestorian Church centered in Persia. From the early 6th century the Nestorian Church was active in missionary work and established Christian settlements in Arabia. The church persists to this day, primarily in the mountains of Kurdistan.

Christ warned the church at Ephesus, saying, *"Remember therefore from where you have fallen, and repent and do the deeds you did at first; or else I am coming to you, and will remove your lamp stand out of its place—unless you repent"* (2:5) Today, the church in which the Council of Ephesus met is in ruins. After the conquest by Islam, the church of Ephesus became nonexistent. The lamp stand, which represents the church, has apparently been removed. Christ says: *"He who has an ear, let him hear what the Spirit says to the churches. To him who overcomes, I will grant to eat of the tree of life, which is in the Paradise of God"* (2:7). Jesus said to His disciples: *"Do not judge lest you be judged"* (Matthew 7:1), but He also said, *"Do not judge according to appearance, but judge with righteous judgment"* (John

7:24). The Apostle John also warns us in 1 John 4:1, saying, *"**Beloved, do not believe every spirit, but test the spirits to see whether they are from God; because many false prophets have gone out into the world.**"* We must not repeat the mistakes of Ephesus. We must continue to test the spirits to discern which are of God and which are false, and we must not tolerate evil men or false apostles in our midst. For if we do, our fate will be the same as that of the church of Ephesus—we will be corrupted from within and our lamp stand removed.

Letter to Smyrna (2:8-11)

To the church in Smyrna Christ is described as: *"**The first and the last, who was dead, and has come to life**"* (2:8). This description is extremely revealing and important because the church of Smyrna will suffer unspeakable persecution and tribulation because of their steadfast faith in Jesus Christ. Therefore, even Christ's opening greeting is filled with reassurance, because if Christ is forever and has suffered death but came to life, then those who put their faith in Him may have hope of eternal life as well. Christ identifies with their trial, saying, *"**I know your tribulation and your poverty (but you are rich), and the blasphemy by those who say they are Jews and are not, but are a synagogue of Satan**"* (2:9). The church in Smyrna finds its counterpart in the martyr church of the second and third centuries. The Caesar cult had emerged and the Christians suffered a great deal because they would not worship Caesar. Polycarp, the bishop of the church, was martyred by fire there in 156 AD because he refused to call Caesar "Lord." The Smyrna church members were fed to the lions at Rome while multitudes cheered. Christ's accusation against the Jews in Smyrna is likely associated with the fact that the Jews there resented the Christians and often conspired with the Roman authorities, contributing to the Christians' persecutions.

The letter to Smyrna is different in that it does not contain a condemnation or judgment against the church, but instead, seeks to reassure those who will undergo great suffering. Christ says to them: *"**Do not fear what you are about to suffer. Behold, the devil is about to cast some of you into prison, that you may be tested, and you will have tribulation for ten days. Be faithful until death, and I will give*** *you the crown of life"* (2:10). Christ is promising them life in the face of death. We do not know with any certainty what is represented by the "ten days." Some scholars believe that the ten days of persecution consisted of ten literal periods of suffering found in history. The number "10" is also sometimes seen as representing things "worldly" as opposed to heavenly. Ten days also reassures us that suffering will be for a "limited" time.

Christ concludes saying, **"He who has an ear, let him hear what the Spirit says to the churches. He who overcomes shall not be hurt by the second death"** (2:11). According to Revelation 20:14 and 21:8, the "second death" is the final death which comes from being cast into the "lake of fire" along with Satan and his angels. Christ is assuring us that if we persevere in our faith to the very end, even though we physically die, yet shall we gain eternal life in Him. Regardless of what comes, we must remain faithful always. Jesus said, **"I am the resurrection and the life; he who believes in Me shall live even if he dies, and everyone who lives and believes in Me shall never die"** (John 11:25-26). The devil may be able to kill our bodies but our souls belong to our Lord, Jesus Christ, and those who persevere shall live with Him forever.

Letter to Pergamum (2:12-17)

To the church in Pergamum Christ is described as: **"The One who has the sharp two-edged sword"** (2:12), previously mentioned in verse 1:16. Again, Hebrews 4:12 portrays the two-edged sword as the **"Word of God"** and as able to **"judge the thoughts and intentions of the heart."** The implication is that there is good and bad in Pergamum, just as there was in Ephesus, which will be separated (cut apart) by the Lord.

Also as with Ephesus, the Lord begins with praise for the good in Pergamum, stating: **"I know where you dwell, where Satan's throne is; and you hold fast My name, and did not deny My faith, even in the days of Antipas, My witness, My faithful one, who was killed among you, where Satan dwells"** (2:13). The reference to "Satan's throne" has been widely debated. It could refer to the "Great Altar of Pergamum" in the enormous temple of Zeus which was erected on a hill and stood 800 ft. above the city. Pergamum was also the center for worship of Asclepius, the god of healing. The "serpent" was Asclepius' symbol, and it is still depicted in the rod of Asclepius, the insignia of many medical associations. The symbol is similar to that described in Numbers 21:6-9 which was used to heal people bitten by serpents. Others believe "Satan's throne" refers to the emperor worship centered at a temple to the goddess Roma and Emperor Augustus erected there. Pergamum was also a Babylonian religious headquarters. Because the name Pergamum has the same root from which we get our English words "bigamy" and "polygamy," it is even possible that Satan's throne could be associated with the materialism, self-indulgence and worldliness that existed there and suggests a mixed marriage of the church and the world. Consistent with this, Pergamum was a center of commerce and was renowned for its library, which rivaled the famous library at Alexandria, and has left a monument to that the city's name in our word "parchment" derived from "Pergamum." In any case, the Christians there were under great pressure and persecution from numerous hostile influences, but had remained faithful and had not denied Christ. Regarding the martyr Antipas, little is known about him but tradition holds that he was ordained by the Apostle John as Bishop of Pergamum and was martyred in 92 A.D. by burning in a brazen bull-shaped altar used for casting out demons worshiped by the local population. Clearly, his witness was a great inspiration to the Christians of Pergamum and his great faith recognized by the Lord.

This leads us to the problem the Lord identifies within the church there, stating, **"But I have a few things against you, because you have there some who hold the teaching of Balaam, who kept teaching Balak to put a stumbling block before the sons of Israel, to eat things sacrificed to idols, and to commit acts of immorality"** (2:14). The story of Balaam and Balak can be found in Numbers, chapters 22 through 24. After being delivered out of Egypt and as the Israelites approached Moab, out of fear of Israel Balak summoned Balaam, a diviner, to come and curse Israel so that he could defeat them. Balaam first refused to go but when offered great gifts and wealth was persuaded to go. Still, he refused to curse Israel and ended up blessing them instead three times. But ultimately, Balaam gave Balak evil council, pointing out how he could lead them into sexual immorality and idolatry, thus bringing about their downfall. This teaching of immorality and idolatry is the teaching that the Lord is condemning in the church at Pergamum. This is reinforced by the next verse, which adds, *"Thus you also have some who in the same way hold the teaching of the Nicolaitans"* (2:15). Remember that the Nicolaitans were those Christians who wanted to retain or return to pagan rituals such as eating food sacrificed to idols and temple fornication. To put it simply, God condemned them for succumbing to self-indulgent and worldly influences.

Christ now warns them, saying, *"Repent therefore, or else I am coming to you quickly, and I will make war against them with the sword of My mouth"* (2:16). Again we see the two-edged sword as the word of God pronouncing judgment. If the Christians who are practicing self-indulgence and idolatry do not repent the Lord will wage war against them. Clearly, the message of Pergamum is that we must be careful not to practice self-indulgence or allow anything to come between us and the Lord. Materialism and worldliness are our enemy because, as Christ said so clearly, *"No one can serve two masters; for either he will hate the one and love the other, or he will hold to one and despise the other. You cannot serve God and mammon"* (Matthew 6:24).

Christ's closing words to Pergamum, state: *"To him who overcomes, to him I will give some of the hidden manna, and I will give him a white stone, and a new name written on the stone which no one knows but he who receives it"* (2:17). Just as God provided manna in the wilderness to sustain His people, He will provide food that sustains those who remain faithful to Him. The meaning of the white stone and the name upon it is obscure, but in ancient times, white stones were given by jurors as a vote for acquittal. Also, a white stone with the engraved name of a deity was sometimes used as a mark of membership. Regarding the name that no one knows except those who will "receive" it, in the Gospel of John, Jesus tells us, *"And I will ask the Father, and He will give you another Helper, that He may be with you forever; that is the Spirit of truth, whom the world cannot receive, because it does not behold Him or know Him, but you know Him because He abides with you, and will be in you"* (John 14:16-17). Only the faithful can receive and know the name. Revelation 3:12b will add concerning those who overcome: *"I will write upon him the name of My God, and the name of the city of My God, the new Jerusalem, which comes down out of heaven from My God, and My new name."* All who remain faithful to the Lord will receive the mark for eternal life and will bear His holy name, whether they are physically alive or dead, yet shall they live.

Letter to Thyatira (2:18-29)

To the church of Thyatira Christ is described as, *"The Son of God, who has eyes like a flame of fire, and His feet are like burnished bronze"* (2:18). This is significant in its association because the guardian divinity of this prosperous city was Apollo, the son of Zeus. All of the emperors were identified as Apollo incarnate and each, like him, the son of Zeus. Therefore the celestial Christ, the "Son of God," is set over, against and above the emperor, who as the incarnate Apollo was seen as the "son of Zeus."

As typical in all the letters to the churches, the Lord next extends His praise for what the church is doing right. The Lord says, *"I know your deeds, and your love and faith and service and perseverance, and that your deeds of late are greater than at first"* (2:19). The Lord's words depict a church serving and growing. Not only are they excelling in many areas but they are doing more now than in their beginning. The phrase "deeds of late" literally means "last deeds."

The church in Thyatira is not without its problems and so the Lord immediately follows His praise with His warning, saying, *"But I have this against you, that you tolerate the woman Jezebel, who calls herself a prophetess, and she teaches and leads My bondservants astray, so that they commit acts of immorality and eat things sacrificed to idols"* (2:20). Who was Jezebel? In the Old Testament a woman of that name married Ahab, one of the kings of the northern kingdom of Israel. She was a Sidonian and a worshiper of Baal. She influenced Ahab to build an altar to Baal in Samaria and to worship the false god. This self-appointed prophetess brought Baalism into Israel as a new religion and seduced God's servants to commit fornication and to eat things sacrificed to idols. This constituted the breaking of God's commandments against creating graven images and idols, and committing adultery (Exodus 20:4, 5 and 14). She also systematically murdered the prophets of God in Israel and even attempted to murder Elijah. She was perhaps the wickedest woman of her day. Ultimately,

God pronounced judgment upon her that she would be killed and eaten by dogs, which was fulfilled and she became *"as dung on the face of the field in the property of Jezreel"* (2 Kings 9:37). The story of Jezebel is told in 1 Kings, chapters 16, 18, 19 and 21, and in 2 Kings, chapter 9. As Balaam was used as a "type" of the false prophet, his female counterpart, Jezebel, the immoral and idolatrous queen, is the type of false prophetess who teaches the Christians to commit fornication and to eat food sacrificed to idols. Here, fornication is not simply sexual immorality, but in a special way is equated with idolatry, particularly emperor worship.

Verses 21 through 23 warn of what will happen within the church if it fails to repent. First, the Lord expresses His willingness to be patient and allow time for repentance, saying, *"And I gave her time to repent; and she does not want to repent of her immorality"* (2:21). Unfortunately, He also lets us know that those who were sinning did not want to repent. Next, the Lord reveals the form His punishment will take upon those who fail to repent, saying, *"Behold, I will cast her upon a bed of sickness, and those who commit adultery with her into great tribulation, unless they repent of her deeds"* (2:22). It would seem clear that the Lord is saying that if the church fails to repent He is going to make it sick and bring upon it great tribulation or distress. But in verse 23 the Lord reminds us that He makes a distinction between those who sin and those who remain faithful, saying, *"And I will kill her children with pestilence; and all the churches will know that I am He who searches the minds and hearts; and I will give to each one of you according to your deeds"* (2:23). Surely God will punish the wicked—those churches and individuals who allow the immoral and adulterous influence of Jezebel in their midst. But God knows the mind and the heart of everyone and will give to each one according to their deeds. We have learned from the letter to Smyrna that the death of the martyrs guarantees their blessed immortality in the New Jerusalem, and that those who die as idolaters are to be cast into the lake of fire for an eternity of punishment (21:8). Now we hear that no sinner can escape the searching look of Christ with *"eyes like a flame of fire"* (2:18) who *"searches the minds and hearts"* (2:23) of all. The Lord sees all, knows all, and judges all according to their deeds, that is to say, how they live their faith.

The message now turns from condemnation for the unrepentant to assurance for those who remain faithful. The Lord now says, *"But I say to you, the rest who are in Thyatira, who do not hold this teaching, who have not known the deep things of Satan, as they call them—I place no other burden on you"* (2:24). For those who do not succumb to Jezebel's theological follies or fall into the fornication and idolatry propagated by the false Babylonian religion, Christ will not add additional burdens. Apparently, what they have already endured in holding to the faith is heartache enough. In regard to the reference to the phrase *"who have known the deep things of Satan,"* this may be an attack upon "Gnosticism." Gnostics were those who professed having received "secret knowledge" regarding the "deep things of God" revealed to them by the Holy Spirit. While Gnosticism may seem similar to traditional Christian belief because of its claim that the Holy Spirit reveals knowledge of God, it has been condemned by the Church. The distinctive difference and problem with Gnosticism is found in the word "secret" in that the knowledge is only given to a few who claim to speak for God and is withheld from the community. Christ teaches us that He is the Light and we have been given His Light and instructed to let it shine so all can see Him. Cults keep secrets but Christians bear witness to all who will listen to the Truth and follow the Way.

Verse 25 is short but reveals much. Christ says, *"Nevertheless what you have, hold fast until I come."* We are to hold fast in the faith as it has been revealed to us though Jesus Christ until His return. The church of Thyatira, or the church type for which it represents, will continue to exist all the way until the time of His return. The faithful church can be defined as the church with deeds of *"love and faith and service and perseverance"* (2:19) which are even greater at the end than at the beginning.

Verses 26 through 28 proclaim Christ's reward and promise to those who overcome and keep His deeds until the end. The Lord says, *"And he who overcomes, and he who keeps My deeds until the end, to him I will give authority over the nations; and he shall rule them with a rod of iron, as the vessels of the potter are broken to pieces, as I also have received authority from My Father; and I will give him the morning star"* (2:26-28). Apparently at the time of Christ's return there will be a reversal of worldly authority, where the faithful will no longer be persecuted by the unfaithful but will rule over the nations of the world. Some believe this is a reference to the Millennium—the 1,000 years of peace when Christ and the faithful will reign over the earth before final judgment is executed (See Revelation 20:4). One thing is certain. There can be no mistake that this passage is pointing back to Psalm 2, where it is written regarding those who devise plans against God and His people, *"Thou shall break them with a rod of iron, Thou shalt shatter them like earthenware"* (Psalm 2:9). The power that overcomes and destroys evil is Christ. This is reinforced in verse 28 when Christ will *"give the morning star"* to those who overcome and keep His deeds. What is the morning star? Revelation 22:16 says, *"I, Jesus, have sent My angel to testify to you these things for the churches. I am the root and the offspring of David, the bright morning star."* Jesus Christ is Himself the morning star who fills us with His Light. The message found in 2 Peter 1:19 is similar, when Peter says: *"And so we have the prophetic word made more sure, to which you do well to pay attention as to a lamp shining in a dark place, until the day dawns and the morning star arises in your hearts."* Another interpretation is that the "morning star" which appears at dawn is representative of the "eternal life" that comes through faith in Christ. This understanding can be seen in Daniel 12:3, which speaking of the faithful at the time of the end says, *"And those who have insight will shine brightly like the brightness of the expanse of heavens, and those who lead the many to righteousness, like the stars forever and ever."* In reality they are the same. Christ Jesus is the Light which gives us eternal life. Though the world remain in darkness, may the Light of our Lord Jesus Christ arise and burn brightly within us until His return and for all eternity.

Letter to Sardis (3:1-6)

To the church of Sardis Christ is described as, *"He who has the seven Spirits of God, and the seven stars"* (3:1). This statement is simple and seems to reference back to the greeting in (1:4) which stated: *"Grace to you and peace, from Him who is and who was and who is to come; and from the seven Spirits who are before His throne."* From this statement we learn that the seven Spirits are before the throne of God, but who are the seven Spirits and the seven stars? Remember, that

Christ revealed that *"the seven stars are the angels of the seven churches"* in (1:20), and because angel means messenger, then the seven stars are messengers of the seven churches. Looking ahead to Revelation 4:5 and 5:6 we gain additional critical insight. First, in (4:5b) we learn that the *"seven lamps of fire burning before the throne"* are *"the seven Spirits of God."* Remember, that in (1:20) the Lord said that *"the seven lamp <u>stands</u> are the seven churches."* Revelation 5:6 reveals even more insight, saying, *"And I saw between [in the midst of] the throne (with the four living creatures) and the elders a Lamb standing, as if slain, having seven horns and seven eyes, which are the seven Spirits of God, sent out into all the earth."* Remember from (1:4) that God is the One *"who is and who was and who is to come."* From all of these references we can conclude that the "seven Spirits" are the Holy Spirit of God that comes from God into the world to indwell the seven churches, to shine through the seven churches as the Light of God, and to convey to the churches the Word (message of truth) from God. Jesus said in John 14:26, *"But the Helper, the Holy Spirit, whom the Father will send in My name, He will teach you all things, and bring to your remembrance all that I said to you."* When the Holy Spirit was poured forth as Jesus promised, moved by the Holy Spirit, Peter proclaimed the message first heard through the prophet Joel, saying, *"And it shall be in the last days,' God says, 'That I will pour forth of My Spirit upon all mankind"* (Acts 2:17a). The significance of all of this relative to the church at Sardis is that the Spirit, i.e., the Light no longer shines through the church and the church has fallen asleep, therefore the Lord is calling for it to "Wake up!"

 The praise for Sardis is barely praise at all. Christ says to the church, *"I know your deeds, that you have a name that you are alive, but you are dead"* (3:1b). Simply being a church by name and saying one is alive does not give one life. If the Holy Spirit is not shining from a church it is dead and only appears to be alive. This does not mean that all hope is lost or that the Spirit is absent. Hence, the Lord's call, saying, *"Wake up, and strengthen the things that remain, which were about to die; for I have not found your deeds completed in the sight of My God"* (3:2). Obviously there is still an opportunity for the church to rekindle the Spirit and finish the work for which God has called it. The

Lord continues his warning, saying to the church, **"Remember therefore what you have received and heard; and keep it, and repent. If therefore you will not wake up, I will come like a thief, and you will not know at what hour I will come upon you"** (3:3). Is what they **"have received and heard"** the Holy Spirit of God? If they will not wake up, will the Lord's coming be **"like a thief"** because in the absence of the Spirit they cannot perceive His coming? Or, in the absence of the Spirit, will Satan come with his lies and steal their very souls? Jesus said in Matthew 24:43, **"But be sure of this, that if the head of the house had known at what time of the night the thief was coming, he would have been on the alert and would not have allowed his house to be broken into."**

Just as we first heard in the letter to Thyatira, the Lord will make a distinction between those who remain faithful and those who do not. The Lord continues speaking but now directs His attention to the remaining faithful in Sardis, saying, **"But you have a few people in Sardis who have not soiled their garments; and they will walk with Me in white; for they are worthy"** (3:4). In Revelation 7:14, John will be told that the people he sees in heaven standing before the throne of the Lamb are the ones who **"have washed their robes and made them white in the blood of the Lamb."** Jesus said, **"If anyone loves Me, he will keep My word; and My Father will love him, and We will come to him, and make Our abode with him"** (John 14:23). Notice that Jesus says **"make <u>Our</u> abode with him."** When we remain faithful, the Lord and the Spirit of God abide in us. Jesus went on to say, **"If anyone does not abide in Me, he is thrown away as a branch, and dries up; and they gather them, and cast them into the fire, and they are burned"** (John 15:6). As with the church at Sardis, we must remain faithful and abide in the Lord so that the Spirit of God will abide in us, guiding (eyes seeing the way) and empowering (horns represent power) us in our walk with the Lamb. (See Revelation 5:6).

Finally we receive the promise. The Lord says, **"He who overcomes shall thus be clothed in white garments; and I will not erase his name from the book of life, and I will confess his name before My Father, and before His angels"** (3:5). Revelation 20:12 informs us that anyone who is not recorded in the Book of Life will be thrown into the fire. The Lord is providing assurance that all who remain alert and do not become complacent or allow their faith to fall asleep will continue to abide in Him and live. We must keep the Spirit of God within us burning and be on fire for the Lord, if we are to escape the flames of judgment.

Letter to Philadelphia (3:7-13)

To the church of Philadelphia Christ is described as, *"He who is holy, who is true, who has the key of David, who opens and no one will shut, and who shuts and no one opens"* (3:7b). You will note that beginning with the church in Philadelphia the Lord stops using portions of the vision described in Revelation 1:12-16. Instead, the Lord provides a three-fold description of Himself as "holy," "true," and as having the "key of David" and who opens and shuts what no one else can shut or open. In a manner of speaking, the Lord Jesus Christ seems to be referring to Himself as the only One who can provide or deny access to heaven. This is supported by other Scripture. As we look at each of the three parts of the description we can see evidence of this.

In the first part Christ speaks of His holiness. The book of Hebrews speaks of Christ as the great high priest that intercedes for us and is the only One pure enough and holy enough to provide the sacrifice that cleans us of our sins and allows us entrance into heaven. Hebrews 7:26 states: *"For it was fitting that we should have such a high priest, holy, innocent, undefiled, separated from sinners and exalted above the heavens."* The pure and innocent Lamb of God is the only One holy enough to pay for our sin.

In the second part Christ speaks of Himself as "True." In this we may be reminded of His declaration in John 14:6, saying, *"I am the way, and the truth, and the life; no one comes to the Father, but through Me."* The truth is that Christ is the only way to God.

In the final part Christ speaks of Himself as the "key of David" and as the One *"who opens and no one will shut, and who shuts and no one opens"* (3:7b). The Lord seems to be quoting or pointing to a passage in Isaiah where the Lord speaks of the authority He will give the king He has chosen. Isaiah 22:22 states: *"Then I will set the key of the house of David on his shoulder, when he opens no one will shut, when he shuts no one will open."* The One on whom God places authority has ultimate authority. In John 10:9 Jesus says of Himself, *"I am the door; if anyone enters through Me, he shall be saved, and shall go in and out, and find pasture."* And in Revelation 22:16 Jesus will remind us of His relation to David, saying, *"I am the root and the offspring of David."* Clearly what the Lord is saying is that He and only He provides us access to heaven.

Apparently, like the Church in Smyrna, the church in Philadelphia has remained true to Him and therefore He offers only praise without any condemnation for faults. Christ says to them: *"I know your deeds. Behold, I have put before you an open door which no one can shut, because you have a little power, and have kept My word, and have not denied My name"* (3:8). Jesus promises to open the door for those who genuinely seek Him, as He says in Matthew 7:7-8: *"Ask , and it shall be given to you; seek, and you shall find; knock, and it shall be opened to you. For everyone who asks receives, and he who seeks finds, and to him who knocks it shall be opened."* Likewise, Jesus makes it clear that in the absence of a genuine relationship with Him and if we have not prepared ourselves for Him the door will remain shut when we knock. In the parable of the ten virgins found in Matthew 25:10b-12, Jesus says, *"And those who were ready went in with him to the wedding feast; and the door was shut. And later the other virgins also came, saying, 'Lord, Lord, open up for us.' But he answered and said, 'Truly I say to you, I do not know you.'"* The key here is the phrase "I do not know you." Knowing of Christ and even believing that Jesus is the Christ is not enough, even *"the demons also believe and shudder"* (James 2:19). We must have a personal relationship with Him. We must know Him and He know us on a personal level. The fact that Jesus has *"an open door which no one can shut"* (3:8) for them indicates they are the people of the church who have such a relationship with Him. Christ's statement that they have only a *"little power"* (3:8) is likely not an indication of fault or weakness but of relative size. The number who are faithful is small as compared to those who are not, so the church has little power over those who oppose it. In the end, the Church Universal will find itself dwarfed by the unbelieving and unfaithful world in which it resides with little power to change it, but the key is to remain faithful even in the midst of such overwhelming darkness. What Christ says the church of Philadelphia did that was most admirable was that they *"have kept My word, and have not denied My name"* (3:9). Remember what Jesus said in Matthew 10:32-33, *"Everyone therefore who shall confess Me before men, I will also confess him before My Father who is in heaven. But whoever shall deny Me before men, I will also deny him before My Father who is in heaven."* Likewise in Mark 8:38, speaking of His return Jesus said, *"For whoever is ashamed of Me and My words in this adulterous and sinful generation, the Son of Man will also be ashamed of him when He comes in the glory of His Father with the holy angels."* Clearly, those who remain faithful to His word and name and continue to confess Him, even when it is unpopular and considered shameful to do so, He will ultimately honor.

Next, Christ continues with words of reassurance that those who are faithful to Him until the end will ultimately prevail. He says, *"Behold, I will cause those of the synagogue of Satan, who say that they are Jews, and are not, but lie—behold, I will make them to come and bow down at your feet, and to know that I have loved you"* (3:9). Again as in the letter to the Smyrna church the Lord mentions the *"synagogue of Satan"* and *"those who say they are Jews and are not"* (2:9). In Galatians 3:7, Paul makes the distinction that it is not blood lines but faith that make one a son of Abraham, saying, *"be sure that it is those who are of faith who are sons of Abraham."* This verse may be saying that the Jews who did not accept but denied that Jesus was the Messiah will end up bowing down before the Christians, who while not descendants of Abraham by birth, became descendants through their faith in Christ. The Jews will ultimately have to recognize and acknowledge God's love for the Gentile believers in His Son. What was said to Abraham will be fulfilled: *"And in you all the families of the earth shall be blessed"* (Genesis 12:3b). God has never limited His salvation to one people and Christ's sacrifice on the cross was intended to purchase salvation for all who would believe in and accept Him as their Lord and Savior. Scripture clearly says that the Jews were God's chosen people and that He will ultimately fulfill all His promises to them. But even the Jews will have to recognize and acknowledge the love of God for the Christian when it is finally revealed to them that Jesus was and is the Messiah, the Son of the Living God.

Following the reassurance of verse 9 is a promise of deliverance in verse 10. The Lord promises: *"Because you have kept the word of My perseverance, I also will keep you from the hour of testing, that hour which is about to come upon the whole world, to test those who dwell upon the earth"* (3:10). Because the preposition that we translate as "from" has a meaning in the Greek of "out from" or "away from," many believe this is a reference to a pre-tribulation Rapture—the removal of the church prior to the great tribulation. Likewise, the word we translate as "testing" can also be translated as "temptation," perhaps meaning that it will be so difficult to endure as a Christian during the tribulation that Christians will be "tempted" to deny their faith to survive, which in reality, is a test of faith. Regarding the belief that this passage supports the Rapture, this view is not shared by all Christians and quite honestly it doesn't matter how God is going to protect His children from testing. What matters is that God will keep His promise, regardless of which way He chooses to do so. Psalm 91:1-3 helps us see a picture of this, saying, **"He who dwells in the shelter of the Most High will abide in the shadow of the Almighty. I will say to the Lord, 'My refuge and my fortress, my God, in whom I trust!' For it is He who delivers you from the snare of the trapper, and from the deadly pestilence."** Whether God shall choose to pluck His Church from the face of the earth or protect His children wherever they are as He did Lot when He destroyed Sodom and Gomorrah (Genesis 19), God will keep His promise.

Again, in verse 11 we hear echoes of the letter to Smyrna. The Lord says, **"I am coming quickly; hold fast what you have, in order that no one take your crown."** The martyrs of Smyrna were told: **"Be faithful until death, and I will give you the crown of life"** (2:10). Now those of Philadelphia are told to "hold fast" so that no one "take their crown." These words remind us of Paul's statement in 2 Timothy 4:7-8, when he says, **"I have fought the good fight. I have finished the course, I have kept the faith; in the future there is laid up for me the crown of righteousness, which the Lord, the righteous judge will award me on that day; and not only to me, but also to all who have loved His appearing."** The "crown" seems to represent God's reward for the righteous who hold fast to Him to the end. It may equate to God's gift of internal life or only to the treasures that await the faithful. Regarding the phrase, **"I am coming quickly,"** as was discussed regarding verse 1:3, this does not mean coming soon, but when He comes it will happen quickly.

Finally in verse 12, just as Jesus described Himself with a three-fold description in the opening to the letter to Philadelphia, now He promises a three-fold reward to those who remain faithful. Christ says, *"He who overcomes, I will make him a pillar in the temple of My God, and he will not go out from it anymore; and I will write upon him the name of My God, and the name of the city of My God, the new Jerusalem, which comes down from out of heaven from My God, and My new name."* Revelation 21:22 tells us that the Lord God Almighty (Father) and the Lamb (Son) are the temple of the new Jerusalem, for speaking of the new Jerusalem John says, *"And I saw no temple in it, for the Lord God, the Almighty, and the Lamb, are its temple"* (21:22). The three-fold promise is first, that those who overcome will be made a part of the city of God, the new Jerusalem, never to leave it again. Second, they will be marked with God's name, as among those who belong to God. And third, they will be marked with the name of the Lamb, the Lord Jesus Christ. Of course, we cannot know with absolute certainty the meaning of the "new name." Based on context it seems logical that it is associated with the Lord Jesus Christ because this is the "Revelation of Christ" and He refers to the name saying, "My new name." Also consistent with the church of Philadelphia being lifted up so that others bow down before it, the reference to a "crown" and "new name" are words found in Isaiah 62:2-3, which reads, *"And the nations will see your righteousness, and all kings your glory; and you will be called by a new name, which the mouth of the Lord will designate. You will also be a crown of beauty in the hand of the Lord, and a royal diadem in the hand of your God."* The church of Philadelphia is often viewed as the missionary church, and of course, the "missio Dei" or the "mission of God" is for the church to make disciples for Jesus Christ. To do this we must not hide from the world but bear witness in the world, which necessitates being faithful to His word and not denying His name. For those who are not overcome by the world but boldly bear witness until the end God promises great reward.

Letter to Laodicea (3:14-22)

To the church of Laodicea Christ is described as, *"The Amen, the faithful and true Witness, the Beginning of the creation of God"*

(3:14b). As in the letter to the church of Philadelphia we have a new description not found in the opening vision. Again we have Christ described three-fold, as first, *"The Amen"* which literally means "truly indeed." Christ is the Truth (John 14:6) and God's Holy Spirit is called the *"Spirit of Truth"* (John 14:17). This first description is reinforced by the second stating the Christ is the *"faithful and true Witness."* This is to say that He is the One we can trust to tell us the truth and bear witness to the truth. While there are more references than we could possibly have time to review, just think of how many times Jesus said to His disciples *"Truly, truly, I say to you."* Therefore, Christ is the Truth and bears witness to the truth. And third, Christ refers to Himself as the *"Beginning of the creation of God."* I am reminded of Paul's description of Christ in Colossians 1:15-16, which states, *"And He is the image of the invisible God, the first-born of all creation. For by Him all things were created, both in the heavens and on the earth, visible and invisible, whether thrones or dominions or rulers or authorities—all things have been created by Him and for Him."* In the context of the letter to Laodicea, what makes this description so important is that Christ is the Truth and speaks the truth and is the beginning of everything, but unless the church changes and repents, the truth is that it will be cast out.

There is no praise for this church, but only condemnation. The church represents the apostate church of the last days. The church is neither filled with faith or a lack of faith but straddles the fence and lacks any real commitment. Verses 3:15-16 state: *"I know your deeds, that you are neither cold nor hot; I would that you were cold or hot. So because you are lukewarm, and neither hot nor cold, I will spit you out of My mouth."* The description is so much like so many churches today, neither hot or cold but only lukewarm with a severe lack of passion or commitment. Churches go through the motions of worship and ministry believing they do God's work while at the same time adhering to the world's socially and politically correct standards. The church cannot be of God and of the world. The church cannot remain neutral and compromise God's truth in order to avoid conflict with the world. Christ says I will *"spit you out of My mouth."* The word "spit" here is of the same Greek root as the English word "emetic." What is interesting is that an emetic is given to one who has swallowed poison in order to make him regurgitate (vomit). In other words, the lukewarm, uncommitted church is repulsive to Christ and makes Him sick enough to vomit it out. This is certainly not the church we want to be.

Historically, we know that the city of Laodicea was extremely wealthy and was both a banking center and contained a famous medical school. The city was so wealthy and proud of its self-dependence, that after it was devastated by an earthquake of 61 A.D. it refused financial assistance from the Roman government, and out of its own resources and by its own efforts eventually rebuilt the city. This is consistent with what Jesus says next in verses 17 and 18: *"Because you say, "I am rich, and have become wealthy, and have need of nothing," and you do not know that you are wretched and miserable and poor and blind and naked, I advise you to buy from Me gold refined by fire, that you may become rich, and white garments, that you may clothe yourself, and that the shame of your nakedness may not be revealed; and eye salve to anoint your eyes, that you may see."* The truth is, worldly wealth can blind us from seeing what is truly of value. The truth is, worldly knowledge can blind us from understanding true wisdom. The truth is, fancy clothes cannot hide the naked shame of our unrighteousness. God longs to help us see, but we must step into His Light and be willing to look through the eyes of His Spirit rather than through our worldly vision. Without God's Light everything is gray and what is right cannot be easily distinguished from what is wrong, what is good cannot be distinguished from what is bad. God calls us to make a choice. We must put Him first or yield to our own selfish interests. But we cannot save ourselves because salvation comes only through the Lord Jesus Christ. Truly, no one can serve two masters (Matthew 6:24), and God will ultimately separate the sheep from the goats (Matthew 25). If we choose to remain lukewarm, we choose against God and will be cast out of His presence. The once wealthy and prosperous city of Laodicea today lies in complete ruins.

Next, the Lord reminds us that love is accompanied by discipline, saying, *"Those whom I love, I reprove and discipline; be zealous therefore, and repent"* (3:19). As Jesus said, *"If you love Me, you will keep My commandments"* (John 14:15). If we love God we will repent of our sins, turning back to God's commands and discipline ourselves to be obedient to His Word. Just as we discipline our children because we love them and want them to grow up safe and knowing the difference between right and wrong, so God disciplines His children to teach them all they must know to obtain His righteousness.

Jesus awaits our response to His call, desiring we invite Him into our lives. While Jesus is the door that opens into heaven, He does not force Himself upon us. We must open the door and invite Him into our lives, and be willing to dine with Him, be in a relationship with Him. Verse 20 states: *"Behold, I stand at the door and knock; if anyone hears My voice and opens the door, I will come in to him, and will dine with him, and he with Me."*

And finally, verse 21 contains a promise for those who overcome their complacency, their lack of commitment, those who repent and rekindle their fire for God and return to a relationship with the Lord. Christ says to them, *"He who overcomes, I will grant to him to sit down with Me on My throne, as I also overcame and sat down with My Father on His throne."* Christ overcame the temptation of sin, and suffered and died for the sake of the unrighteous that we might obtain the righteousness of God through His sacrifice. If we too are willing to give up everything for Him we too can share in His inheritance and take our place with Him in heaven.

The words spoken to the seven churches are true. They speak to all churches in all ages. They speak to the Church which is the body of Christ. He has given the Church His Spirit to be in our midst and to illuminate God's purpose for us, and to empower us to do God's will. All of the book of Revelation must be viewed as a message to the Church, as a message to all who are members of Christ's Church. The messages for the churches are for us. If we heed them we will receive the promises and rewards God has promised. If we fail to heed their warnings, then we will receive the punishments and consequences that they reveal. God is "revealing" His Truth to us. Will we listen?

Examples or History?

As previously stated, the seven churches found in Revelation were local churches that actually existed in Asia Minor at the time Revelation was written, but each may also be representative of a particular age in church history. Therefore, in a very marvelous way, the Lord could be taking churches currently existing at that time, and comparing their behavior and their circumstances with certain epochs which were yet to appear in the history of the church. The Lord may be writing the history of the future as well as providing instruction relevant to both the original hearers and all future generations.

The church of **Ephesus** may correspond to the apostolic church, which began with the birth of the Church at Pentecost (33 AD) and ended with the death of the Apostle John (about 100 AD), but also continues to call the Church to rekindle its beginning passion.

The church of **Smyrna** may find its counterpart in the martyr church of the second and third centuries, the greatest period of persecution in all Christianity (100 to 312 AD). But Christians of every age who suffer persecution for their faith can find hope and reassurance in this letter.

The church of **Pergamum** may represent the state church, beginning with Constantine (312 AD) and continuing to the end. Some scholars limit this church period to ending in 606 AD, seeing this period as a time when materialism, self-indulgence and worldliness invaded the Church. Because these characteristics continue to plague the institutional church to this day, others see the representation as continuing until the end.

The church of **Thyatira** has the features of the firmly established church that is not only a church but state, such as the Vatican which is indeed both. It begins with Gregory the Great (590 AD) and continues to the end. Again, some scholars limit this church period to ending in 1540 AD, seeing the developing Protestant Reformation as a shift away from the dominate state-church into a church of the people.

The church in **Sardis** may be a picture of the Reformation church, beginning in the sixteenth century (around 1540 AD) and continuing into the Tribulation to the end. The Reformation Church is identified by some with dead churches, lacking in fervor and spirit that need to wake up.

The church in **Philadelphia** sets forth the characteristics of the missionary church, beginning with the rise of modern missions under William Carey who founded the English Baptist Missionary Society in 1792 AD. Carey also translated all or portions of the Bible into over 29 languages and dialects. The missionary church is seen as continuing until the end, but as in the example of the letter to Philadelphia, its influence may be small compared to other world influences as the end approaches.

The church in **Laodicea** may portray the apostate church of the last days—a church which has become corrupt and rejects fundamental doctrines of the Christian faith. Certain church theologians of the 4th and 5th centuries considered apostasy to be as serious as adultery and murder. In the 20th century, the Roman Catholic Code of Canon Law still imposed the sanction of excommunication for those whose rejection of the faith fitted the technical definition of apostasy. But the absence of civil sanctions and an increasing tolerance of divergent viewpoints have tended increasingly to mitigate the reaction of believers to those who reject Christianity. In other words, beginning in the 20th century, the church has tolerated the rejection of many beliefs previously viewed as fundamental to all Christians, while also allowing previously viewed heretical beliefs to be taught as acceptable Christian teachings. This has led to the secularization of the Church where there is less distinction between Christian doctrinal views and worldly views within the church. This Church continues but no longer lives out its purpose. These churches lack a commitment to the truth.

In summary, what was then and what was to become of the seven churches cited in Revelation, can be viewed as examples of both historic periods of the Church, and characteristics or types that can be found in many churches. The lessons within the letters, proven true in church history, provide examples of both how churches anywhere and at any time can error and/or prosper. The seven churches provide examples of what can go wrong in any church. Any church is capable of losing the love and passion for ministry it may have had at its beginning (Ephesus). Any church can encounter fear and suffering (Smyrna). Any church can be subject to doctrinal compromise (Pergamum). Any church can slide into moral compromise (Thyatira). Any church can over time become spiritually dead (Sardis). Any church can find itself engaged in a struggle to hold fast against great opposition (Philadelphia). And any church can become lukewarm, going through the motions but no longer serving its purpose (Laodicea). The Lord helps us understand both what causes failure and success within the Church. If we will listen and obey the teachings found in these letters we can both avoid mistakes and become the Church the Lord desires we be. Failing to learn the lessons of the letters leads only to repeating the mistakes and our ultimate destruction. *"Blessed is he who reads and those who hear the words of the prophecy, and heed the things which are written in it; for the time is near"* (Revelation 1:3).

PART 3

Introductory Visions

Chapter 1 provided an introduction and a miraculous vision as testimony of the validity of all that would follow and be revealed in the book of Revelation. Chapters 2 and 3 contained seven distinct letters written to seven churches that actually existed at the time of Christ's Revelation to John, and within these letters, we saw revealed a view of the future history of Christ's Church up until His second coming.

Beginning in chapter 4 our view is shifted from earthly to heavenly. We will now also shift our view from what was and was to be in the earthly Church to what is already known in heaven and will happen in the future. The main body of the Book of Revelation is still before us and is seemingly composed of seven series of eschatological visions with seven visions in each series. Chapters 4 and 5 serve as a fitting introduction to this series of apocalyptic scenes. Chapters 4 and 5 provide two visions, one of God (chapter 4) and one of Christ (chapter 5), in all their majesty, splendor, and power. God and Christ are depicted as far removed from the earth and its inhabitants, which during this present evil age are under the domination of Satan and his demonic forces, both supernatural and human. But we are assured that God and Christ are not unaware of our desperate plight, are not without deep concern about our sorrows and tribulations, and are not powerless to rescue us from our enemies and to save us out of this age of evil and wickedness. On the contrary, these two scenes portray them in all of their majestic might as a pledge that very soon they will intervene in the affairs of this world, will defeat and overpower Satan and his followers, will terminate his dominion, and will institute a new age under their own control for the benefit of the faithful.

Vision of Adoration of God in Heaven (4:1-11)

In my research I have found two widely different views regarding the significance of the vision described in chapter 4. Some see this as the point in Revelation when the Church is raptured—taken from earth into heaven—where it will escape the punishment which is described in the following chapters. Others only see John being taken into heaven in order to see, and then witness what he sees so we can learn from it and escape punishment through repentance and adherence to Christ's teachings. Rather than reading from a particular theological view point let us simply listen to what has been written.

Revelation 4:1 states: *"After these things I looked, and behold, a door standing open in heaven, and the first voice which I had heard, like the sound of a trumpet speaking to me, said, "Come up here, and I will show you what must take place after these things.""* The key to interpretation of this verse is how one defines "these things." Those who believe this is a reference to the "rapture" define "these things" as the completed history of the Church, therefore, "after these things" is seen as saying after the history of the church on earth is over because the Church has now been removed into heaven. A more conservative definition simply views "these things" as the future history of the Church on earth which has just been revealed to John, and now John will be shown additional things in heaven. What we can surmise with some certainty is that it is Christ who is speaking to John and who is inviting him into heaven. From Revelation 1:10 we know that the "first voice" was Christ's voice and only Christ can open the door to heaven. Without adding additional meanings it seems clear that verse 1 describes Christ inviting John into heaven to see things which are in heaven and/or will occur in the future.

Revelation 4:2 states: *"Immediately I was in the Spirit; and behold, a throne was standing in heaven, and One sitting on the throne."* This verse reinforces the view that it is John rather than the entire Church being transported to heaven at this point because John refers only to himself. John's reference to being "in the Spirit" is generally interpreted as meaning his spirit rather than his body has been transported to heaven and/or what he is seeing that is in heaven is being revealed through the Spirit of God. The very first thing John sees is a throne with a being sitting on it. Based on the description in the following verse it is generally assumed that the being is God (Father).

Revelation 4:3 states: *"And He who was sitting was like a jasper stone and a sardius in appearance; and there was a rainbow around the throne, like an emerald in appearance."* Revelation 21:11 describes the jasper as "crystal-clear" and a sardius is a red stone like a ruby. Some see the clear jasper representing the purity of God. The color red could represent God's righteousness or fire, symbolic for the Holy Spirit or the wrath of punishment to come. The "rainbow" around the throne can also be translated as a "halo," therefore, this could either represent the holiness and glory of God, or be a reminder of God's promise to Noah not to destroy the world again by flood. We will revisit this image when we discuss verse 5.

Revelation 4:4 states: *"And around the throne were twenty-four thrones; and upon the thrones I saw twenty-four elders sitting, clothed in white garments, and golden crowns on their heads."* These twenty-four thrones and elders are mentioned again in Revelation 4:10, 5:8, 11:16 and 19:4. The elders are not identified anywhere but twelve of them are believed to be Jesus' disciples. Regarding the disciples, in Matthew 19:28, when Jesus was speaking to His disciples He said, "Truly I say to you, that you who have followed Me, in the regeneration when the Son of Man will sit on His glorious throne, you also shall sit upon twelve thrones, judging the twelve tribes of Israel." Revelation 20:4 speaks of an undisclosed number of thrones on which people sit and pass judgment. Some believe the twenty-four elders are a combination of the twelve apostles and the twelve tribes of Israel. Others believe they represent the twenty-four groups or orders within the Levitical priesthood. All we can know for certain, using Jesus' words from Matthew is that they are from those who follow Him.

Revelation 4:5 states: *"And from the throne proceed flashes of lighting and sounds and peals of thunder. And there were seven lamps of fire burning before the throne, which are the seven Spirits of God."* The description of lighting and thunder are similar to other theophanies (appearances of God) such as in Exodus 19:16 and Ezekiel 1:13. Combined with the description given in Revelation 4:3 above with a clear jasper in the center, I am reminded of the similarity of what my late wife was shown in one of her visions. In a vision of heaven Jesus showed her a large white stone throne, on which she describes the One sitting on the throne, saying, *"The center of His Being was clear as crystal, and through Him, I could see the white throne on which He sat. Shooting out were rays of brilliant light, first transparent, then bright white, then blinding white the further it got from His center."*

(Carolyn Rene' Dailey's drawing of God on His throne.)

Regarding the seven lamps of fire burning before the throne, we are told these are the seven Spirits of God. Similar descriptions can be found in Exodus 25:37 and Zechariah 4:2-6. The seven Spirits before the throne of God were already mentioned in Revelation 1:4. Revelation 1:20 informed us that the seven lampstands are the seven churches and from this we derived that the Spirit of God dwells in the Church. Therefore, what we are beholding is the Presence of God and the Spirit of God.

Revelation 4:6a continues, saying, *"and before the throne there was, as it were, a sea of glass like crystal."* What is the sea of glass like crystal that appears "before" the throne of God in heaven? Let us look elsewhere in scripture. Ezekiel 1:22, 26 describes an *"expanse, like the awesome gleam of crystal"* (1:22) and *"above the expanse that was over their heads there was something resembling a throne"* (1:26). Ezekiel 10:1 connects the *"crystal expanse"* with a *"sapphire stone, in appearance resembling a throne."* It would seem that the prophet Ezekiel was seeing the same thing as John only instead of a crystal sea being "before" the throne, Ezekiel looking upward from below, saw the throne "above" the crystal expanse. John's point of view is from *heaven* and Ezekiel's is from *earth*. So what is the crystal sea? Ezekiel saw it between him and the throne and John sees it before or below the throne, therefore it seems to be a barrier or separation between heaven and earth. Ezekiel calls it an "expanse" which might provide us a vital clue. Genesis 1:6-8a states: *"Then God said, 'Let there be an expanse in the midst of the waters, and let it separate the waters from the waters.' And God made the expanse, and separated the waters which were below the expanse from the waters which were above the expanse; and it was so. And God called the expanse heaven."* The crystal sea and the expanse may be the same thing—a barrier God has placed between heaven (dwelling of God), and earth (dwelling of mankind). Perhaps this is something like what mystics call the "veil" that separates the unseen spiritual world from the physical world we live in. The view from above describes the sea as "like glass" which is the appearance of a sea void of waves and turbulence. It could be that in heaven all is calm and full of God's peace. Another clue might be derived from Revelation 15:2, which states: *"And I saw, as it were, a sea of glass mixed with fire, and those who had come off victorious from the beast and from his image and from the number of his name, standing on the sea of glass, holding harps of God."* Those who have escaped the beast through Christ find themselves "on" the sea of glass, perhaps meaning that they have been raised from below to above the sea into heaven.

<u>Revelation 4:6b-8</u> states: *"and in the center around the throne, four living creatures full of eyes in front and behind. And the first creature was like a lion, and the second creature like a calf, and the third creature had a face like that of a man, and the fourth creature was like a flying eagle. And the four living creatures, each one of them having six wings, are full of eyes around and within; and day and night they do not cease to say, "Holy, holy, holy, is the Lord God, the Almighty, who was and who is and who is to come.""* Now we encounter our first great mystery of meaning. What or who are these strange creatures who

stand in the presence of God? They will be mentioned in nine other verses in Revelation, always near His throne and almost always in continuous worship of God (Revelation 5:6, 8:14, 6:1, 6 and 11, 14:3, 15:7 and 19:4). In Revelation they are called "four living creatures." Similar creatures are described in Ezekiel 1:5-12 and 10:1-22 which he calls "four living beings" and "cherubim." The creatures Ezekiel describes each had four faces, resembling the faces of a man, a lion, a bull and an eagle, and four wings. They each were associated with wheels that were full of eyes. Isaiah 6:1-7 also describes beings he calls seraphim, but he doesn't say how many there are. They are with God and worshiping God and have six wings, but with two of their wings they cover their face so we don't know what they look like. The description of the "four living creatures" of Revelation, the cherubim in Ezekiel and the seraphim in Isaiah, although similar, each have distinct differences so we cannot assume they are the same. There has been much speculation regarding the symbolic meaning of these creatures and their various parts. Generally, the "eyes in front and behind" are seen to represent that these creatures see everything, past and future. Some see the four different faces representing leadership; the lion leader of the wild beasts, bull or calf leader of domestic beasts, eagle leader of the birds of the air, and man as leader of all. These four creatures may have some connection with the four signs of the zodiac, which include the Bull, the Lion, the Scorpion (frequently depicted with a manlike face), and the Eagle (a nearby constellation substituted for Aquarius). They could also represent the four powers at the four ends of the earth and be related to the four points of the compass and the four winds. All of this is pure speculation because in reality we simply do not know what they represent. What we do know is that they are consistently portrayed as being near God and continuously praising Him. Their function seems clearly to praise God, perhaps representing all life that has breath praising God as their Creator. They provide us with a good example to follow.

<u>Revelation 4:9-11</u> states: ***"And when the living creatures gave glory and honor and thanks to Him who sits on the throne, to Him who lives forever and ever, the twenty-four elders will fall down before Him who sits on the throne, and will worship Him who lives forever and ever, and will cast their crowns before the throne, saying, "Worthy are***

Thou, our Lord and our God, to receive glory and honor and power; for Thou didst create all things, and because of Thy will they existed, and were created.'" Now the four living creatures praise and honor God, and when they do so, all the elders join in to praise and honor God. The act of falling down before God and casting their crowns before Him is symbolic for both their submission to God and their acknowledgement that all of their rewards (their crowns) belong to God, i.e., they would not have them if it were not for God. This is reinforced by their words, acknowledging that God created all things and that everything exists (including themselves) because it was God's will for them to exist. God deserves praise and honor for He is the source of all that is worthy of praise and honor. Their praise and words are also further assurance that God is in control over all creation, and will soon make His great power evident to all. Perhaps this scene is intended as evidence that God is about to do away with the present creation and create a new and perfect one for all who honor Him.

Vision of Adoration of the Lamb of God (5:1-14)

It is important to understand that the division of the Bible into chapters and verses only came into existence about 500 years ago and there were no such divisions in the original text. While chapters and verses assist us greatly in finding and referencing particular scriptures they are not necessarily divinely inspired and are sometimes arbitrary. With that said, chapters 4 and 5 should probably not have been separated into two separate units. The scene John is witnessing in heaven continues from chapter 4 into chapter 5 in a seamless fashion. What does change is the focus of our attention, which shifts from God on His throne to the Lamb of God who is worthy to open the scroll in God's hand. The emphasis shifts with the scroll from God the Father to God the Son, and likewise, the worship in heaven shifts from God the Father to God the Son, the Lamb of God. With the introduction to the scroll in chapter 5 we begin a transition which is preparing us to hear what has been written by God and will come to pass as the seals on the scroll are opened and the contents of the scroll revealed.

Revelation 5:1 states: *"And I saw in the right hand of Him who sat on the throne a book written inside and on the back, sealed up with seven seals."* Our attention is drawn to a book (scroll) which is held in the hand of God. It is sealed with seven seals and in such a way that one portion of it can be unrolled at a time. As previously stated, seven is often symbolic for perfection and/or completeness. We are told that both sides of the scroll contain writing, both "inside and on the back." This sealed scroll may be referenced three places in the Old Testament. First, there may be a reference to it in Isaiah 29:11 which speaks of a sealed book (scroll) as part of a warning against Jerusalem. The book cannot be read because the people are unworthy to read it. In Ezekiel 2:9-10 we are told of a book (scroll) written on front and back which contains lamentations of mourning and woe. And finally, in Daniel 12:4, Daniel is instructed to seal up words he has been given regarding the end of time. All of these accounts are consistent in that they speak of a sealed book or sealed words that speak of terrible things that will happen at the end of time.

Revelation 5:2 states: *"And I saw a strong angel proclaiming with a loud voice, "Who is worthy to open the book and to break the seals?""* As a prelude to the termination of Satan's reign, it is necessary to find someone who can open the book so as to release the seven plagues it contains, that God's judgment may take place and be delayed no longer.

Revelation 5:3 states: *"And no one in heaven, or on the earth, or under the earth, was able to open the book, or to look into it."* In this verse we are simply being informed that there is no one in heaven or on earth among humans and/or angels who is worthy to open or look into the book. No one in heaven and earth is good enough or worthy to know the secrets of God or to administer over God's punishment of the wicked.

Revelation 5:4-5 states: *"And I began to weep greatly, because no one was found worthy to open the book, or to look into it; and one of the elders said to me, "Stop weeping; behold, the Lion that is from the tribe of Judah, the Root of David, has overcome so as to open the book and its seven seals.""* John weeps because of his disappointment that no one was found worthy to open or look into the book, which would allow evil to continue its reign unpunished and delay the reward of the faithful. But John is reassured by one of the elders on the twenty-four thrones around God. The question asked in verse 5:2 was rhetorical in that the answer was known in heaven even before the question was asked. Only the One who has "overcome" is worthy to open the seals. We are told that this person is the "Lion that is from the tribe of Judah, the Root of David." The titles apply to the Christ and in Revelation 22:16 Jesus Himself states: *"I am the root and offspring of David."* Our attention is now focused with anticipation on the only One who is worthy, our Lord and Savior Jesus the Christ.

Revelation 5:6 states: *"And I saw between the throne (with the four living creatures) and the elders a Lamb standing, as if slain, having seven horns and seven eyes, which are the seven Spirits of God, sent out into all the earth."* We see a shift from one type of animal imagery to another relating to Christ, from the Lion to the Lamb. The Lamb imagery reminds us of the Passover where a lamb is slain for the sake of God's people. We are reminded that Jesus Christ, the Son of God and Lord of Lords (Lion), has willingly sacrificed Himself (Lamb) for our sake, and through His sacrifice has "overcome" sin and death and become "worthy" to open the seals. Regarding the imagery of the seven horns and seven eyes, the horns are symbolic of complete power (the omnipotence of God) and the eyes are symbolic of complete awareness and knowledge (the omniscience of God). In numerous passages in the Old Testament "horns" are portrayed as symbols of power. In Matthew 28:18 Jesus declares, *"All authority has been given to Me in heaven and on earth."* Likewise, as we have discussed regarding the four living creatures, "eyes" are often portrayed as symbols of seeing, which equate both to perceiving and knowing. The imagery is very similar to that found in Zechariah, chapter 4, which speaks of a vision of a lamp stand with seven lamps and seven flames, which are equated with the Spirit of God. Referencing the seven, Zechariah is told *"these are the eyes of the Lord which range to and fro throughout the earth"* (Zechariah 4:10b). In reference to Jesus, Hebrews 4:13 states: "And there is no creature hidden from His sight, but all things are open and laid bare to the eyes of Him with whom we have to do."

Revelation 5:7 states: *"And He came, and He took it out of the right hand of Him who sat on the throne."* Perhaps symbolic, but in the passing of the scroll which will release judgment upon the earth, we see the passing of authority to administer that judgment from God the Father to God the Son. Jesus taught His disciples, saying, *"For not even the Father judges anyone, but He has given all judgment to the Son, in order that all may honor the Son, even as they honor the Father. He who does not honor the Son does not honor the Father who sent Him... For just as the Father has life in Himself, even so He gave to the Son also to have life in Himself; and He gave Him authority to execute judgment, because He is the Son of Man"* (John 5:22-23, 26-27). I believe this verse represents the central and pivotal point in chapters 4 and 5. Prior to this point we see the four living creatures and the twenty-four elders which surround the throne of God worshipping God (Father). After this point we now witness them worshipping the Lamb, our Lord and Savior Jesus Christ (Son).

Revelation 5:8 states: *"And when He had taken the book, the four living creatures and the twenty-four elders fell down before the Lamb, having each one a harp, and golden bowls full of incense, which are the prayers of the saints."* Beginning with verse 8 we see a three-fold acknowledgement and praising of the Lamb which has begun with those closest to the throne of God—the four living creatures and twenty-four elders. In verse 11-12 we will hear all the angels of heaven add to the chorus, and in verse 13, all of creation both in heaven and on earth will add their praise.

Revelation 5:9-10 states: *"And they sang a new song, saying, "Worthy art Thou to take the book, and to break its seals; for Thou wast slain, and didst purchase for God with Thy blood men from every tribe and tongue and people and nation. And Thou hast made them to be a kingdom and priests to our God; and they will reign upon the earth."* By the words contained in their "new" song it is clear that they sing about Christ who has purchased for God through His blood people of all tribes, tongues and nations. Jesus Himself at the Last Supper said to His disciples, *"This is My blood of the covenant, which is poured out for many"* (Mark 14:24). Speaking of Christ, Paul will add clarity to this image in his own words, saying, *"For it was the Father's good pleasure for all the fullness to dwell in Him, and through Him to reconcile all things to Himself, having made peace through the blood of His cross; through Him, I say, whether things on earth or things in heaven"* (Colossians 1:19-20).

Revelation 5:11-12 states: *"And I looked, and I heard the voice of many angels around the throne and the living creatures and the elders; and the number of them was myriads of myriads, and thousands of thousands, saying with a loud voice, "Worthy is the Lamb that was slain to receive power and riches and wisdom and might and honor and glory and blessing."* The acknowledgement of Christ's worthiness and praise for Him continues to radiate out from the throne to now include thousands of thousands of angels in heaven.

Revelation 5:13 states: *"And every created thing which is in heaven and on the earth and under the earth and on the sea, and all things in them, I heard saying, "To Him who sits on the throne, and to the Lamb, be blessing and honor and glory and domination forever and ever."* Ultimately, all of creation joins in and sings praise to the Father and the Lamb. In Isaiah 45:23 God declares through the prophet Isaiah, saying, *"I have sworn by Myself, the word has gone forth from My mouth in righteousness and will not turn back, that to Me every knee will bow, every tongue will swear allegiance."* And Paul, inspired by the Holy Spirit, will declare to us, saying, *"Therefore also God highly exalted Him, and bestowed on Him the name which is above every name, that at the name of Jesus every knee should bow, of those who are in heaven, and on earth, and under the earth, and that every tongue should confess that Jesus Christ is Lord, to the glory of God the Father"* (Philippians 2:9-11).

Revelation 5:14 states: *"And the four living creatures kept saying, "Amen." And the elders fell down and worshiped."* As chapter 4 began with praise for God the Father, chapter 5 ends with praise for both Father and Son. The four living creatures closest to the throne of God keep saying "Amen" which adds certainty to the message. And what is the message of chapters 4 and 5? Clearly, God the Father and His Son, Jesus Christ, are to be at the center of our worship, for they alone are worthy of our worship. And that authority to administer judgment has been given to Jesus, the Lamb of God, for the Father has given Him this authority and only Jesus is worthy to administer God's justice—a justice that will punish the wicked and reward the righteous.

PART 4

The Seven Seals

Chapter 6 marks the beginning of judgments being released upon the earth, which is generally viewed as the "Great Tribulation." Some scholars believe it also marks the beginning of the "Day of the Lord" when God punishes the world for its wickedness. And some believe it is the beginning of the "Day of Christ" when Christians are "caught up" into heaven to be with the Lord (also called the Rapture). It is important to note that not all who believe in the Rapture agree on its timing. Some believe Christians will be "caught up" prior to the Tribulation and will avoid all suffering. Others believe it will happen at some midway point and that we will have to endure some of the dreadful things which will come upon the earth. And still others see it happening at the end when Christ returns in the clouds with glory immediately before the final punishments are poured out upon the world. Likewise, while almost everyone believes that the "Great Tribulation," the "Day of the Lord," and the "Day of Christ" are all integrally linked, not all believe they are all the same event. Before we can move forward into chapters 6 through 18, which depict great punishments being released upon the earth, we must first sort out the time line of the Tribulation, Day of the Lord, and Day of Christ.

In the letter to the church of Philadelphia in Revelation 3:10 Jesus says: *"**Because you have kept the word of My perseverance, I also will keep you from the hour of testing, that hour which is about to come upon the whole world, to test those who dwell upon the earth.**"* This would indicate that at least some Christians will be taken home prior to the Tribulation or "hour of testing." But it is revealed to us in 1 Peter 4:12 that some will suffer in the "testing." Peter says: *"**Behold, do not be surprised at the fiery ordeal among you, which comes upon you for your testing, as though some strange thing were happening to you; but to the degree that you share the sufferings of Christ, keep on rejoicing;**"*

so that also at the revelation of His glory, you may rejoice with exultation." Peter equates the "testing" as sharing in the "sufferings of Christ." Peter's words could also be seen to suggest that this time of testing will lead up to "the revelation of His glory," which could be seen as His second coming in glory. While this may be completely true at the end, I believe each of us, regardless of the time in which we live, will be tested in our faith and required to demonstrate that we belong to Christ. Our time on earth is our "time of testing" and preparation for the eternity we will live with Christ. Scripture consistently and clearly indicates throughout the Bible that God will always be with us and will at some point deliver us. But Scripture does not give us a clear and certain point in which our deliverance will be accomplished other than the moment of deliverance we all share upon the Cross with Jesus. There is some evidence to suggest that God will deliver us at different times according to His will. What is most important of all is the assurance that <u>God will deliver us</u>.

Regarding the Tribulation period, there is substantial scriptural evidence that this is the period described in chapter 6, immediately "preceding" the "Day of the Lord." The parallel between the breaking of the first six seals and the "Apocalyptic Discourses" found in Matthew 24, Mark 13 and Luke 17 and 21 are very similar. Matthew 24 provides the clearest correlation. The pivotal event of the <u>sixth seal</u> seems to separate the "Great Tribulation" from the "Day of the Lord." In the Old Testament the "Day of the Lord" is always seen as a great and terrible day of punishment. Isaiah 13: 6 and 9 read as follows: *"Wail, for the day of the Lord is near! It will come as destruction from the Almighty...Behold the day of the Lord is coming, cruel, with fury and burning anger, to make the land a desolation; and He will exterminate its sinners from it."* In the New Testament we hear a similar description found in 2 Peter 3:10, saying, *"But the day of the Lord will come like a thief, in which the heavens will pass away with a roar and the elements will be destroyed with intense heat, and the earth and its works will be burned up."* Clearly, the "Day of the Lord" is not simply a time of "testing" but a time of utter "destruction." Joel 2:31 gives us insight into the division point between the "Tribulation" period and the "Day of the Lord," saying, *"The sun will be turned into darkness, and the moon into blood, <u>before</u> the great and awesome day of the Lord* *comes."* Matthew 24:29-30 gives us our most definitive sign regarding the separation between "Tribulation" and the "Day of the Lord." Jesus says: ***"But immediately <u>after the tribulation</u> of those days the sun will be darkened, and the moon will not give its light, and the stars will fall from the sky, and the powers of the heavens will be shaken, and then the sign of the Son of Man will appear in the sky, and then all the tribes of the earth will mourn, and they will see the Son of Man coming on the clouds of the sky with power and glory."*** The people of the earth mourn because the glory of Christ is now revealed and the time of punishment has arrived. During the Tribulation Christians will suffer at the hands of non-believers, but afterward Christ will be revealed to the whole world, and then the believers will be "gathered up" and the non-believers punished.

I have already said that many Christians believe that God will "Rapture" them off the earth prior to any of the events listed in the book of Revelation. Others believe that they will have to enter this time of trial and testing but will ultimately be delivered by God. Psalm 91 testifies that God will protect His children from harm <u>during</u> a time of punishment of the wicked. This may be describing the "Day of the Lord" in Revelation. Psalm 91:1, 5-8 reads: ***"He who dwells in the shelter of the Most High will abide in the shadow of the Almighty… You will not be afraid of the terror by night, or of the arrow that flies by day; of the pestilence that stalks in darkness, or of the destruction that lays waste at noon. A thousand may fall at your side, and ten thousand at your right hand; but it shall not approach you. You will only look on with your eyes, and see the recompense of the wicked."*** This description does not sound like a view from heaven but from someone on earth witnessing the destruction up close. We must remember that God is consistent throughout the Bible in both word and action. In the story of the destruction of Sodom and Gomorrah, Lot cannot reach the safety of the mountains so God grants him safety in the small town of Zoar located within the valley of Sodom and Gomorrah. God protects him where he "is" even though it is within the valley of destruction (Genesis 19). Likewise, when God rained down the ten plagues upon Egypt to force Pharaoh to release God's people, the first three plagues were suffered by all, both Egyptians and Hebrews. But beginning with the fourth plague God made a distinction and protected

God's people from the plagues which from that point on would only afflict the Egyptians (Exodus 9:4). Therefore, through the lens of the Old Testament we can see that God sometimes allows His own children to suffer in the process of separating what is His from what is wicked. But at some point God always protects His own and punishes the wicked. With all of this in mind let us now enter the sixth chapter of the book of Revelation and discover the time of testing we may have to suffer through before God delivers us or protects us from the wrath He will pour out upon the wicked.

First Seal: The White Horse and Rider (6:1-2)

Revelation 6:1, states: *"And I saw when the Lamb broke one of the seven seals, and I heard one of the four living creatures saying as with a voice of thunder, "Come!""* It may be important to point out that many early manuscripts read, *"Come and see!"* rather than just *"Come!"* This applies also to Revelation 6:3, 5 and 7. The distinction in meaning would suggest that rather than the plague being called forward to occur, John is being called forward to see what is going to happen in the future. It is also important to note the similar pattern in the breaking of the first four seals, each having a different living creature declaring, *"Come!"* or *"Come and see!"* This may distinguish the first four seals and plagues as a set, and indeed each of the first four bring forth something destructive intended to hurt and perhaps also "test" the people of the earth, separating those who believe from those who do not believe in Jesus as their Lord.

Revelation 6:2, states: *"And I looked, and behold, a white horse, and he who sat on it had a bow; and a crown was given to him; and he went out conquering, and to conquer."* When Jesus' disciples asked Him, *"What will be the sign of your coming, and of the end of the age?"* (Matthew 24:3), Jesus answered them with a series of events or signs that would come. These signs have a strong correlation with the events described in the breaking of the seals in Revelation 6. The first sign Jesus provides His disciples is a warning, saying, *"See to it that no one misleads you. For many will come in My name, saying, 'I am the Christ,' and will mislead many"* (Matthew 24:4-5). Satan does not create but often attempts to duplicate God in order to confuse and mislead God's people. In the case of the Exodus from Egypt, remember that Pharaoh's magicians were able to duplicate many of the early signs which came from God in order to discredit God. In Revelation 19:11 we will hear that Christ will return on a "white horse." The rider of the white horse in 6:2 is believed to represent the "antichrist," who comes pretending to be Christ in order to deceive many and lead them into destruction. The antichrist comes "conquering, and to conquer" but he cannot prevail as "conqueror" because he is not the Christ, who is Lord of Lords and King of Kings. Therefore, the first seal and the first plague is not a physical plague which destroys the body but a spiritual plague that destroys souls. This influence may not come through a single "man" but as a "spiritual movement."

It is important to note that the first horseman of the apocalypse, which is widely believed to be the antichrist, may not be a "future" event but may have already begun. We know from Scripture that John believed the "spirit of the antichrist" to already be present in the world. John warned his contemporaries, saying, **"Children, it is the last hour; and just as you heard that antichrist is coming, even now many antichrists have arisen; from this we know that it is the last hour"** (1 John 2:18). John clarifies that the antichrist is recognized by its opposition to Jesus, saying, **"and every spirit that does not confess Jesus is not from God; and this is the spirit of the antichrist, of which you have heard that it is coming, and now it is already in the world"** (1 John 4:3). And just as Jesus had warned of deceivers who would come, John verifies, saying, **"For many deceivers have gone out into the world, those who do not acknowledge Jesus Christ as coming in the flesh. This is the deceiver and the antichrist"** (2 John 1:7). While it seems clear that the "spirit" of antichrist has been present from the time John lived, this does not mean the first horseman has been riding all this time. John sees the release of the horseman as a future event, beyond his own time. The breaking of the first seal must "release" a more powerful presence or personification of the antichrist, a deceptive force which will deceive many people over a more compressed time frame. Paul speaks of a coming of the "man of lawlessness" who is the "son of destruction" and is in Paul's time "restrained." In 2 Thessalonians 2:1-10, Paul writes: **"Now we request you, brethren, with regard to the coming of our Lord Jesus Christ, and our gathering together to Him, that you** *may not be quickly shaken from your composure or be disturbed either by a spirit or a message or a letter as if from us, to the effect that the day of the Lord has come. Let no one in any way deceive you, for it will not come unless the apostasy comes first, and the man of lawlessness is revealed, the son of destruction, who opposes and exalts himself above every so-called god or object of worship, so that he takes his seat in the temple of God, displaying himself as being God. Do you not remember that while I was still with you, I was telling you these things? And you know what restrains him now, so that in his time he may be revealed. For the mystery of lawlessness is already at work; only he who now restrains will do so until he is taken out of the way. And then that lawless one will be revealed whom the Lord will slay with the breath of His mouth and bring to an end by the appearance of His coming; that is, the one whose coming is in accord with the activity of Satan, with all power and signs and false wonders, and with all the deception of wickedness for those who perish, because they did not receive the love of the truth so as to be saved."* Does the appearance or coming of the "man of lawlessness" and "son of destruction" coincide with the first horseman of the apocalypse? One could argue that we live in such a time when the "spirit of the antichrist" is manifesting itself in a multitude of ways and is wreaking havoc, causing many to fall away from the faith. Most Christians can clearly see the spirit of the one who opposes Christ is present in the world. Does that mean the lawless one has appeared? Does the antichrist have to be identified as a "specific" person for his presence not to be recognized? Is lawlessness and rebellion against God not already present as our secular society (mankind) redefines the rules regarding what is right or wrong, rather than depending on God's Word for truth? Does the first horseman already ride?

Second Seal: The Red Horse and Rider (6:3-4)

Revelation 6:3-4, states: *"And when He broke the second seal, I heard the second living creature saying, "Come!" And another, a red horse, went out; and to him who sat on it, it was granted to take peace from the earth, and that men should slay one another; and a great sword was given to him."* The second sign given in Matthew 24 involves war.

Jesus says in Matthew 24:6-7a: *"And you will be hearing of wars and rumors of wars; see that you are not frightened, for those things must take place first, but that is not yet the end. For nation will rise against nation, and kingdom against kingdom..."* What I believe Jesus is saying is that His disciples should not be afraid when they hear of wars and/or wars come because this is not the sign. The sign will be when war breaks out between "nations and kingdoms," which many interpret to mean "world wars" such as those we experienced in the Twentieth Century. More people died in these wars than all the wars which came before. And regarding God's chosen people, the Jews, within this time we witnessed the Holocaust, an attempt to exterminate the Jewish people. But this correlation is reinforced by the fact that the events of WW-1 and WW-2 led to the restoration of Israel as a nation, which is also a "sign" to proceed the return of Christ. Wars have always been with us, but beginning with WW-1 and following, the scale and scope of war, and its resulting death and destruction is unprecedented in all of human history. And as a direct result of these world wars we saw the rebirth of the Jewish nation. These events are linked.

Third Seal: The Black Horse and Rider (6:5-6)

Revelation 6:5-6, states: *"And when He broke the third seal, I heard the third living creature saying, "Come!" And I looked, and behold, a black horse; and he who sat on it had a pair of scales in his hand. And I heard as it were a voice in the center of the four living creatures saying, "A quart of wheat for a denarius, and three quarts of barley for a denarius; and do not harm the oil and the wine.""* Again, going back to Matthew 24, the next words Jesus spoke to His disciples were, *"and in various places there will be famines..."* (Matthew 24:7b). The quote contained in verse 6 above provides evidence that the third plague will be famine. A denarius was a small silver coin which was equivalent to the ordinary wage for a day's labor (Matthew 20:2). The wage for a day's labor would provide enough for a man to feed his entire family. A denarius as the price for a quart of wheat or three quarts of barley would be 8 to 16 times the normal price. These are famine prices and the scale held by the rider perhaps an indication that grain was so scarce and dear that it had to be weighed very carefully. Regarding the scales, the prophet Ezekiel speaks of hard times when food is so scarce it will be measured, saying, *"And your food which you eat shall be twenty shekels a day by weight; you shall eat it from time to time. And the water you drink will be the sixth part of a hin by measure; you shall drink it from time to time... Moreover, He said to me, "Son of man, behold, I am going to break the staff of bread in Jerusalem, and they will eat bread by weight and with anxiety, and drink water by measure and in horror"* (Ezekiel 4:10, 11 & 16). Regarding the reference to not harming the oil and the wine, these are items only the wealthy could afford. The implication may be that the rich and the wealthy will continue to have plenty but the poor will suffer. The prophet Amos speaks of a time when the rich will cheat the poor, saying, *"When will the new moon be over, so that we may sell grain, and the Sabbath, that we may open the wheat market, to make the bushel smaller and the shekel bigger, and to cheat with dishonest scales, so as to buy the helpless for money and the needy for a pair of sandals, and that we may sell the refuse of the wheat?"* (Amos 8:5-6). It could be surmised that during the tribulation period the poor in poor nations will suffer the greatest due to famine, while the rich in rich nations will not suffer at all. Billy Graham in his book, "Storm Warning" states that there is more famine in the world today than ever before, but if the money we currently spend on weapons was used to feed the hungry, all would have plenty to eat. When I hear Amos' words, crying out: *"When will the new moon be over, so that we may sell grain, and the Sabbath, that we may open the wheat market..."* I am reminded of the old "Texas Blue Law" that prohibited commerce on Sundays. It was repealed that commerce may take place on the Lord's Day. Has the time Amos spoke of arrived? Do we live in a time when the rich are becoming richer, and the poor becoming poorer?

Fourth Seal: The Pale Horse and Rider (6:7-8)

Revelation 6:7-8, states: *"And when He broke the fourth seal, I heard the voice of the fourth living creature saying, "Come!" And I looked, and behold, an ashen horse; and he who sat on it had the name Death; and Hades was following with him. And authority was given to them over a fourth of the earth, to kill with sword and with famine and with pestilence and by the wild beasts of the earth."* The color of the horse translated here as "ashen" which actually means sickly pale or the greenish color of a bloodless corpse. Also important in the imagery is the fact that the riders name is "Death" and that "Hades" follows closely behind. Revelation 20:14, states: *"And death and Hades were thrown into the lake of fire. This is the second death, the lake of fire."* We are told that authority was given to them, both Death and Hades to kill a fourth of those living on the earth. The inclusion of Hades may imply that this will be both a physical and spiritual death event in that those who die will die separated from Christ. We already know that war and famine have already come preceding the fourth plague. Death is the anticipated result of war and famine, but the implication is that even more will be involved. People will die from war, famine and "pestilence" which can include "plague." There are two modern worldwide pandemics we should reflect upon. The first being the influenza pandemic which occurred at the close of WW-1, killing over 50 million people. And the second being the COVID-19 pandemic which began in late 2019, and at the time of this writing continues having already killed about 4 million people worldwide.

Also, returning again to Matthew 24, we hear Jesus say: *"And at that time many will fall away and will deliver up one another and hate one another. And many false prophets will arise, and will mislead many. And because lawlessness is increased, most people's love will grow cold"* (Matthew 24:10-12). This sounds like a time of deception and death, both physical and spiritual. Within our own society and around the world we have seen a sharp increase in lawlessness and people acting like wild beasts without conscience as they abuse and prey on one another. In the current pandemic, the fighting over wearing facemasks or being vaccinated could be a perfect example of this coming lawlessness. Are we not seeing a continuing breakdown of moral values leading to an increase in pain and suffering? While physical death of a fourth of the earth may not be apparent, spiritual death seems wide spread and increasing within the world we live.

The four judgments revealed in the breaking of the first four seals are not something new which has never been revealed before. God has previously spoken of these things. One of the clearest accounts, which is consistent both with Matthew 24 and Revelations 6 is found in Ezekiel

14:21, which says, *"For thus says the Lord God, "How much more when I send My four severe judgments against Jerusalem: sword, famine, wild beasts, and plague to cut off man and beast from it!""* It is important to note that Jerusalem was the center of the Jewish faith and the location of God's temple and throne. To be cut off from Jerusalem would equate to being cut off from God. Therefore, beginning with the first seal marking the coming of the antichrist or antichrists spiritual movement, and proceeding to the fourth seal when Death and Hades work together, this will be a period of time that will result in death to many peoples' faith in God. It will be a time of great testing and persecution for Christians. Do we live in that time today?

<u>Fifth Seal</u>: Lament of the Martyrs (6:9-11)

<u>Revelation 6:9-11</u>, states: *"And when He broke the fifth seal, I saw underneath the altar the souls of those who had been slain because of the word of God, and because of the testimony which they had maintained; and they cried out with a loud voice, saying, "How long, O Lord, holy and true, wilt Thou refrain from judging and avenging our blood on those who dwell on the earth?" And there was given to each of them a white robe; and they were told that they should rest for a little while longer, until the number of their fellow servants and their brethren who were to be killed even as they had been, should be completed also."* Returning again to Matthew 24 we hear Jesus tell His disciples: *"Then they will deliver you to tribulation, and will kill you, and you will be hated by all nations on account of My name"* (Matthew 24:9). The breaking of the fifth seal clearly informs us that Christians will be alive and many will be put to death during the Tribulation period. We should also understand that death may not simply come through execution by non-believers because we are Christian. Rather, because we are called to be a living sacrifice (Romans 12:11), we will often put ourselves in harm's way out of love for Christ. For example: a missionary may travel to an unsafe and dangerous place because of their love for Christ. Doctors may expose themselves to deadly disease in order to bring healing to the sick. And in a multitude of other ways, we who trust in the Lord will take risks and be willing to sacrifice ourselves for the sake of others. Relative to

Revelation 6, Paul's words in Romans 8 take on new meaning, when he says, **"Who shall separate us from the love of Christ? Shall tribulation, or distress, or persecution, or famine, or nakedness, or peril, or sword? Just as it is written, "For Thy sake we are being put to death all day long; we were considered as sheep to be slaughtered." But in all these things we overwhelmingly conquer through Him who loved us"** (Romans 8:35-37). The fifth seal calls for patience, to allow time for all who will receive our Lord Jesus Christ to be saved and have the opportunity to live or sacrifice their lives for Him who sacrificed Himself that they might gain eternal life.

Depending on one's own personal interpretation one could say that none or all of the signs depicted in the first four seals has already come about. While a particular individual has not been identified as the Antichrist, the spirit of the antichrist is present in the world and we have seen many pretenders come forward claiming to be Christ. Two world wars have killed tens of millions. Famine, both as a result of war and climate change has spread throughout the world, but amazingly has spared the wealthiest of nations. Two world-wide pandemics have claimed millions more. Christians and Christianity have come under attack, and persecution in many places on the earth seems to be increasing. We see some of this manifesting itself in Islamic fundamentalists who wage a war of terrorism against both Christians and Jews. What is clear is that we have not seen the final sign revealed in the sixth seal. Therefore, if we have entered the Tribulation period we have not reached the end, which means we can expect things to get worse before the Lord intercedes for the sake of the elect. Let us now examine the final sign before the great and terrible Day of the Lord arrives.

Sixth Seal: Cosmic Woes (6:12-17)

Revelation 6:12-14, states: *"And I looked when He broke the sixth seal, and there was a great earthquake; and the sun became black as sackcloth made of hair, and the whole moon became like blood; and the stars of the sky fell to the earth, as a fig tree casts its unripe figs when shaken by a great wind. And the sky was split apart like a scroll when it is rolled up; and every mountain and island were moved out of their places."* This will truly be a cosmic event that will shake heaven and earth. It is hard to image destruction so massive and wide spread that "every island and mountain" will be "moved out of their places." In Matthew 24:29 Jesus says, *"But immediately after the tribulation of those days the sun will be darkened, and the moon will not give its light, and the stars will fall from the sky, and the powers of the heavens will be shaken."* From Jesus' words in Matthew we know that this sign comes after, or at the end of the Great Tribulation. From Joel 2:31 we learned that it precedes the coming of the "great and awesome day of the Lord." Therefore, we can see this sign as a time of transition, and based on what is revealed in verses 15 through 17 which follow, it will also be a sign of recognition. In other words, when this sign is revealed many will recognize their error in denying or rejecting Christ, and that punishment is at hand. God's judgment is about to be released on the world and the wicked are about to receive their deserved punishment. But even now, mercy accompanies judgment, for punishment will come in a series of escalating events, perhaps leaving room and time for repentance.

Revelation 6:15-17, states: *"And the kings of the earth and the great men and the commanders and the rich and the strong and every slave and free man, hid themselves in the caves and among the rocks of the mountains; and they said to the mountains, "Fall on us and hide us from the presence of Him who sits on the throne, and from the wrath of the Lamb; for the great day of their wrath has come; and who is able to stand?""* The greatest and most powerful of the earth now hide in caves and are filled with terror because they know the time has come to face the consequences of their choice of rejecting Christ. They now realize and are faced with the fact that all that God has revealed through His Word is true. They can no longer deny His name or His truth. There is no place to hide from the One who sees all and has authority over all. They are doomed and now await the execution of their fate. Why do they not repent?

First Interlude (7:1-17)

Chapter 7 provides a brief interlude between the sixth and seventh seals, and mentions two distinct groups that will be saved. The first group are descendants of Israel, and the pause in the destruction is to provide opportunity for them to be marked as servants of God. This process of marking before the release of judgment is very similar to that described in Ezekiel 9. The second group is a great multitude that have come out of the Great Tribulation because they have washed their robes and made them white in the blood of the Lamb. We could perhaps say that they have "marked" themselves with the blood of the Lamb, and by doing so, have gained salvation. Many believe those in the second group have sealed themselves through their own blood, meaning they have died during the Great Tribulation for the Lord's sake, died because of their belief in Jesus Christ. Because this second group is designated as having come out of every nation, tribe and tongue, it is generally distinguished as gentiles. Thus, the first group is Jews, marked by God as His servants, and the second group gentiles, who have marked themselves as servants of God through the blood of the Lamb, our Lord Jesus Christ. We should remember that the blood of lambs was used to mark the doors of the homes of God's people to protect them when God poured out judgment upon the first born of Egypt.

Sealing of the Martyrs (7:1-8)

Revelation 7:1-3, states: *"After this I saw four angels standing at the four corners of the earth, holding back the four winds of the earth, so that no wind should blow on the earth or on the sea or on any tree. And I saw another angel ascending from the rising of the sun, having the seal of the living God; and he cried out with a loud voice to the four angels to whom it was granted to harm the earth and the sea, saying, "Do not harm the earth or the sea or the trees, until we have sealed the bond-servants of our God on their foreheads."* In the breaking of the first six seals we have seen a rapidly escalating physical and spiritual destruction, but between the sixth and seventh seals we see a pause for the marking and/or revealing of those marked by God for salvation. In Revelation 7:1 we have four angels at the four corners of the earth holding back destruction. The implication is not that the earth is square with corners but corresponds to the four points of the compass. The destruction will be complete and extend to all of the earth. The fifth angel is ascending (coming up) from the rising of the sun (coming at the beginning of a new day). This angel brings a message to the other four that they are to delay destruction until God's people are marked. The angel uses the plural "we" regarding those who will do the sealing. It is not clear if the four angels are to participate in the sealing or the ascending angel is not alone and has others to help. In any case, what is important is that the servants of God will be sealed or marked. The reason they are marked is not given, but it can be presumed that they are being distinguished so that they will be excluded from the wrath of God which will punish and bring destruction.

Further evidence that the seal or mark is to exclude God's servants from harm can be found in Ezekiel 9:1-6, which is as follows: *"Then He cried out in my hearing with a loud voice saying, "Draw near, O executioners of the city, each with his destroying weapon in his hand." And behold, six men came from the direction of the upper gate which faces north, each with his shattering weapon in his hand; and among them was a certain man clothed in linen with a writing case at his loins. And they went in and stood beside the bronze altar. Then the glory of the God of Israel went up from the cherub on which it had been, to the threshold of the temple. And He called to the man clothed in linen at whose loins was the writing case. And the Lord said to him, "Go through the midst of the city, even through the midst of Jerusalem, and put a mark on the foreheads of the men who sigh and groan over all the abominations which are being committed in its midst." But to the others He said in my hearing, "Go through the city after him and strike; do not let your eye have pity, and do not spare. Utterly slay old men, young men, maidens, little children, and women, but do not touch any man on whom is the mark; and you shall start from My sanctuary." So they started with the elders who were before the temple."* In Ezekiel we have six destroyers and a seventh man in linen who marks God's people who *"sigh and groan over all the abominations."* Ezekiel's vision teaches us that there will be no escape for the wicked, not even for women and children. Only those who are marked will be spared. Evidently, the same will be true when God pours out final punishment and judgment on the earth.

Revelation 7:4-8, states: *"And I heard the number of those who were sealed, one hundred and forty-four thousand sealed from every tribe of the sons of Israel: from the tribe of Judah, twelve thousand were sealed, from the bribe of Reuben twelve thousand, from the tribe of Gad twelve thousand, from the tribe of Asher twelve thousand, from the tribe of Naphtali twelve thousand, from the tribe of Manasseh twelve thousand, from the tribe of Simeon twelve thousand, from the tribe of Levi twelve thousand, from the tribe of Issachar twelve thousand, from the tribe of Zebulun twelve thousand, from the tribe of Joseph twelve thousand, from the tribe of Benjamin, twelve thousand were sealed."* Clearly those to be sealed and spared are Jews, Israelites, and descendants of the sons of Israel. We are told the number is 144,000 comprised of 12,000 from each tribe. This does not mean that only 144,000 will be sealed and saved. The total of 144,000 is derived from the formula of (12 x 12 x 1,000). This formula and number is often seen as "all inclusive" or as "representative" of all who will be saved. God may be saying that He will save all of the devote Jews still alive at the end, or the number may only represent the total who will be saved. Because I believe God is always consistent in His teachings, I believe not all Jews will be sealed as in the example found in Ezekiel's vision and many other examples in Scripture. The description could even be literal in that the 144,000 represent the final remnant that God will save as He has always promised to preserve a "remnant" of His chosen people. We should not however confuse the sealing of the 144,000 with the salvation of the gentiles. Clearly, in Revelation 7 God is making a clear distinction between two different groups who will be saved from God's wrath and punishment. The Jews are listed first and now we will examine the second group.

Glorified Multitude in Heaven (7:9-17)

Revelation 7:9, states: *"After these things I looked, and behold, a great multitude, which no one could count, from every nation and all tribes and peoples and tongues, standing before the throne and before the Lamb, clothed in white robes, and palm branches were in their hands."* This description makes it clear that this group is not limited to any national, cultural or ethnic group, but is comprised of people from all the earth. We are told that this multitude is so large no one could count them, which would suggest there will be many more than the 144,000 counted out of the Israelites. This group wears white robes, which we were told in Revelation 6:11 were given to the martyrs when they were told to wait until the number who would die for Christ was complete. These people are no longer under the throne so perhaps we can surmise the number of martyrs is now complete. They hold palm branches in their hands, which according to Leviticus 23:40 are held and waved with joy on the first Day of Atonement—the celebration of the sacrifice for sins and the reconciliation between God and man. Therefore, all elements of the description point to the multitudes being Christians who have lived and/or died for Christ. Looking back at Revelation 6:11, the assumption is that they have died for Christ rather than having been raptured (taken up) by Christ. But it is possible that the multitude in white robes comprise all Christians, both those who had died and those still alive at the end of the Tribulation period of testing. If the description of protection in the midst of destruction provided in Psalm 91 is in reference to Jews alone, then it could be true that God has removed Christians from the earth. If the Psalm 91 description pertains to all who find refuge in Christ, Jew and Christian alike, then it is possible that Christians, sealed by the blood of Christ, may still be upon the earth, but will be protected from the destruction which is about to take place.

Revelation 7:10-12, states: *"and they cry out with a loud voice, saying "Salvation to our God who sits on the throne, and to the Lamb." And all the angels were standing around the throne and around the elders and the four living creatures; and they fell on their faces before the throne and worshiped God, saying, "Amen, blessing and glory and wisdom and thanksgiving and honor and power and might, be to our God forever and ever. Amen."* Those who have been saved now cry out salvation to God and to the Lamb. This may seem odd because we see God as the *source* of our salvation rather than the *recipient*. This scene is similar to that of Revelation 4:10 when the twenty-four elders cast their crowns before God. God's grace provided them the crowns, and God does not need their crowns, yet they cast them before God. The act of giving to God what God has given us is an act of worship and acknowledgment that God is the source of the gifts we have received. The multitude, along with the twenty-four elders, the angels and the four living creatures, now praise and honor God. We believe God is worthy of blessing and glory and wisdom and thanksgiving and honor and power and might forever. And we add salvation to our list. He is the source of salvation!

Revelation 7:13-14, states: *"And one of the elders answered, saying to me, "These who are clothed in the white robes, who are they, and from where have they come?" And I said to him, "My lord, you know." And he said to me, "These are the ones who come out of the great tribulation, and they have washed their robes and made them white in the blood of the Lamb."* Here we see put to rest any remaining question regarding who the multitude are who stand before the throne in white robes. The question is raised to John, which he cannot answer to indicate he is not the source of this revelation. Then the elder provides the answer, advising that these people come out of the great tribulation and have made their robes white by the blood of Christ. Therefore, most Bible scholars see them as the last of the martyrs whose numbers were not yet complete in Revelation 6:11. They have received salvation through the blood of Christ—by His merits and His perfection and His sacrifice, they have become clean and worthy to stand before the throne of God. Many would say they have shared in a baptism of blood, following Christ as the first martyr, being willing to shed their own blood as a testimony of their faith in Christ. Perhaps there will be a distinction for those who die for Christ in that they will be given the honor to serve and worship immediately before the throne of God and Christ. But Scripture teaches us that not only those who die for Christ will join with Him in heaven but also those who live for Christ—are a living sacrifice. Paul urges us to be such in Romans 12:1, saying, *"I urge you therefore, brethren, by the mercies of God, to present your bodies a living and holy sacrifice, acceptable to God, which is your spiritual service of worship."* We are each called to die to sin and be reborn through the blood of Christ. Through baptism and the profession of our faith in Jesus Christ we are washed clean of our sin by the blood of Christ—our robes are made white. Personally, I must question if truly living our lives for Christ is not the same as giving our lives for Christ. Whether in living or dying, let us each be willing to sacrifice our lives for Christ—live our lives for Christ.

Revelation 7:15, states: *"For this reason, they are before the throne of God; and they serve Him day and night in His temple; and He who sits on the throne shall spread His tabernacle over them."* This verse provides the basis for those who believe God distinguishes martyrs with the special honor of serving before His throne. The act of *"spreading His tabernacle over them"* could be seen as making them priests in His temple because only priests were allowed to enter the temple. All others had to stand outside in the courtyard of the temple and worship. On the other hand, Revelation 21:22 informs us that in the New Jerusalem there is no temple *"for the Lord God, the Almighty and the Lamb, are its temple."* Likewise, in 1 Peter 2:9-10 we are told: *"But you are a chosen race, a royal priesthood, a holy nation, a people for God's own possession, that you may proclaim the excellencies of Him who has called you out of darkness into His marvelous light; for you once were not a people, but now you are the people of God; you had not received mercy, but now you have received mercy."* Perhaps God's spreading *"His tabernacle over them"* means that God extends His house to include those who <u>live</u> and <u>die</u> for Him.

<u>Revelation 7:16-17</u>, states: *"They shall hunger no more, neither thirst anymore; neither shall the sun beat down on them, nor any heat; for the Lamb in the center of the throne shall be their shepherd, and shall guide them to springs of the water of life; and God shall wipe every tear from their eyes."* These final verses are likely provided as an assurance that persecution will come to an end. During times of persecution, Christians were and are deprived of those things that sustain physical life such as food and drink. They are also forced to suffer the "heat" of persecution. God is promising that someday the Lamb will be their shepherd and lead them to springs of the water of life. Likewise, someday God will wipe every tear from their eyes for they will no longer suffer under persecution or have any reason to cry.

PART 5

The Seventh Seal and the Seven Trumpets

In Part 4 we covered the breaking of the first six seals (Chapter 6) and the interlude between the sixth and seventh seal (Chapter 7). You will note that the plagues associated with the first four seals were primarily earthly, and although caused by the influence of Satan through the "spirit of the antichrist," they are inflicted by people following his influence. During this time of tribulation many will not recognize or acknowledge that Satan is the root cause. War, famine and death have always been a part of this world, and therefore do not require belief in invisible forces of good and evil, of God and Satan. Part 5 will consist of chapters 8 through 11, which cover the breaking of the seventh seal, and the seven trumpets that follow. The breaking of the seventh seal seems to be in stark contrast with that of the sixth, causing not massive destruction or cosmic disturbances, but bringing only silence in heaven. The breaking of the seventh seal is grouped with the seven trumpets because they seem integrally connected, and many scholars see the seven trumpets as part of the seventh seal.

The wrath being poured out upon the earth will now shift from being man-made to cosmic and supernatural in nature. The first four trumpets will cause destruction to rain down upon the earth from the heavens destroying a third of the plants, a third of the sea and all that lives in it, poisoning a third of the waters that provide us drink, and darkening a third of the sun, moon and stars. The darkening of the sun, moon and stars may create some confusion because with the previous sixth seal the sun was already darkened, the moon turned to blood and the stars had fallen from the sky. We will address this seeming contradiction later. The first four trumpets are horrific, but those that follow are much worst and are given more extensive descriptions. The fifth trumpet unleashes the horror of darkness and affliction from the bottomless pit. Likewise, the sixth trumpet unleashes the four angels of destruction and an army of 200 million supernatural warriors to kill a third of mankind that have survived to this point. The final and seventh trumpet is like the seventh seal. It does not bring further destruction but marks another transition.

It heralds the announcement that the reign of Christ will now begin. Let us now examine these chapters searching for answers and meaning that will inform our faith. May we also find further assurance that even in God's administration of justice, He continues to provide opportunity for repentance and mercy to those who will turn back to Him.

Seventh Seal: Preparation for Trumpets (8:1-6)

Chapter 8 describes the breaking of the seventh seal, which seems to be the doorway through which the seven trumpets enter. The seventh seal could actually be the seven trumpets. The plagues associated with the first four seals could be assumed to stretch over a period of time or could happen rapidly. They may already be happening, or have already happened. War and the famine and death that follow take time to take their toll. Some believe the breaking of the seals marks the first three and half years of the Tribulation, which is also understood to be the less severe portion. The trumpets seem to occur at a much faster rate, and it is clearly implied they will be much worse.

Revelation 8:1, states: ***"And when He broke the seventh seal, there was silence in heaven for about half an hour."*** The breaking of the sixth seal brought forth cosmic events in the heavens and an earthquake that moved every mountain and island out of their places. But with the breaking of the seventh seal we are given only ***"silence in heaven."*** We are not told that the earth is silent but only heaven. Perhaps heaven stands in silent anticipation of all that is about to follow. Some believe the silence is provided to allow God to hear the praises and petitions of the saints requesting that final judgment be administered. Silence can also be clearly symbolic for death. Psalm 115:17 reads: ***"The dead do not praise the Lord, nor do any who go down into silence."*** Perhaps God waits in silence listening for the voice of repentance, but the souls of the unrepentant are dead and the dead make no sound of praise or repentance. Note that the time is limited to only about half an hour. How much time this represents is unknown. God will no longer allow delay. It is time for the wicked to be punished.

Revelation 8:2, states: ***"And I saw the seven angels who stand before God; and seven trumpets were given to them."*** This is the first mention of "seven angels" standing before God, but there have been several references to the seven Spirits of God. The only previous reference to seven angels in Revelation were the seven angels of the seven churches, which we were told were represented as seven stars in the right hand of the One upon the throne. But we have seen how all of these are interconnected in that God sent His seven Spirits to dwell in the seven churches, which are seven golden lamp stands, which hold seven lamps, which are the seven Spirits of God. Revelation 1:20, stated: *"As for the mystery of the seven stars which you saw in My right hand, and the seven golden lamp stands: the seven stars are the angels of the seven churches, and the seven lamp stands are the seven churches."* Revelation 4:5 completed the circle stating: *"And there were seven lamps of fire burning before the throne, which are the seven Spirits of God."* We cannot be certain but perhaps the seven angels are the seven angels of the churches empowered by the seven Spirits of God.

Revelation 8:3-4, states: *"And another angel came and stood at the altar, holding a golden censer; and much incense was given to him, that he might add it to the prayers of all the saints upon the golden altar which was before the throne. And the smoke of the incense, with the prayers of the saints, went up before God out of the angel's hand."* In Revelation 5:8 we were told that the four living creatures and the twenty-four elders before the throne of God were given *"golden bowls of incense, which are the prayers of the saints."* A censer is a device which holds fire and on which incense is placed. The fire heats the incense creating a sweet smelling smoke. A censer with incense was used in the worship of God, and these are still used by many churches. In some cases a censer with incense was used to intercede with God. Such is the example found in Numbers 16:46 when Moses ordered Aaron to use one to make atonement for the congregation to prevent them from suffering God's wrath because they had grumbled against Moses and Aaron. In this case, the prayers of the saints may contain their petitions for justice such as we heard in their voices in Revelation 6:10.

Revelation 8:5, states: *"And the angel took the censer; and he filled it with the fire of the altar and threw it to the earth; and there followed peals of thunder and sounds and flashes of lightning and an earthquake."* Wow, what a contrast! The same censer that has just been used to offer the prayers of the saints to God is now refilled with fire from the altar and thrown to the earth. The thunder, lightning and earthquake also stand in stark contrast to the half-hour of silence. The prayers have been heard and punishment is about to be heralded through seven trumpets.

Revelation 8:6, states: *"And the seven angles who had the seven trumpets prepared themselves to sound them."* Some see the seven trumpets as something separate from the seventh seal, but others believe the seven trumpets represent the sevenfold calamity of the seventh seal, seven woes spoken against the wicked. I use the term "spoken" because as we heard in Revelation 1:10 and 4:1, God's voice is like the sound of a trumpet. I believe the seven trumpets are seven woes resulting from the breaking of the seventh seal. I believe they are directed at the wicked and not the righteous. I am not convinced that all of God's children will be taken to heaven through a Rapture event. I believe this is possible, but I am inclined to believe that righteous witnesses will remain on earth until the very end. And I am absolutely certain, even though many righteous may suffer and die during this time for their faith, that in the end God will protect His children wherever they are.

First Trumpet: Hail and Fire (8:7)

Revelation 8:7, states: *"And the first sounded, and there came hail and fire, mixed with blood, and they were thrown to the earth; and a third of the earth was burned up, and a third of the trees were burned up, and all the green grass was burned."* The rain of hail and fire is similar to the seventh plague which fell upon Egypt as found in Exodus 9:13-26. This plague did not only destroy grass and trees but killed people and livestock which were not brought under cover. God warned His people before the plague came so only those who disbelieved became victim of the plague. Likewise, God made a distinction, having the plague fall upon Egypt but not upon Goshen where the sons of Israel were. Therefore, if any of God's children remain on the earth at this time, it is equally likely that they will be protected from this event. The mix of blood was not mentioned in Exodus. This plague in Revelation could be much more severe, and the blood could be a reference to the death that will come upon those who disbelieve and do not seek shelter from the hail storm. It could also be connected to the blood of the saints which cried out for justice and for the wicked to be punished. It should be noted that while only a third of the earth was burned up, all of the grass was burned. Grass is the food of livestock, so it might be implied that this plague on the land is intended to cut off the food we receive from the land, both meat and vegetation.

Second Trumpet: **Mountain falls into Sea** (8:8-9)

Revelation 8:8-9, states: *"And the second angel sounded, and something like a great mountain burning with fire was thrown into the sea; and a third of the sea became blood; and a third of the creatures, which were in the sea and had life, died; and a third of the ships were destroyed."* The description of a great mountain burning with fire leads many to believe this will be like a meteor or asteroid, but the emphasis is not placed on the destruction such an impact would cause, but a poisoning of the sea. Whatever strikes the sea will destroy ships, so there will be a physical destruction associated with its striking, but it will also change the water into blood and kill one third of all sea life. In the first plague against Egypt as found in Exodus 7:19-21, the waters were turned to blood, but this was the Nile River and not the sea. The real implication, like with the first trumpet above, is that a third of our food from the sea will be cut off. With each trumpet blast our source of food provided by God from the creation of the world is diminished. What God provided to mankind to sustain us is being systematically taken away at the end.

Third Trumpet: **Star falls into Sea** (8:10-11)

Revelation 8:10-11, states: *"And the third angel sounded, and a great star fell from heaven, burning like a torch, and it fell on a third of the rivers and on the springs of waters; and the name of the star is called Wormwood; and a third of the waters became wormwood; and many men died from the waters, because they were made bitter."* This is the third time that something burning with fire has fallen from heaven. Peter says, *"The present heavens and earth by His word are being reserved for fire, kept for the day of judgment and destruction of ungodly men"* (2 Peter 3:7). The first fire destroyed the plants, the second destroyed the fish of the sea, and now the third will poison a third of the drinking waters of the earth. This plague seems to fulfill God's promise through the prophet Jeremiah regarding how He will punish those who spread false prophecy or false teachings. God said, *"Therefore thus says the Lord of hosts concerning the prophets, 'Behold, I am going to feed them wormwood and make them drink poisonous water, for from the prophets of Jerusalem pollution has gone forth into all the land"* (Jeremiah 23:15). We do not know the form of this pollution, but we may have a clue in the word "Chernobyl," from the Ukraine Bible, which means "Wormwood." The nuclear accident at Chernobyl polluted the ground water, and the radiation caused thousands to die, and tens of thousands to become sick. Will some future nuclear accident or use of nuclear weapons pollute one third of the drinking waters of the world?

Forth Trumpet: Darkening of Sun, Moon and Stars (8:12)

Revelation 8:12, states: *"And the fourth angel sounded, and a third of the sun and a third of the moon and a third of the stars were smitten, so that a third of them might be darkened and the day might not shine for a third of it, and the night in the same way."* It is difficult to know exactly how to reconcile this scene with the previous description of the sun being darkened, the moon being turned to blood, and the stars falling from the sky which occurred with the breaking of the sixth seal in Revelation 6:12-13. We can only assume that these signs were temporary, and the lights of the sky have reappeared. What is different this time is that the light is not dimmed (a reduction of quantity) but cut back in length (a reduction of time). In other words the day and night have become one-third shorter. Because in the creation God gave us the sun, moon and stars to measure <u>time</u> and seasons, the message here may be that "time is being shortened." With the sounding of the third trumpet, all food and water had been reduced by one third. Is the punishment perhaps fitting? The wicked have starved the righteous and shed their blood. Now the wicked will go hungry and be forced to drink blood (water turned bitter by wormwood). Time is growing shorter for the wicked!

The Eagle's Warning (8:13)

Revelation 8:13, states: *"And I looked, and I heard an eagle flying in midheaven, saying with a loud voice, "Woe, woe, woe, to those who dwell on the earth, because of the remaining blasts of the trumpet of the three angels who are about to sound!"* The first four trumpets have rendered only partial destruction falling down upon the earth. All have fallen from the sky and may be supernatural rather than natural events. Some believe that it is angels who have fallen; bringing and spreading the plagues. This would make sense in that the plagues are not localized, as could be expected if a natural object such as a meteor struck the earth from space. The nature of these first three trumpets is not to kill but cause suffering, even though we are told some will die as a result of these plagues. Perhaps God does not want the wicked to escape through death but to suffer. After all, with the breaking of the sixth seal, we are told the wicked wanted to die to escape God's wrath (6:16). Or, is God providing a continuing opportunity for repentance. Verse 13 provides a second interlude, and a warning that the three remaining plagues will be much more severe. It is hard for us to believe that in light of all of these signs and plagues, people would not repent and turn to God for safety. Perhaps by this time, the separation of good from evil will be so complete, that no one will be willing to change. Perhaps the pride of the wicked runs so deep that they would rather die than change… would rather curse God than surrender to Him and receive life.

Chapter nine contains the description of the fifth and sixth trumpets, which are the first two of the final three and the most severe punishments. The fifth trumpet opens the bottomless pit and releases locust-like creatures which torment mankind for five months. The sixth trumpet releases four angels and their supernatural army of two hundred million who will kill a third of mankind still remaining. It is very important to note that the torture and death inflicted by these two events is not directed to the faithful but the unrepentant. Chapter 9 ends stating that the people did not repent but continued to worship demons and idols and live immoral lives.

Fifth Trumpet: **Plague of Demonic Locust** (9:1-12)

Revelation 9:1, states: *"And the fifth angel sounded, and I saw a star from heaven which had fallen to the earth; and the key of the bottomless pit was given to him."* You will note that the key to the bottomless pit is given to *"a star from heaven which had fallen to the earth."* It seems clear that this must be a fallen angel and perhaps even Satan himself who is leader over the fallen angels. Part of our interpretation of this can be supported by words found in Isaiah 14:12-15, which states: *"How you have fallen from heaven, o star of the morning, son of the dawn! You have been cut down to the earth, you who have weakened the nations! But you said in your heart, 'I will ascend to heaven; I will raise my throne above the stars of God, and I will sit on the mount of assembly in the recesses of the north. I will ascend above the heights of the clouds; I will make myself like the Most High. Nevertheless you will be thrust down to Sheol, to the recesses of the pit."* While Isaiah is actually speaking about the king of Babylon, he may also be speaking of the evil one who influences and leads earthly kings against God's people. One thing is certain. God is in control. The fallen angel cannot open the pit unless he is given the key or the permission of God. This is similar to the story of Job, when Satan could not inflict hardship upon Job without God's permission and could only harm Job to the degree God allowed.

Regarding the pit, some scholars believe this is neither Sheol, the temporary dwelling of the spirits of the dead from the Old Testament, nor is it the place of final and eternal punishment, which in Revelation is described as the lake of fire, the equivalent of Hell. They believe it is a holding place where demons are imprisoned. For example, Revelation 20:1 speaks of an abyss where Satan will be bound in chains for a thousand years. In Luke 8:31 the demons possessing the man asked Jesus to cast them into the pigs rather than *"command them to depart into the abyss."* Also supporting this place as a place where fallen angels are sent, in 2 Peter 2:4 Peter states: *"God did not spare the angels when they sinned, but cast them into hell and committed them to chains of deepest darkness to be kept until the judgment."* Of course, we find ourselves at this point in Revelation at the time of "the judgment," so this may also imply that what is released from the pit are fallen angels, which we better know as demons.

Revelation 9:2, states: *"And he opened the bottomless pit; and smoke went up out of the pit, like the smoke of a great furnace; and the sun and the air were darkened by the smoke of the pit."* As stated above, the bottomless pit, also translated as the abyss, is a place where angels are held awaiting the judgment of God. It is a terrible place of fire and smoke, therefore when it is opened, smoke rises from this place blocking out the sun and creating even more darkness.

Revelation 9:3, states: *"And out of the smoke came forth locusts upon the earth; and power was given them, as the scorpions of the earth have power."* We are reminded of the eighth plague, which was the plague of locusts that fell upon Egypt, causing the sky to darken (Exodus 10:4-15). Likewise, swarms of locusts are predicted in Joel 1:2-11 and 2:1-11 as precursors of the Day of the Lord. These are not ordinary locusts but have been given the power or perhaps permission to sting and torment mankind.

Revelation 9:4, states: *"And they were told that they should not hurt the grass of the earth; nor any green thing, nor any tree, but only the men who do not have the seal of God on their foreheads."* Don't be confused or distracted by the command not to hurt the grass, remembering that the grass was burned up by the first trumpet. The point here is that normal locusts eat green vegetation and do not sting or harm people. These locusts are commanded by God not to harm plants, but to inflict pain on people who do not have the seal of God on their foreheads. Their purpose is only to inflict pain and torment on the unrepentant. This also implies that there still remains people with the "seal of God" on the earth. We do not know if these people are only Jews, part of the 144,000 previously sealed, and/or also include Christians sealed by the blood of Christ.

Revelation 9:5, states: *"And they were not permitted to kill anyone, but to torment for five months; and their torment was like the torment of a scorpion when it stings a man."* Here we hear the limitations that are placed on the locusts. They cannot kill but only torment, and they can do so for only five months. The sting of a scorpion is very painful and feels like a great burning, but is rarely fatal. This plague will be terrifying in that mankind will be inflicted with terrible pain which comes out of, or is perhaps hidden in darkness for five months. I do not know if the "five month" length of time is significant and can find no similar reference in Scripture other than that Elizabeth was in seclusion for "five months" after she became pregnant with John the Baptist.

Revelation 9:6, states: *"And in those days men will seek death and will not find it; and they will long to die and death flees from them."* The torment of this time will indeed be severe if men will prefer to die than to suffer it, but they will not be able to escape it through death. This seems clearly a supernatural event because even suicide is no longer an option. People cannot end their physical lives—they cannot escape punishment through death. Verses 20-21, which will follow, might suggest that this time of torture without death is a final time given to allow man to repent of his sins.

Revelation 9:7-10, states: *"And the appearance of the locusts was like horses prepared for battle; and on their heads, as it were, crowns like gold, and their faces were like the faces of men. And they had hair like the hair of women, and their teeth were like the teeth of lions. And they had breastplates like breastplates of iron; and the sound of their wings was like the sound of chariots, of many horses rushing to battle. And they have tails like scorpions, and stings; and in their tails is their power to hurt men for five months."* The locusts are described as armored and winged cavalry horses with long hair, large teeth, human faces, and stinging tails. They are not real locusts but supernatural beings and most likely demons who have been given power to harm men. The gold crowns they wear may be symbolic of the authority they have been given to do harm.

Revelation 9:11, states: *"They have as king over them, the angel of the abyss; his name in Hebrew is Abaddon, and in the Greek he has the name Apollyon."* The literal meaning of the names "Abaddon" and "Apollyon" are respectively, "destruction" and "destroyer." The Hebrew word "Abaddon" is found six times in the Old Testament. In Job 31:12 it means "destruction" or "ruin." In Job 28:22 it equates to "death." In Psalm 88:11 it is comparable to the "grave." In Job 26:6 and Proverbs 15:11 and 27:20 it refers to the region of the damned. The Greek equivalent word of "Apollyon" has very similar meaning, but rather than "destruction" or "death" it more literally means "the destroyer," which is a good description of Satan. In any case, the king of the locusts is certainly one who brings destruction.

Revelation 9:12, states: *"The first woe is past; behold, two woes are still coming after these things."* As we have seen numerous times throughout Revelation, some verses are set as boundaries, marking the completion of one event and warning of what will follow. Of the final three woes brought about through the seven trumpets, one is now complete, and the other two are about to follow. These announcements indicate a pattern of warnings by which man has opportunity to reflect on what has happened and repent.

Sixth Trumpet: Destroying Horseman (9:13-21)

Revelation 9:13-14, states: *"And the sixth angel sounded, and I heard a voice from the four horns of the golden altar which is before God, one saying to the sixth angel who had the trumpet, "Release the four angels who are bound at the great river Euphrates."* It is not clear if these four angels are the same four angels found in Revelation 7:1-2 who were *"holding back the four winds of the earth"* and were *"granted to harm the earth and the sea."* These angels are bound, or held back from releasing their destruction at the great river Euphrates, which is located north and east of Israel. This river ran through ancient Babylon and today runs through the regions of Kuwait, Iraq and Syria. This may mean that the area around the Euphrates River is where destruction will begin, come from, or be centered. Two Old Testament Scriptures seem to connect with Revelation 9:13-14. First, in reference to the deliverance of Israel in a day when a "great trumpet" will be blown, Isaiah 27:12-13 states: *"And it will come about in that day, that the Lord will start His threshing from the flowing stream of the Euphrates to the brook of Egypt; and you will be gathered up one by one, O sons of Israel. It will come about also in that day a great trumpet will be blown; and those who were perishing in the land of Assyria and who were scattered in the land of Egypt will come and worship the Lord in the holy mountain at Jerusalem."* This passage seems to support the notion that final punishment will begin in the Middle East in the nations which today are predominately Islamic and enemies of Israel. At the same time God will gather and protect the people of Israel, and they will worship on His holy mountain in Jerusalem. The second reference centers on punishment which will come upon the arrival of the great Day of the Lord. Jeremiah 46:10 states: *"For that day belongs to the Lord God of hosts, a day of vengeance, so as to avenge Himself on His foes; and the sword will devour and be satiated and drink its fill of their blood; for there will be a slaughter for the Lord God of hosts in the land of the north by the river Euphrates."* Again, this passage seems to indicate that punishment will begin or be focused in the Middle East near the Euphrates River. Also in reference to Islam, Hebrews provides evidence that judgment will be most fierce against those who have rejected the Son of God. Hebrews 10:28-31 reads: *"Anyone who has set aside the Law of Moses dies without mercy on the testimony of two or three witnesses. How much severer punishment do you think he will deserve who has trampled under foot the Son of God, and has regarded as unclean the blood of the covenant by which he was sanctified, and has insulted the Spirit of grace? For we know Him who said, "Vengeance is Mine, I will repay." And again, "The Lord will judge His people.""*

Revelation 9:15, states: *"And the four angels, who had been prepared for the hour and day and month and year, were released, so that they might kill a third of mankind."* Clearly, God has set a very specific time for punishment. It will begin at a particular hour, day, month, and year that He has chosen. Different from the fifth trumpet which brought about pain without death, the sixth trumpet marks the beginning of a great but still limited slaughter of humankind. We are told the angels are to kill only one third of all humankind, which we presume are those not marked as belonging to God.

Revelation 9:16, states: *"And the number of the armies of the horsemen was two hundred million; I heard the number of them."* The number may be symbolic, being twice ten thousand times ten thousand. Many think this vast army will come from China because it is the only country in the region with a large enough population to produce such a vast army, but the description which follows in verse 17 would suggest that these are not human but supernatural beings. In either case, it is the most massive army that ever marched into battle taking the greatest toll ever afflicted on humankind.

Revelation 9:17, states: *"And this is how I saw in the vision the horses and those who sat on them: the riders had breastplates the color of fire and of hyacinth and of brimstone; and the heads of the horses are like the heads of lions; and out of their mouths proceed fire and smoke and brimstone."* Fire is red, hyacinth is a deep blue and brimstone is associated with sulfur, which is yellow. The significance of these colors is not clear, but a lion was equated as a symbol of power and authority, and thus it is from the mouth of the lion head that destruction comes forth in the form of fire, smoke and brimstone.

Revelation 9:18, states: *"A third of mankind was killed by these three plagues, by the fire and the smoke and the brimstone, which proceeded out of their mouths."* God destroyed Sodom and Gomorrah with a rain of fire and brimstone. It is interesting, that along with smoke, these three elements are designated as "three plagues." Clearly, people are to be killed by fire and by brimstone and by smoke.

Revelation 9:19, states: *"For the power of the horses is in their mouths and in their tails; for their tails are like serpents and have heads; and with them they do harm."* It is important to note that it is not the riders who kill but the horses. Power is in their heads and tails (which have heads). Death comes from the lion heads and harm from the serpent tails. The description we have from verses 17 and 19 do not correlate with any modern soldier or machine of war. We have to stretch the symbolism to make it fit any man made weapon of war we have today. It is more likely that the description is of supernatural beings and possibly demons of some form given permission by God to destroy one third of humankind.

Revelation 9:20-21, states: *"And the rest of mankind, who were not killed by these plagues, did not repent of the works of their hands, so as not to worship demons, and the idols of gold and of silver and of brass and of stone and of wood, which can neither see nor hear nor walk; and they did not repent of their murders nor of their sorceries nor of their immorality nor of their thefts."* These verses give us insight to why God's punishment has been only partial up to this point. Mankind is still being given opportunity to repent and stop sinning against God. But we are told that mankind fails to repent of the *"works of their hands."* This means that man's actions or works continue unrepentant. It is not enough to simply repent with words. Words must become manifest in our actions. As long as we put material things before God we are guilty of idolatry. As long as we act selfishly, harming others and taking from others for personal gain, and as long as we put our faith in things other than God, we remain unrepentant. The message of Revelation continues to be a call for repentance while there is still time, because at some point, time will run out and judgment will be final.

Second Interlude (10:1—11:14)

As the opening of the seventh seal was delayed by two scenes in chapter 7, so the blowing of the seventh trumpet must wait upon two scenes. What we see in chapter 10 are very similar images as those seen in Ezekiel, chapters 1 through 3. Chapter 10 forms an interlude between the sixth and seventh trumpets. Here we have the only thing that remains sealed and is not revealed. When John heard the voice of the seven thunders, he started to write, but he heard a voice from heaven saying to him, *"Seal up the things which the seven peals of thunder have spoken, and do not write them"* (Rev. 10:4). In this chapter, we also read of a little book which was as sweet as honey in John's mouth, but which became bitter in his stomach. Chapter 10 will proclaim that with the seventh trumpet, delay of punishment will end, but what will also end is time and opportunity for repentance.

John Eats the Scroll of Doom (10:1-11)

Revelation 10:1-3, states: *"And I saw another strong angel coming down out of heaven, clothed with a cloud; and the rainbow was upon his head, and his face was like the sun, and his feet like pillars of fire; and he had in his hand a little book which was open. And he placed his right foot on the sea and his left on the land; and he cried out with a loud voice, as when a lion roars; and when he had cried out, the seven peals of thunder uttered their voices."* The imagery in these three verses is similar to imagery found in the first three chapters of Ezekiel.

Regarding the angel coming down out of heaven clothed in a cloud, Ezekiel 1:4 states: *"And as I looked, behold, a storm wind was coming from the north, a great cloud with fire flashing forth continually and a bright light around it, and in its midst something like glowing metal in the midst of the fire."* God has often appeared clothed in a cloud. In Exodus 19:9, 16 we see God clothed in a cloud with flashes of lightning and thunder as He descends upon His mountain to speak through Moses. God also appears and speaks from a cloud during the Transfiguration. Here, the one descending is said to be a strong angel rather than God Himself, but it seems clear that he acts for God.

Regarding the angel's face being like the sun and his feet like pillars of fire and his having a rainbow upon his head, Ezekiel 1:27-28 states: *"Then I noticed from the appearance of His loins and upward something like glowing metal that looked like fire all around within it, and from the appearance of His loins and downward I saw something like fire; and there was a radiance around Him. As the appearance of the rainbow in the clouds on a rainy day, so was the appearance of the surrounding radiance. Such was the appearance of the likeness of the glory of the Lord."* Ezekiel believes the One who appears to him is the Lord. Many see this as a "Christophany" (appearance of Christ in the Old Testament). Again, John says the one who comes down from heaven is a "strong angel" rather than Christ, although some scholars believe that this is Christ. This is further supported by the fact that in Revelation 5:7 Christ has taken the scroll out of the hand of God and has possession of it. Other scholars believe it is more consistent with Scripture that Christ's final descent to earth comes at the end of time when He comes to gather His elect, and therefore, He sends a strong angel in His stead.

Regarding the little book in the hand of the angel, Ezekiel 2:9 states: *"Then I looked, behold, a hand was extended to me; and lo, a scroll was in it."* In Revelation 5:1 we saw God holding a book (scroll) with words front and back and seven seals. In Revelation 5:2 we heard a "strong angel" proclaim with a loud voice, *"Who is worthy to open the book and to break its seals."* Now a "strong angel" (perhaps the same one) cries out again like a lion as he holds a little book. We do not know if this is the same book that was sealed with the seven seals or a different book. Jesus often used the phrase "as it is written" when

83

revealing God's truth. The importance of the scroll in Ezekiel, and the book with seals, and the little book found in chapter 10 is that they contain the Word of God—what God has spoken and therefore either already has or will definitely happen.

Regarding the significance of the angel standing with one foot on the sea and the other on the land, this may simply mean that God has dominion and power over both land and sea, or the truth being revealed will apply everywhere—on both land and sea.

Regarding the seven peals of thunder which utter their voices when the angel cries out, when God speaks from heaven in John 12:28-29 the people around Jesus who heard God's voice said it sounded like thunder. Job 37:5 states: *"God thunders with His voice wondrously, doing great things which we cannot comprehend."* Psalm 29:3 states: *"The voice of the Lord is upon the waters; the God of glory thunders, the Lord is over many waters."* We might be safe to equate the seven peals of thunder with the seven fold voice of God.

Revelation 10:4-7 states: *"And when the seven peals of thunder had spoken, I was about to write; and I heard a voice from heaven saying, "Seal up the things which the seven peals of thunder have spoken, and do not write them." And the angel whom I saw standing on the sea and on the land lifted up his right hand to heaven, and swore by Him who lives forever and ever, who created heaven and the things in it, and the earth and the things in it, and the sea and the things in it, that there shall be delay no longer, but in the days of the voice of the seventh angel, when he is about to sound, then the mystery of God is finished, as He preached to his servants the prophets."* This scene is similar to one found in Daniel 12:7-9, which states: *"And I heard the man dressed in linen, who was above the waters of the river, as he raised his right hand and his left toward heaven, and swore by Him who lives forever that it would be for a time, times, and a half a time; and as soon as they finished shattering the power of the holy people, all these events will be completed. As for me, I heard but could not understand; so I said, "My lord, what will be the outcome of these events?" And he said, "Go your way, Daniel, for these words are concealed and sealed up until the end time."* Both in Daniel and in Revelation we are told that there is a final mystery that will remained sealed and will not be revealed until the very end of time. In Daniel, the angel assures Daniel that the mystery of God will be fulfilled. In Revelation we will hear that with the blowing of the seventh trumpet an assurance that there will be *"delay no longer."* We also hear that with the blowing of the seventh trumpet the *"mystery of God is finished, as He preached to His servants the prophets."* There are many examples throughout the prophets of the Old Testament that God's deliverance and judgment will be heralded by a trumpet blast. In Matthew 24:31 Jesus states: *"And He will send forth His angels with a great trumpet and they will gather together His elect from the four winds, from one end of the sky to the other."* It would appear that the seventh trumpet will complete the trumpets or the seven-fold trumpet of God.

Revelation 10:8 states: *"And the voice which I heard from heaven, I heard again speaking with me, and saying, "Go, take the book which is open in the hand of the angel who stands on the sea and on the land."* In Ezekiel's vision it is the prophet Ezekiel who receives the scroll (book) from the hand of the Lord. In Revelation 5, Jesus Christ, the worthy Lamb of God receives the book with its seven seals from the hand of God the Father. Here it is John who receives a little book from a strong angel sent by God.

Revelation 10:9-11 states: *"And I went to the angel, telling him to give me the little book. And he said to me, "Take it, and eat it; and it will make your stomach bitter, but in your mouth it will be sweet as honey." And I took the little book out of the angel's hand and ate it, and it was in my mouth sweet as honey; and when I had eaten it, my stomach was made bitter. And they said to me, "You must prophesy again concerning many peoples and nations and tongues and kings.""* Again, there is a striking similarity to this event to that found in Ezekiel 3:1-7, 14, which states: *"Then He said to me, "Son of man, eat what you find; eat this scroll, and go, speak to the house of Israel." So I opened my mouth, and He fed me this scroll. And He said to me, "son of man, feed your stomach, and fill your body with this scroll which I am giving you." Then I ate it, and it was sweet as honey in my mouth. Then He said to me, "Son of man, go to the house of Israel and speak with My words to them. For you are not being sent to a people of unintelligible speech or difficult language, but to the house of Israel, nor to many peoples of unintelligible speech or difficult language, whose words you cannot understand. But I have sent you to them who should listen to you; yet the house of Israel will not be willing to listen to you, since they are not willing to listen to Me. Surely the whole house of Israel is stubborn and obstinate... So the Spirit lifted me up and took me away; and I went embittered in the rage of my spirit, and the hand of the Lord was strong on me."* Both in Ezekiel and Revelation the scroll or book is sweet in the mouth but bitter in the stomach.

Eating the book is taking the word (written word) of God into one's self. Hearing God's justice in that He is about to punish the wicked is sweet to the taste, but learning that there are those who claim to belong to God will receive punishment is bitter in the stomach. The scroll or word of God is given to the prophet so that it can be proclaimed that people might hear and repent from their evil ways. In the case of Ezekiel, the word is to be proclaimed to the house of Israel who are an intelligible people who should understand and be able to receive the word, but Ezekiel is told they will not receive and this leaves him bitter. In Revelation, John is given the word that he may prophesy to many peoples and nations and tongues and kings. Again the witness is so that people can hear and repent, but again, they will not. Some believe that John finds the book bitter because he is now aware of the suffering that Christians will have to undergo before God's final judgment. The delay is required to allow all those who will repent opportunity to repent. But the delay causes many Christians to suffer and reminds us that Christ said we must be willing to take up our cross and follow Him. We must be willing to suffer as our Lord Jesus Christ suffered so that as many as possible will have opportunity for repentance and salvation. Finally, Psalm 119:103 states, *"How sweet are Thy words to my taste! Yes, sweeter than honey to my mouth!"* We understand that God's word is sweet to those who receive it and obey it. But for those who reject God's word, they will face the bitterness of punishment. As is said in Jeremiah 4:18, *"Your ways and your deeds have brought these things to you. This is your evil. How bitter! How it has touched your heart!"*

Measuring of the Temple and the Two Witnesses (11:1-14)

In chapter 11 we will finally hear the Seventh Trumpet sound, which heralds the "kingdom of the world" becoming the "kingdom of our Lord." But first we will hear of a measuring of the temple and of two witnesses who will prophesy for 1,260 days. We must remember that the events which are depicted are not necessarily linear or occurring in sequenced fashion one after another. Our human thinking tends to arrange things in order with a desire for laying them out on a progressive time line. Given the interlude which fell between the breaking of the sixth and seven seal, and the interlude we have between the sixth and seventh trumpet, it seems that the Lord is pausing to give us deeper insight and assurance of what is to come. The 1,260 days of prophesy by the two witnesses does not mean that a minimum of 1,260 days will transpire between the sixth and seventh trumpet. On the contrary, Jesus told us in Revelation 1:1 that these things must take place "shortly" which we came to understand as happening quickly once they begin. Revelation seems to depict a number of events occurring in an "overlapping" fashion, some occurring over a longer period of time leading up to and overlapping with a series of sudden and quickly moving events at the end. Both long and short term events are falling into place as God's plan reaches its final destination.

Revelation 11:1-2, states: *"And there was given me a measuring rod like a staff; and someone said, "Rise and measure the temple of God, and the altar, and those who worship in it. And leave out the court which is outside the temple, and do not measure it, for it has been given to the nations; and they will tread under foot the holy city for forty-two months.""* At the time of John's writing of Revelation there is no temple in Jerusalem to measure for it has already been destroyed by the Romans, dismantled stone by stone as Jesus had told His disciples would happen in Matthew 24:2. Therefore, the temple John is asked to measure is not a building built by man. Scripture bears witness that Jesus said that if His temple were destroyed He would rebuild it in three days. The temple He spoke of was not a building but His own body. Likewise, the apostle Paul states in 1 Corinthians 3:16, *"Do you not know that you are a temple of God, and that the Spirit of God dwells in you?"* And Peter also says in 1 Peter 2:5, *"you also, as living stones, are being built up as a spiritual house for a holy priesthood, to offer up spiritual sacrifices acceptable to God through Jesus Christ."* Perhaps the temple which John is being asked to measure is the "Church," but what about the outer court? John is told not to measure the *"court which is outside the temple"* because it will be *"tread under foot"* for a period lasting *"forty-two months."* Speaking of the end times, in Luke 21:24 Jesus says, *"Jerusalem will be trampled under foot by the Gentiles until the times of the Gentiles be fulfilled."* In Daniel 12:7b the length of time is recorded saying, *"it would be for a time, times, and half a time; and as soon as they finish shattering the power of the holy people, all these events will be completed."* The Temple and inner court were reserved for Jews only and the outer court was a place where Gentiles were allowed. From this perspective one might conclude that the Jews are being measured and the Gentiles left outside to be trodden upon for forty-two months. But the separation has become not one of lineage but one of faith. The faithful take refuge in the shelter of God and become part of the body of Christ. The unfaithful are often viewed as those on the outside who do not believe or have rejected the faith.

One clue that may help determine what is happening here is the measuring itself. From Ezekiel 40:3—42-20 and 47:1-12 we see the measurement of the temple taking place just before God restores it and fills it with His Presence. Also in Zechariah 1:16 and 2:2-8, and in Jeremiah 31:39 we see measurement as preparatory to the restoration and rebuilding of the temple. Whether the measurement in Revelation is in reference to the Jews, Christians, or both, it is likely a precursor of God's restoration of His people, which now include Jews and Christians.

Revelation 11:3, states: *"And I will grant authority to my two witnesses, and they will prophesy for twelve hundred and sixty days, clothed in sackcloth."* For a period of 1,260 days, which would be exactly forty-two months under the Jewish lunar calendar, two witnesses are to prophesy prior to final judgment and reward. This witness may be intended as a last chance to hear God's Word and repent, or it may be offered as a final exhortation of all that God has done and why what is about to happen is righteous and just. There has been some speculation regarding the identity of the two witnesses. Some believe they are Enoch (Genesis 5:24, Hebrews 11:5) and Elijah (2 Kings 2:11). Others believe they are Moses and Elijah (Matthew 17:3). The reason some believe it is Enoch and Elijah is because they are the only two people in the Bible that never died, but instead, were taken into heaven by God while still alive. Because God has declared that man is given only one life to live (Hebrew 9:27), many believe that the two witnesses who are killed, must be Enoch and Elijah who have not previously died. Others believe that they are Moses and Elijah, who are seen to represent the Law and the Prophets—the two primary Old Testament witnesses of God's truth. Jesus said that He came *"not to abolish the Law or the Prophets"* but to *"fulfill them"* (Matthew 5:17). Still others believe that the two witnesses are the Church, and within this view perhaps the two witnesses represent the Old and New Testaments, which provide for us the prophetic word fulfilled in Christ. In any case, the fact that they are clothed in sackcloth would indicate a time of lament and mourning and/or a call for repentance.

Revelation 11:4, states: *"These are the two olive trees and the two lampstands that stand before the Lord of the earth."* This is a continuing reference to the "two witnesses" and we look to Zechariah, chapter 4 for explanation. First, the book of Zechariah begins with a call to repentance to God's chosen people, and an expression of His favor and love for them. In the midst of this call God describes a single lampstand with seven spouts between two olive trees. When Zechariah asks about the lamps, God says, *"Not by might nor by power, but by My Spirit"* (Zechariah 4:6) and *"these are the eyes of the Lord which range to and fro throughout the earth"* (Zechariah 4:10). When Zechariah asks: "What are the two olive branches which are beside the two golden pipes, which empty the golden oil from themselves?" (Zechariah 4:12), God answers, saying, *"These are the two anointed ones, who are standing by the Lord of the whole earth"* (Zechariah 4:13). Understandably, the olive tree produces oil that is burned in lamps to produce light. Therefore, the two lamps and olive trees may represent Moses and Elijah as Law and Prophets, or the Old and New Testaments as prophecy and prophecy fulfillment, representing both sources and instruments of the light that illuminates understanding and brings us to repentance. Of course the ultimate source of all that gives light is God Himself, the One who provided the Word and fulfilled the Word when the Word became flesh—the incarnate Jesus Christ. Remember Jesus' words in John 8:12, saying, *"I am the light of the world; he who follows Me shall not walk in darkness, but shall have the light of life."* And Jesus has imparted His Light into the Church as we can hear in His proclamation and instruction to His disciples in Matthew 5:14, 16: *"You are the light of the world..."* and *"Let your light shine before men in such a way that they may see your good works, and glorify your Father who is in heaven."* The two witnesses bear witness to the glory of God.

Revelation 11:5-6, states: *"And if anyone desires to harm them, fire proceeds out of their mouth and devours their enemies; and if anyone would desire to harm them, in this manner he must be killed. These have the power to shut up the sky, in order that rain may not fall during the days of their prophesying; and they have power over the waters to turn them into blood, and to smite the earth with every plague, as often as they desire."* This description provides further support for Moses and Elijah being identified as the two witnesses. Moses, as God's instrument in delivering God's people from Egypt, turned water into blood and brought ten plagues upon Egypt (Exodus 7:17-19). Elijah, as God's prophet, shut up the skies so rain didn't fall for three and a half years, which is forty-two months (1 Kings 17:1; James 5:17). Elijah also brought forth fire from heaven to destroy God's enemies (2 Kings 1:10-13). But in this case, fire comes from their mouths. This seems to be a fulfillment of what is stated in Jeremiah 5:14, which states: *"Therefore, thus says the Lord, the God of hosts, "Because you have spoken this word, behold, I am making My words in your mouth fire and this people wood, and it will consume them."* The similarities are striking but we must remember that Moses and Elijah were only instruments for God, and that it was the power of God's Word spoken through the prophets that shut up the sky, turned the water into blood, and brought forth plagues as witness of His power.

Revelation 11:7, states, *"And when they have finished their testimony, the beast that comes up out of the abyss will make war with them, and overcome them and kill them."* The two witnesses are not only witnesses but also to be "martyrs." The particular Greek word translated as "witnesses" in 11:3 can be equally translated as "martyrs." The beast from the abyss or the bottomless pit arises to wage war against and kill the witnesses of God. This is the first of four depictions we will be given of Satan. The others will be as the dragon in 12:3, the beast with ten horns and seven heads in 13:1, and as the beast with two horns who spoke like a dragon in 13:11. This first appearance of the beast may be best identified as the Antichrist, who wages war with God, Christ, and the Christian Church on earth. This verse may be intended to convey that at some point the beast will defeat the church, or at least it will appear that he has done so.

Revelation 11:8, states, *"And their bodies will lie in the street of the great city which mystically is called Sodom and Egypt, where also their Lord was crucified."* We know the identity of the place the witnesses are killed because we are told it was where the "Lord was crucified" which was in Jerusalem. The "great city" which is "mystically" called "Sodom and Egypt" is likely not a reference to a place but a condition. Sodom was a place of great sin, and Egypt a place of great persecution. Sodom and Egypt probably here represent the characteristics of the evil "great city" which is actually the world which crucified Christ and continues to persecute and kill His witnesses. We might be reminded of Paul's words in Romans 8:36, which state: *"For Thy sake we are being put to death all day long; we were considered as sheep to be slaughtered."*

Revelation 11:9-10, states, *"And those from the peoples and tribes and tongues and nations will look at their dead bodies for three and a half days, and will not permit their dead bodies to be laid in a tomb. And those who dwell on the earth will rejoice over them and make merry; and they will send gifts to one another, because these two prophets tormented those who dwell on the earth."* Only today, in our age of television, satellites, and the internet is it possible for *"peoples and tribes and tongues and nations"* to *"look"* upon such a scene within such a brief time period as *"three and half days."* The two witnesses were sent to "witness" but given power to protect themselves and cause plagues to get the peoples' attention as part of their calling them to repentance. God has frequently used trials to call people to repentance. But the people have not repented and now celebrate the death of God's prophets who *"tormented those who dwell on the earth."* The people are self-centered, celebrating the death of those who caused them discomfort. I believe that all Christians are called to "comfort the afflicted and afflict the comfortable."

Revelation 11:11-12, states, *"And after the three and a half days the breath of life from God came into them, and they stood on their feet; and great fear fell upon those who were beholding them. And they heard a loud voice from heaven saying to them, "Come up here." And they went up into heaven in the cloud, and their enemies beheld them."* Just as Satan may have believed he defeated Christ at the crucifixion, on the third day Jesus rose from the dead, and then ascended into heaven in a cloud. Here, after three and a half days, we see the two witnesses rising from death to life and then ascending into heaven in a cloud. Christ was victorious over Satan through His death and resurrection. Paul states in Romans 8:11: *"But if the Spirit of Him who raised Jesus from the dead dwells in you, He who raised Christ Jesus from the dead will also give life to your mortal bodies through His Spirit who indwells you."* Paul adds in 1 Corinthians 15:54: *"But when this perishable will have put on the imperishable, and this mortal will have put on immortality, then will come about the saying that is written, 'Death is swallowed up in victory.'"* Looking forward to Revelation 12:3 and in reference to the victory God's witnesses will have over Satan, the accuser, we hear: *"And they overcame him because of the blood of the Lamb and because of the word of their testimony, and they did not love their life even to death."* The two witnesses did not die in vain but accomplished their witness both in life and through their death, that God is greater than death and has defeated death.

Revelation 11:13, states, *"And in that hour there was a great earthquake, and a tenth of the city fell; and seven thousand people were killed in the earthquake, and the rest were terrified, and gave glory to the God of heaven."* Regarding the earthquake, Ezekiel 38:19 describes a great earthquake in Israel at the time God's judgment is poured out, saying, *"And in My zeal and in My blazing wrath I declare that on that day there will surely be a great earthquake in the land of Israel."* In regard to *"a tenth of the city fell,"* this may not necessarily be a reference to Jerusalem alone. As you may remember from the explanation of the "great city" in verse 11:8 above, many scholars believe this a reference to the evil world that opposes Christ. Therefore, this could be a reference to an earthquake that starts in Israel and shakes the whole world, causing a tenth to fall. In reference to the *"seven thousand people"* who are killed in the earthquake, a literal translation of the Greek would be, "names of men, seven thousand." Many scholars believe that the seven thousand is not simply everyday people but celebrities—people who have recognized names and are considered important. Again, this may be intended to get people's attention. In our indifferent world no one seems to care when thousands die of hunger in Africa, but when a celebrity dies it is news around the world. Finally, we are told that those who remained *"gave glory to the God of heaven"* but we are not told they repented. They recognize God's power, and they fear God, but they express no evidence of changing their wicked ways as Nineveh did when God pronounced judgment against it through His prophet Jonah. When Nineveh repented, God withheld judgment, but judgment will not be withheld at the time of the end because the people will fail to turn back from their evil ways and repent.

Revelation 11:14, states, *"The second woe is past; behold, the third woe is coming quickly."* In Revelation 8:13 we heard the angel exclaim "woe, woe, woe" before the fifth, sixth, and seventh trumpets would be sounded. The fifth trumpet and first woe came with the opening of the bottomless pit and the plague of demonic locusts. The sixth trumpet and second woe came with the army of 200,000,000 originating at the Euphrates River and killing one fourth of all mankind. The killing and resurrection of the "two witnesses" and the great earthquake that follows "in that hour" now completes the second woe. The third woe we are told will come quickly or without delay.

Seventh Trumpet: Christ's Reign to Begin (11:15-19)

Revelation 11:15, states, *"And the seventh angel sounded; and there arose loud voices in heaven, saying, "The kingdom of the world has become the kingdom of our Lord, and of His Christ; and He will reign forever and ever.""* The seventh trumpet brings the heavenly proclamation that the prayer the Lord Jesus Christ taught us has been answered and is fulfilled. As part of the Lord's Prayer we say: *"Thy kingdom come, Thy will be done, on earth as it is in heaven."* The reign of Christ over heaven and earth will now begin.

Revelation 11:16-17, states, *"And the twenty-four elders, who sit on their thrones before God, fell on their faces and worshiped God, saying, "We give Thee thanks, O Lord God, the Almighty, who art and who wast, because Thou hast taken Thy great power and hast begun to reign.""* Notice in the elders' thanksgiving that something has changed. Before they worshiped the one "who was, who is, and who is to come" (1:4, 8; 4:8), but now they omit the phrase referencing the future—"who is to come." This verse marks Christ coming. From this point onward the future reference is eliminated (16:5).

Revelation 11:18, states, *"And the nations were enraged, and Thy wrath came, and the time came for the dead to be judged, and the time to give their reward to Thy bond-servants the prophets and to the saints and to those who fear Thy name, the small and the great, and to destroy those who destroy the earth."* Notice that the world does not embrace the coming of Christ or His reign, but rather is *"enraged."* The world that is in Satan's control, where God's people are being persecuted and killed, and where non-believers are self-centered rather than God-centered, does not welcome Christ but is angered by His coming. This verse continues to speak of all the things that will come after Christ's return, including: God's wrath; judgment of the dead; reward of the faithful; and final destruction of all that destroyed the earth. <u>This verse, located in the center of the book of Revelation, provides a concise summary of all that has been prophesied to come with Christ's return, and much of which the remaining chapters will depict in detail.</u>

Revelation 11:19, states, *"And the temple of God which is in heaven was opened; and the ark of His covenant appeared in His temple, and there were flashes of lightning and sounds and peals of thunder and an earthquake and a great hailstorm."* The earthly temple curtain was torn in two opening the inner room, holy of holies, when Jesus died on the cross. This earthly symbol represented the removal of the barrier of our sin which separated us from God. Jesus' death on the cross paid the price for our sin and made it possible for us to be restored and redeemed through His sacrifice on the cross. The appearance of the temple of God in heaven being opened marks the completion of what began at the cross. The time of grace and of harvest is coming to a close.

PART 6

Seven Visions of the Dragon's Kingdom

In Part 5 we covered the breaking of the seventh seal and the seven trumpets. With the breaking of the seventh seal there was silence in heaven, a pause that lasted a brief half hour. But with the sounding of the trumpets we witnessed an escalating punishment which moved from cosmic to supernatural. As God in the beginning had given plants and animals for food and water to drink we saw these things progressively taken away. As many who have persecuted Christians have deprived them of food and water, we saw the persecutors deprived of the same. And ultimately in the last three trumpets, we witnessed three great "woes" poured out upon the guilty on the earth. The first tormented, the second brought death to a quarter of mankind, and the third marked the beginning of the reign of Christ on earth. Before the last trumpet sounded two witnesses gave testimony for forty-two months before being killed, raised to life, and raised to heaven. And yet the people continued unrepentant. With every seal and every trumpet there was only limited destruction to allow room and opportunity for repentance. It would seem that God was providing witness of both His mercy and justice. Even the guilty are given opportunity to repent and change, but when they do not, they deserve their punishment.

John has provided witness of his visions of Seven Seals and Seven Trumpets. There was an interlude provided between the sixth and seventh seals where John was shown a vision of the sealing of the martyrs on earth, and the glorified martyrs in heaven. Likewise, between the sixth and seventh trumpets, John was shown a vision of the eating of the scroll of doom, and the two witnesses. We will now enter what some might see as another interlude but it is more than that. In the eighteenth verse of chapter 11 we were provided a summary of all that will follow in the remainder of Revelation, but compressed and without detail. Part 6 will begin a series of visions that will both decompress the rapid events contained in Revelation 11:18, and will also place them in the larger context of the heavenly struggle between good and evil. We will see a number of personalities revealed that will provide insight into unseen things on earth. This wide screen picture of events seems to begin with Christ's first coming, and then progressing to His second coming. During this time the beast, revealed in many forms, wages war against God and all that belong to God. It is a war already won through the blood of Jesus Christ, yet it is a time of battle over the souls of men.

CHAPTER 12:

In chapter 12 we are introduced to five personalities. The first is a woman, who is described as clothed with the sun, with the moon under her feet and a crown of twelve stars on her head. Some believe she is the Church. Others believe she represents Israel and still others, the Virgin Mary (1-2). The second personality is a great red dragon who is identified as the devil or Satan (3-4). The third personality is the child born of the woman, who we know to be Jesus the Christ because we are told He will rule the nations with a rod of iron (5-6). The fourth personality is Michael, the Archangel who protects God's people (7-9). The fifth personality would appear to be the remnant of the Jewish people, assuming the woman represents Israel and these are her offspring. Chapter 12 begins the final struggle that will last to the end. This war seems to begin with the first coming of Christ and will wage on until He ends it with His return. Chapter 12 is only the beginning of this heavenly view, which will continue until the end.

First Vision: Heavenly Mother and Birth of Messiah (12:1-6)

Revelation 12:1-2, states: *"And a great sign appeared in heaven: a woman clothed with the sun, and the moon under her feet, and on her head a crown of twelve stars; and she was with child; and she cried out, being in labor and in pain to give birth."* Some scholars believe the woman clothed with the sun is the Church, but most believe she represents Israel. Jacob was the son of Isaac who was the son of Abraham. God renamed Jacob, giving him the name Israel, which means "he who strives with God." Israel had twelve sons, who would become the twelve tribes of Israel. The youngest of these sons was Joseph, who we are told his father Israel loved the most. Joseph had dreams and was able to interpret dreams. This gift from God would result in him being sold into slavery in Egypt, where he would rise to be a ruler of Egypt, second only to the Pharaoh. Through his position and authority in Egypt, he will save his own family and all of Egypt from starvation. So by now you are asking: What does this have to do with the woman clothed with the sun? The dream that resulted in Joseph's brothers enslaving him to Egypt is found in Genesis 37:9, and is described by Joseph as follows: ***"Lo, I have had still another dream; and behold, the sun and the moon and eleven stars were bowing down to me."*** As can be seen in his families reaction to his dream, they perceived the "sun, moon and seven stars" to represent Joseph's "father, mother and seven brothers." They believed that Joseph was exhorting himself as greater than them, but actually, the dream was an accurate depiction of events to come, when God would give him power and authority that would save the whole family, and set the stage for God to deliver His people. God's chosen family will enter Egypt through Joseph, but 430 years later, God's chosen people will be delivered out of Egypt through Moses.

Now let us consider the ancient symbolic understanding of the sun and the moon. While we do not put our faith in astrology but the spoken Word of God, Scripture teaches that God can speak to us through heavenly signs. Psalm 19:1-4 states: ***"The heavens declare the glory of God; the skies proclaim the work of His hands. Day after day they pour forth speech; night after night they display knowledge. There is no speech or language where their voice is not heard. Their voice goes out into all the earth, their words to the ends of the world."*** Zoroastrian priests who believed in one true God, the existence of angles and demons, and other understandings similar to the Jewish and Christian faith, considered the sun to be symbolic of the supreme father and the moon to be associated with birth. Astrologically, a person's "moon sign" still derives from which constellation the moon is in at the time of their birth. The magi, who many believe were Zoroastrian, traveled to Judah following a star at the time of Jesus' birth, and to worship who they believed to be a divine king to be born in Israel.

Based on modern computer generated star maps of what was happening in the heavens about the time of Christ's birth, we know that there were extremely rare planetary conjunctions occurring in the constellations Leo and Virgo. The symbol for the constellation Leo is the lion which is also the symbol of Judah (Israel). The symbol for Virgo is the "virgin." Some scholars now believe the magi traveled to Judah because they interpreted the extremely rare events they witnessed in the stars as pointing to the virgin birth of a divine King in Israel. What is most remarkable is that on September 11, 3 B.C., the sun was "clothed" (located in the middle of) the constellation Virgo (the Virgin), while the moon was located under the feet of Virgo, and the constellation Leo with its twelve stars (representative of Israel), was located above the head of Virgo. This dramatic sign in heaven could have marked the date of the conception of Jesus Christ. We relegate this particular sign to the conception because an even more spectacular heavenly sign occurred nine months later on June 17, 2 B.C., perhaps reflecting the date of Jesus' birth. And finally, a third sign, when Jupiter, the king planet, entered retrograde and came to a complete stop directly over Bethlehem on December 25, 2 B.C. This event fits the legend and biblical account of the arrival of the magi in Bethlehem. This extraordinary series of astrological events coincides with the words found in Isaiah 7:10, which state: ***"Therefore the Lord Himself will give you a sign: Behold, a virgin will be with child and bear a son, and she will call His name Immanuel."*** Yes, the date we celebrate Christ's birth on December 25th was set by the Church because there is no historical record indicating Jesus' actual birth date. Also, we know that the Magi did not visit on the date of Christ's birth, but afterward when the family is living in a house and not a stable. But God controls the heavens, and therefore these date alignments based on heavenly events appearing so long ago could provide insight and should be taken seriously.

Now move forward in time to an event foretold in Ezekiel, which many scholars view as an unmistakable sign of the end times—the rebirth of Israel as a nation in "one day" on May 14, 1948. Compare this to Isaiah 66:7-8, which reads: ***"Before she travailed, she brought forth; before her pain came, she gave birth to a boy. Who has heard such a thing? Who has seen such things? Can a land be born in one day? Can a nation be brought forth all at once? As soon as Zion*** *travailed, she also brought forth her sons."* Are the sons brought forth the twelve tribes of Israel reborn as the modern nation of Israel, no longer divided as depicted in Ezekiel 37:21-22, but one unified nation? Do we hear interwoven in these first two verses both the "signs" of Christ's first coming and of His return? Is the Virgin Mary the woman clothed with the sun, or perhaps Son, and through which Christ Jesus was born? It is perhaps no coincidence that the three young children in the village of Fatima, Portugal in 1917 will see the Virgin Mary appear to them, as they describe, *"clothed with the sun, with the moon at her feet, and a crown of twelve stars above her head."* These children will be shown visions and given three secrets which are said to be warnings calling for our repentance before the "end comes."

Revelation 12:3, states: ***"And another sign appeared in heaven: and behold, a great red dragon having seven heads and ten horns, and on his heads were diadems."*** The words we translate as red and as dragon only appear in the book of Revelation. The color red is actually fiery red as is the color of fire and is the same color as the second horse of the apocalypse which brought war. The dragon is understood as a form of giant and horrible serpent, and figuratively a representation of the devil or Satan. The seven heads may be symbolic for great wisdom. In Ezekiel 28 we see this serpent as full of wisdom, and the same one who was in the Garden of Eden, and as one who once dwelled in a special place on the holy mountain of God. God says: ***"You had the seal of perfection, full of wisdom and perfect in beauty. You were in Eden, the garden of God;... You were the anointed cherub who covers, and I placed you there. You were on the holy mountain of God; you walked in the midst of the stones of fire"*** (Ezekiel 28:12b, 13a and 14). The "anointed cherub who covers" may mean that he was a "guardian angel." Regarding the ten horns, Daniel 7 describes a great beast with ten horns coming up out of the sea (Daniel 7:7). In Daniel 7:24 we gain insight into what the horns may represent, for the "Son of Man" interprets the vision saying: ***"As for the ten horns, out of this kingdom ten kings will arise; and another will arise after them, and he will be different from the previous ones and will subdue three kings."*** This reference seems to imply a series or group of leaders or nations which will come up perhaps out of the sea of humanity to oppose God. Because the number ten is often seen as representing the world just as the number three is representative of God in reference to the Holy Trinity, this beast likely represents worldly and not religious leaders. The seven diadems or crowns on the horns of the beast probably represent the beast's dominion, power and/or authority over the world. Some identify the red dragon with Russia and China and the rise of Communism in these blatantly atheistic nations. There is actual Scriptural basis for this identity. Ezekiel speaks of nations from the north who will attempt to destroy Israel. Ezekiel 39:1 states: *"And you, son of man, prophesy against Gog, and say, 'Thus says the Lord God, "Behold, I am against you, O Gog, prince of Rosh, Meshech, and Tubal."* Gog is a word for ruler, which literally means the man on top. Gog is the chief prince of the land of Magog and the "prince of Rosh, Meshech, and Tubal" (Ezekiel 38:2). "Rosh" in the Hebrew is also an ancient name for Russia. Joseph Stalin said, *"We have deposed the czars of the earth and we shall now dethrone the Lord of heaven."* There is no doubt that Russia's atheistic government under Communism opposed God. Concerning "Meshech" and "Tubal" mentioned with Gog and Rosh, Genesis 10:1-2 informs us that of the three sons of Noah, that three of Japheth's sons would be named: "Magog, Tubal, and Meshech." Ethnologist—historians who track the migrations of people—tell us that after Noah's flood, the Japhethites (sons of Jephath and their tribes) migrated from Asia Minor to the north, beyond the Caspian and Black Seas. They settled in the area of Rosh that we know today as Russia. The Greek name *Moschi*, derived from the Hebrew name *Meshech*, is the source of the name of the city Moscow which is the capital of Russia.

<u>Revelation 12:4</u>, states: *"And his tail swept away a third of the stars of heaven, and threw them to the earth. And the dragon stood before the woman who was about to give birth, so that when she gave birth he might devour her child."* We cannot know for certain the meaning of the dragon's tail sweeping away a third of the stars of heaven. Many believe this is a reference to fallen angels who aligned themselves with Satan and were cast to the earth with him to become demons, supported by verse 9 which follows. Others believe this statement depicts a third of Christians being persecuted and/or killed by the dragon. We will address this further in our discussion of verse 9.

Regarding the woman, she is most likely Israel, and perhaps even a personification of the Virgin Mary, for the Messiah comes out of the Jewish people and specifically, Jesus was born of the Virgin Mary. What is interesting is that the dragon does not attack the woman but waits to attack the Child she will bear. This should remind us of God's declaration in the Garden of Eden to Eve, the mother of mankind, and to the serpent, the deceiver. God declares in Genesis 3:15, saying, *"And I will put enmity between you* [serpent] *and the woman, and between your seed and her seed; He* [Christ] *shall bruise you* [serpent] *on the head, and you* [serpent] *shall bruise him* [Christ and/or His followers] *on the heel."* I have inserted identifiers as most scholars believe are implied. Truly, Scripture consistently informs us that Christ will crush the head of Satan, but Satan's infliction upon Christ and His followers will not compare to Satan's ultimate destruction and punishment. In either case, what is clear is that the descendants of the "woman" will be in conflict with those who descend or are influenced by Satan. We can clearly see this depiction played out in King Herod's attempt to destroy the Christ child after His birth. As it is recorded in Matthew 2:16, saying, *"Then when Herod saw that he had been tricked by the magi, he became very enraged, and sent and slew all the male children who were in Bethlehem and in all its environs, from two years old and under, according to the time which he had ascertained from the magi."* From the beginning, Satan has used those under his control to wage war with God and all who serve Him.

Revelation 12:5, states: *"And she gave birth to a son, a male child, who is to rule all the nations with a rod of iron; and her child was caught up to God and to His throne."* There seems to be a strong correlation between this passage and Psalm 2. First, the Psalm portrays a picture of those who stand in opposition to God and His Christ, stating, *"Why are the nations in an uproar, and the peoples devising a vain thing? The kings of the earth take their stand, and the rulers take counsel together against the Lord and against His Anointed"* (Psalm 2:1-2). Psalm 2:9 references a "rod of iron" as it speaks of the power God will give to Christ over those who oppose Him, saying, *"Thou shalt break them with a rod of iron, Thou shalt shatter them like earthenware."* This Psalm also reinforces the premise that the red dragon of verse 3 represents worldly kingdoms or nations that oppose God.

Regarding the Child being "caught up" to God and to His throne, the Greek verb translated here means to take by force or take with power. It is the same verb used in 2 Corinthians 12:4, when Paul is "caught up into Paradise" to hear inexpressible words. It is the same verb root used in 1 Thessalonians 4:17, when those who remain alive in Christ are "caught up" in the clouds to meet the Lord in the air at the time of His return. King Herod failed to kill Christ as a baby because God intervened, warning Joseph in a dream to take Jesus and Mary and flee to Egypt (Matthew 2:13). The Roman governor Pontius Pilate, backed by the Jewish Sanhedrin, and the King Herod of Jesus' time, condemned Christ to die, but He defeated death, rose from the grave and ascended into heaven to take His place on the throne of God.

Second Vision: Michael's Victory Over the Dragon (12:7-9)

Revelation 12:6, states: *"And the woman fled into the wilderness where she had a place prepared by God, so that there she might be nourished for one thousand two hundred and sixty days."* It would be easy to compare this verse to Matthew 2:13, when God warned Joseph to take the holy family and escape from King Herod to Egypt, but this doesn't explain the 1,260 days. Again, most scholars identify the woman with Israel although some identify her with the Church. What is clear is that God will guide her to a place He has prepared in the wilderness and provide for her there for 1,260 days or 3-1/2 years. Is this the final and most terrible 3-1/2 year period of the Tribulation when Satan overpowers the saints who are martyred for the Word of God? If the woman represents Israel, everything makes perfect sense. In Revelation 7:3-8 we witnessed the sealing of 144,000 from the twelve tribes of Israel, so that they might not be harmed as destruction is released upon the earth. Jeremiah 30:7 speaks of a great and terrible time when God will protect His own, saying, *"Alas! for that day is great, there is none like it; and it is the time of Jacob's distress, but he will be saved from it."* Likewise, in Daniel 12:1 we are told: *"Now at that time Michael, the great prince who stands guard over the sons of your people, will* arise. *And there will be a time of distress such as never occurred since there was a nation until that time; and at that time your people, everyone who is found written in the book, will be rescued."* Is it during the final 3-1/2 years of the Tribulation that Satan makes his final attempt to destroy the Jews but God steps in to protect and deliver them?

Revelation 12:7-8, states: *"And there was war in heaven, Michael and his angels waging war with the dragon. And the dragon and his angels waged war, and they were not strong enough, and there was no longer a place found for them in heaven."* In Daniel 10:13 and 21 we are shown that there are struggles being waged between angels and heavenly forces that effect our lives here on earth. A heavenly messenger speaks to Daniel about the heavenly forces defending God's people in Daniel 10:21, saying, *"However, I tell you what is inscribed in the writing of truth. Yet there is no one who stands firmly with me against these forces except Michael your prince."* As we learned from Daniel 12:1 above, Michael is "the great prince who stands guard over the sons" of Israel. The apostle Paul also speaks of this unseen heavenly struggle in Ephesians 6:12, saying, *"For our struggle is not against flesh and blood, but against the rulers, against the powers, against the world forces of this darkness, against the spiritual forces of wickedness in the heavenly places."* Perhaps Michael stands guard over both Jews and Christians, but it is clear that we struggle against more than evil men.

Revelation 12:9, states: *"And the great dragon was thrown down, the serpent of old who is called the devil and Satan, who deceives the whole world; he was thrown down to the earth, and his angels were thrown down with him."* The prophet Isaiah speaks of Satan's fall from heaven, saying, *"How you have fallen from heaven, O star of the morning, son of the dawn! You have been cut down to the earth, you who have weakened the nations!"* (Isaiah 14:12). Likewise, we hear of this fall in Ezekiel 28, where it is written: *"By the abundance of your trade you were internally filled with violence, and you sinned; therefore I have cast you as profane from the mountain of God. And I have destroyed you, O covering cherub, from the midst of the stones of fire... By the multitude of your iniquities, in the unrighteousness of your trade, you profaned your sanctuaries. Therefore I have brought fire from the midst of you; it has consumed you, and I have turned you to ashes on the earth in the eyes of all who see you. All who know you among the peoples are appalled at you; you have become terrified, and you will be no more"* (Ezekiel 28:16, 18-19). While the implication is that Satan was cast from heaven long ago, when the seventy disciples Jesus sent out returned claiming that demons were subject to them in His name, He answered saying, *"I was watching Satan fall from heaven like lightening"* (Luke 10:18). We cannot see what is happening in heaven, and future events are often proclaimed in Scripture long before they actually occur. We have no way of knowing the exact time that Satan is cast from heaven along with His angels. We do know that the serpent deceived Adam and Eve in the very beginning and that Jesus and His disciples cast out demons, so Satan and his rebellious angels have had access to the earth for a long time. Also, we know Satan has also had access to heaven because Satan was allowed to come before God in heaven and accuse Job (Job 1:6; 2:1). Is it possible that Satan has retained at least some access to heaven until the very near end?

Third Vision: Song of Woe and Rejoicing (12:10-12)

Revelation 12:10, states: *"And I heard a loud voice in heaven, saying, "Now the salvation, and the power, and the kingdom of our God and the authority of His Christ have come, for the accuser of our brethren has been thrown down, who accuses them before our God day and night."* In this verse we find an answer to the previous question. Satan has continued to have access to heaven, accusing our brethren day and night. When the sixth seal was broken John said: *"and the stars of the sky fell to the earth"* (Revelation 6:13). And, when the fifth trumpet sounded John declared: *"I saw a star from heaven which had fallen to the earth; and the key of the bottomless pit was given to him"* (Revelation 9:1). How can Satan have fallen but not fall until the end? Perhaps we can resolve some of the confusion by separating spiritual from physical. Satan has "spiritually" fallen from grace, having been cast down from his position of service and power in the presence of God long ago because of his pride. The old adage is true that "pride comes before a fall." But now, in the final 3-1/2 years before final judgment and punishment are rendered, Satan is "physically" expelled from heaven and will no longer be allowed to be the accuser who accuses those who are faithful to God. Another way of looking at this is to understand the physical and spiritual realms, not as two places in different locations, but two realms which can occupy the same space. Scripture provides evidence that around us may exist things seen and unseen. Angles and demons may be near, respectively, providing protection or temptations. We cannot see them because they exist in the spiritual realm while we are in the physical realm. Scripture informs us that evil cannot stand in God's presence, therefore, Satan's fall may also be equated as a separation from God and a loss of access to God's presence.

Revelation 12:11, states: *"And they overcame him because of the blood of the Lamb and because of the word of their testimony, and they did not love their lives even to death."* Here we are told how the two witnesses of Revelation 11:1-6 could persevere against the beast and a hostile world for 3-1/2 years. Here we find the reason all who remain faithful to the Lord can persevere the trials and tribulations of this world. It is because of the saving blood of Jesus Christ. It is because of their testimony for Christ. It is because of their willingness to die for their belief in Christ and His Word. Let us not forget Jesus' declaration found in Mark 8:34-35, saying, *"If anyone wishes to come after Me, let him deny himself, and take up his cross, and follow Me. For whoever wishes to save his life shall lose it; but whoever loses his life for My sake and the gospel's will save it."*

Revelation 12:12, states: *"For this reason, rejoice, O heavens and you who dwell in them. Woe to the earth and the sea, because the devil has come down to you, having great wrath, knowing that he has only a short time."* After deceiving Adam and Eve in the Garden of Eden, the Lord cursed the serpent, saying, *"Because you have done this, cursed are you more than all cattle, and more than every beast of the field; on your belly shall you go, and dust shall you eat all the days of your life"* (Genesis 3:14). Satan is now truly confined to the dust of the earth. He will now suffer more than the cattle who are bred for slaughter, or the beast who live a life of burden. His time grows short before he is crushed by Christ. In the short time remaining, he is filled with wrath and the destroyer of lives seeks only to destroy everything created by God. But there is rejoicing in heaven because he has access to heaven no more.

Fourth Vision: The Woman and her Other Children (12:13-17)

Revelation 12:13, states: *"And when the dragon saw that he was thrown down to the earth, he persecuted the woman who gave birth to the male child."* We have seen plenty of evidence of his persecution of the woman. If the woman truly represents Israel and the Jewish people, clearly the Jews have suffered great persecution since the death and resurrection of Christ. We have especially seen evidence of this in the past century in the holocaust, witnessing the extermination of millions of Jews. Many nations gather now in the Middle East, and supported by Russia, conspire to eliminate Israel from the face of the earth.

Revelation 12:14, states: *"And the two wings of the great eagle were given to the woman, in order that she might fly into the wilderness to her place, where she was nourished for a time and times and half a time, from the presence of the serpent."* God declared to His people after delivering them from Egypt and leading them to the wilderness at Mount Sinai, saying, *"You yourselves have seen what I did to the Egyptians, and how I bore you on eagles' wings, and brought you to Myself"* (Exodus 19:4). God also nourished them in the wilderness, providing food for His people for 40 years. In Psalm 91 we see the image of God protecting His own under His wings. It is written: *"He who dwells in the shelter of the Most High will abide in the shadow of the Almighty... He will cover you with His pinions, and under His wings you may seek refuge; His faithfulness is a shield and bulwark"* (Psalm 91:1 and 4). It is also interesting to note, that the first nation of the world that recognized modern Israel as a nation when it declared itself such in May of 1948 was the United States of America, whose national symbol is the eagle.

Revelation 12:15-16, states: *"And the serpent poured water like a river out of his mouth after the woman, so that he might cause her to be swept away with the flood. And the earth helped the woman, and the earth opened its mouth and drank up the river which the dragon poured out of his mouth."* God used a flood of water that fell from the heavens and flowed up "out of the earth" (Genesis 7:11) to destroy the wicked of the world in the time of Noah. It is ironic that the earth swallows the flood poured out by Satan to destroy the woman of the righteous. There is a strong parallel found in "The Song of Moses and Israel" located in Exodus 15. The song depicts Pharaoh's pursuit of God's people which ends with Pharaoh and his army being swallowed by the waters of the Red Sea (remember the red dragon comes out of the sea). In Exodus 15:9-12, Moses sings: *"The enemy said, 'I will pursue, I will overtake, I will divide the spoil; my desire shall be gratified against them; I will draw out my sword, my hand shall destroy them.' Thou didst blow with Thy wind, the sea covered them; they sank like lead in the mighty waters. Who is like Thee among the gods, O Lord? Who is like Thee, majestic in holiness, awesome in praises, working wonders? Thou didst stretch out Thy right hand, the earth swallowed them."* Speaking of God's deliverance, Isaiah 25:8 states, *"He will swallow up death for all time, and the Lord God will wipe tears away from all faces, and He will remove the reproach of His people for all the earth; for the Lord has spoken."* It seems that the death that Satan pours forth will be swallowed up as the earth swallowed up the Egyptians. And finally, speaking of the evil one to come who brings desolation in the final week, Daniel 9:26b states: *"And its end will come like a flood; even to the end there will be war; desolations are determined."* The 144,000 of Israel sealed in Revelation 7:4-8 are under God's protection.

Revelation 12:17, states: *"And the dragon was enraged with the woman, and went off to make war with the rest of her offspring, who keep the commandments of God and hold to the testimony of Jesus."* Because the dragon is prevented from venting his wrath on the woman, he instead makes war with the rest of her offspring. Her "offspring" are defined as those who "keep the commandments of God and hold to the testimony of Jesus." This is a fairly good description of Christians and/or Messianic-Jews, which are Jews who hold to their Jewish heritage but believe that Jesus is the Messiah. In either case, the implication is that there are still at this point Christians or those who believe in Jesus Christ as the Messiah on the earth to wage war against.

CHAPTER 13:

In chapter 13 we are introduced to two beasts, one that comes up out of the sea and one that comes up out of the earth. These two beasts, combined with the dragon, form an unholy trinity of evil. Satan often mocks God with his own twisted imitations. In this unholy trinity, Satan is the counterpart of God the Father in heaven. The beast from the sea is generally seen as the Antichrist and a worldly leader (13:1-10). We are told three times (13:3, 12 & 14) that he has a fatal wound that has been healed; therefore, it is apparent that he is the intended counterpart of Jesus the Christ, who died and was raised from the dead. The beast from the earth is revealed as the "false prophet" (16:13; 19:20 & 20:10), and is a religious leader because he causes people to worship the beast—the Antichrist (13:11-13). Just as Christ's Church is filled with the power of God's Holy Spirit, the false prophet is given power by the beast to create great signs and wonders in order to cause the people of the earth to worship the beast. He then uses his influence to deceive the people of the earth into making an image of the beast, thus causing them to break God's second commandment and commit the sin of idolatry (13:14). The false prophet is then given power to bring the image to life so that it can speak, and cause those who do not worship the image of the beast to be killed (13:15). And finally, the false prophet through the power of the beast, requires people to be marked with the mark of the beast in order to conduct any commerce (13:16-17). Essentially, we see Satan's "worldly" influence requiring people to "bear his mark," and Satan's "religious" influence requiring people to "worship his image." The chapter concludes with the revealing of the number of the beast, which we are told is "that of a man," and is 666 (13:18). Clearly, the beast intends to be lord over both the secular and religious world, so that no one can live without being marked by him and worshiping him.

Fifth Vision: The Beast from the Sea (13:1-4)

Revelation 13:1, states: *"And he stood on the sand of the seashore. And I saw a beast coming up out of the sea, having ten horns and seven heads, and on his horns were ten diadems, and on his heads were blasphemous names."* The he who stands on the seashore is likely the dragon spoken of in the previous verse 12:17, and is enraged and will now make war with the rest of the woman's offspring using the two beasts he will bring forth. As for the first beast which comes up out of the sea, most scholars see this as a man, a worldly leader, and the personified Antichrist, coming out of the sea of humanity. We have discussed the ten horns and seven heads in our examination of 12:3 above, but there are new insights to consider from the book of Daniel. Remember that the meaning of the ten horns on the beast that Daniel saw were explained by the angel, who said, ***"As for the ten horns, out of this kingdom ten kings will arise"*** (Daniel 7:24). The question is: "Out of what kingdom do these ten kings arise?" In his explanation of the vision of the great statue, Daniel tells King Nebuchadnezzar that God is revealing mysteries of ***"what will take place in the end of days"*** (Daniel 2:28). Daniel describes the head of gold as the kingdom of Babylon (1), the breast and two arms of silver as representing the Medes and the Persians (2), the stomach of brass as the Greeks (3), the two legs of iron as the Roman Empire in its strength (4), and finally the two feet of iron mixed with clay as the Roman Empire in its later corrupted state and weakened condition (5). Some scholars see these depicting five of the heads of the beast. The sixth head is seen as coming at the end time. The sixth head being comprised of ten kings or nations which come out of Rome, or western civilization. These are associated with the ten toes on the feet of iron and clay. The final and seventh head may be perceived as the Antichrist, or the final manifestation of all that stands in opposition to Christ and His followers. Later in Revelation 17:10-12, we will see another depiction of seven heads, which we are told are seven kings, as well as ten horns which are ten kings. There it will be revealed that five of the seven have already fallen, that one is, and another is to come. This could correlate with Daniel's vision in that the five kingdoms of Babylon through Rome, which we are told have previously fallen. The ten kings, ten horns, ten toes, if equated with western civilization, exists now, and the Antichrist led worldly and religious overthrow of power are coming.

Regarding the ten diadems, as previously stated, these depict crowns and are symbolic of authority, power and dominion. Again, the number 10 is also symbolic of the world and depicts this beast and his dominion as worldly, or as a world leader.

Regarding the "blasphemous names" on the seven heads, while we translate the word "names" into English in the plural because of the seven heads, the Greek noun is singular, and should be translated as "name." This may mean that the name on all seven heads that is considered blasphemous is the same on all seven. Looking back at the kingdoms described by Daniel, their leaders all held one thing in common; they all claimed to be divine. Each demanded to be worshiped by their people. This was just as true for King Nebuchadnezzar of Babylon as it was for the emperors of Rome. I believe this is the key insight to the end times. It is a time when mankind puts himself above God, and the self-made man worships his creator, he worships himself. The beast out of the sea may also represent the rising influence of the age of "enlightenment" (17th and 18th centuries) when scientific discovery led mankind to believe we can know all things and can do all things through science. This was the beginning of the end of trusting Scripture as the ultimate source of truth, with human reasoning beginning to be elevated above God's Word. Not man, but only God, knows all and can do all.

Revelation 13:2, states: *"And the beast which I saw was like a leopard, and his feet were like those of a bear, and his mouth like the mouth of a lion. And the dragon gave him his power and his throne and great authority."* The description of the beast from the sea resonates with Daniel's vision of the four beasts found in Daniel 7. Regarding these beast Daniel sees, *"The first was like a lion"* (Daniel 7:4), the second one *"resembling a bear"* (Daniel 7:5), and the third was *"like a leopard"* (Daniel 7:6). While not apparently included in the description of 13:3 above, Daniel's fourth beast is described as *"dreadful and terrifying and extremely strong; and it had large iron teeth"* (Daniel 7:7). These four beasts are seen in Daniel to correlate with the first four parts of the great statue, representing the Babylonian (Lion), Medo-Persian (Bear), Greek (Leopard) and Roman (Strong beast with iron teeth) Empires. Again, seemingly to mock God and His Son, Jesus Christ, who is Incarnate, God in the flesh of man, the dragon (Satan) gives the beast his power, and throne, and great authority. Jesus declared in Matthew 28:18, saying, *"All authority has been given to Me in heaven and on earth."* And in Luke 22:69, Jesus proclaimed: *"But from now on the Son of Man will be seated at the right hand of the power of God."* The Antichrist, or spirit of the antichrist dwelling in mankind, will be the incarnate Satan, doing his evil will in the world as Jesus did the good will of His Father. While it may appear that this beast is a particular entity or a particular person, his manifestation may not be so clear that it is recognized as a particular person. The Antichrist may actually dwell in all men who put themselves above God and oppose God.

Revelation 13:3-4, states: *"And I saw one of his heads as if it had been slain, and his fatal wound was healed. And the whole earth was amazed and followed after the beast; and they worshiped the dragon, because he gave his authority to the beast; and they worshiped the beast, saying "Who is like the beast, and who is able to wage war with him?""* Again, seemingly to mock and imitate the death and resurrection of the true Christ, we hear that one of the heads of the beast from the sea will appear to have *"been slain, and his fatal wound was healed."* This will be emphasized three times in all, first here and then in 13:12 and 13:14. Just as the resurrection of Jesus Christ from the dead will result in Christians believing in the Lord and following Him, the *"whole earth was amazed and followed after the beast."* To the world the beast is seen as having power over death, therefore, the world worships the source of the beast's power, the dragon, and the beast who has apparently conquered death. The world does not believe that anyone can wage war against such power. The truth is that the power is false, a deception and lie, which is Satan's stock and trade as the great deceiver. We might ask ourselves, which is believed more today in the world we live in, that the true source of healing comes from scientific advances in medicine by men, or from faith in God?

Sixth Vision: The Beast from the Sea Exercises His Authority (13:5-10)

Revelation 13:5, states: *"And there was given to him a mouth speaking arrogant words and blasphemies; and authority to act for forty-two months was given to him."* Jesus was accused of blasphemy when He claimed to be the Son of God. At Jesus' trial before the Sanhedrin the high priest asked Him if He was the Christ, the Son of God. Jesus answered, saying, *"I am; and you shall see the Son of Man sitting at the right hand of Power, and coming on the clouds of heaven."* The high priest responded by tearing his clothes and saying, *"You have heard the blasphemy"* (Mark 14:60-64). Blasphemy is when one claims to be God who is not God. Jesus is God and His words were not blasphemy. The Antichrist, or spirit of antichrist dwelling in mankind, will claim to be what he is not and his mouth will be full of blasphemies. He will be allowed to speak arrogant words for forty-two months. Does man claim to be, or act as if he is God today?

Revelation 13:6, states: *"And he opened his mouth in blasphemies against God, to blaspheme His name and His tabernacle, that is, those who dwell in heaven."* In Daniel 7:8 it says that the beast was given *"a mouth uttering great boasts."* Notice that the Antichrist blasphemies against God, His name, and His tabernacle. Regarding the name of God, speaking of the "name" of Jesus Christ, the apostle Peter in Acts 4:12 proclaims: *"And there is salvation in no one else; for there is no other name under heaven that has been given among men, by which we must be saved."* Jesus Himself speaks of the importance of the "name" when He says: *"He who believes in Him is not judged; he who does not believe has been judged already, because he has not believed in the name of the only begotten Son of God"* (John 3:17). The "name" is the name "Jesus," and this is the name that the Antichrist speaks against and profanes. The Antichrist also blasphemies *"His tabernacle,"* which we are told is comprised of *"those who dwell in heaven."* This may be a reference to the angels who have forced him from heaven, and those who have been saved that he can no longer tempt and attack. But Scripture proclaims that God *"gave the right to become children of God, to those who believe in His name"* (John 1:12). The Antichrist cannot touch those who dwell in heaven so he shifts his focus to those who claim the name of Christ, who still dwell upon the earth. And let us not forget that Christ dwells in the hearts of Christians, therefore, we are a tabernacle (temple) of Christ. This means that Christians living on earth can expect to come under Satan's attack.

Revelation 13:7, states: *"And it was given to him to make war with the saints and to overcome them; and authority over every tribe and people and tongue and nation was given to him."* Just as the beast was allowed to kill the two witnesses in 11:7, a time will come when he will be allowed to make war and overcome the saints. He will also be given for a short time authority over every tribe and people and tongue and nation. Yes, God is in control but He will never take away our freedom of choice. Daniel 7:25 says the beast will *"wear down the saints of the Highest One, and he will intend to make alterations in times and in law; and they will be given into his hand for a time, times, and half a time."* In the last three and half years of the Tribulation, God may allow the beast to attack the saints directly, and the beast may overcome them, but he can only kill their mortal bodies, as he did the two witnesses. Those who remain true to God will have victory even in death. My late wife, in one of her many visions, saw Satan who proclaimed he had power over her. With a strength that she acknowledged came from God, she answered Satan with defiance declaring to him that he had no power over her except what she gave him. She then commanded him to leave in the name of Jesus Christ and Satan fled screaming. Truly, Satan has no power over us except what we give him, but he strives to deceive us into surrendering power to him. Perhaps he will wear some down, but let it not be you. Remember that Satan has no power over Christ, so remain faithful to Christ even unto death, and know that you already have gained your victory through the blood of Jesus Christ.

Revelation 13:8, states: *"And all who dwell on the earth will worship him, everyone whose name has not been written from the foundation of the world in the book of life of the Lamb who has been slain."* We must be careful each time we see the phrase, *"all who dwell on the earth"* because I don't believe it means all that physically live on the earth. Otherwise, why would the distinction be added referencing *"everyone whose name has **not** been written from the foundation of the world in the book of life"*? What is actually being said is that all those who live on the earth, AND are not believers in Jesus Christ, worshiped the beast. Speaking of those who lived by faith in God before the first coming of Jesus Christ, Hebrews 11:13 and 16 states: *"All these died in faith, without receiving the promises, but having seen them and having welcomed them from a distance, and having confessed that they were strangers and exiles on the earth… But as it is, they desire a better country, that is a heavenly one. Therefore God is not ashamed to be called their God; for He has prepared a city for them."* The words in Hebrews seem to imply that those who died in their faith saw not the earth but heaven as their home. I also believe that the moment we accept Jesus Christ as our Lord and Savior, the earth is no longer our home even though we still live here. At that moment we become both children of God and citizens of heaven, living as strangers in exile on the earth. In another of my late wife's visions the Lord Jesus Christ stood with her in the clouds facing the earth below. He pointed to the earth and said to her, *"This is not your home anymore."* He then showed her a magnificent golden city in heaven, and pointing to it said to her, *"This is your home now."* He then again pointed toward the earth and said to her, *"Now go and bring others home with you."* As Satan makes war against the saints, the earth may become a living hell, but to Christians, heaven will be our home. Remember, that Christ will never abandon you and that Jesus said to His disciples in Matthew 28:20, *"I am with you always, even until the end of the age."*

Revelation 13:9-10, states: *"If anyone has an ear, let him hear. If anyone is destined for captivity, to captivity he goes; if anyone kills with the sword, with the sword he must be killed. Here is the perseverance and the faith of the saints."* Verse 9 sounds a warning, and a call to pay special attention. This phrase came at the end of each of the seven letters to the churches in chapters 2 and 3. A time will come when God's people will suffer because of the sins of others. In Jeremiah 15:2, speaking of the judgment which will come on God's people because of the evil deeds of their king, God tells Jeremiah to tell them: *"And it shall be that when they say to you, 'Where should we go?' then you are to tell them, 'Thus says the Lord: "Those destined for death, to death; and those destined for the sword, to the sword; and those destined for famine, to famine; and those destined for captivity, to captivity."* Christians are not to resort to violence in their defense but put their faith in the Lord. When Peter drew his sword to defend Jesus, cutting off the ear of the slave of the high priest, Jesus responded saying, *"Put your sword back into its place; for all those who take up the sword shall perish by the sword"* (Matthew 26:52). The final sentence should remind us of the letter to the church at Smyrna. This was the blasphemed and persecuted church. Jesus told them, *"Do not fear what you are about to suffer. Behold, the devil is about to cast some of you into prison, that you may be tested, and you will have tribulation for ten days. Be faithful until death, and I will give you the crown of life"* (Revelation 2:10). What we are being told is that some Christians will be destined for captivity, persecution and martyrdom. This will be their fate, for they have been chosen, and *"written from the foundation of the world in the book of life of the Lamb who has been slain"* (13:8).

Through their sacrifice they honor the One who sacrificed Himself that they may have life eternal with Him in heaven.

Seventh Vision: The Beast from the Earth (13:11-18)

Revelation 13:11, states: *"And I saw another beast coming up out of the earth; and he had two horns like a lamb, and he spoke as a dragon."* While the first beast came up out of the sea, the second comes up out of the earth. The first is a worldly leader, but the second seems clearly to be a religious leader. This is supported by the fact that he causes people to worship the first beast, and because in Revelation 16:13, 19:20 and 20:10 he is referred to as the "false prophet." We are told that he has two horns "like a lamb." This second beast and third person of the satanic trinity seems to mock the roll of Christ in the Holy Trinity, being "like a lamb" but he is not the Lamb of God. He is definitely of Satan for he speaks "as a dragon," which we know to be Satan.

Revelation 13:12, states: *"And he exercises all the authority of the first beast in his presence. And he makes the earth and those who dwell in it to worship the first beast, whose fatal wound was healed."* As Jesus received His authority from His heavenly Father, this second beast "exercises all the authority of the first beast." He makes people worship the first beast. Essentially, this beast functions as priest, or the evil counterpart of the Christian Church. The Christian Church follows, worships, and witnesses for Jesus Christ, who was raised from the dead. This "false prophet" makes people "in the earth" worship the "worldly" beast out of the sea. Perhaps we see his presence in the secularization of religion and the Church. Perhaps he is the force that moves the Church from being centered in Christ to embracing the relativism of the world. We could also equate this with atheism and every belief or religion that stands opposed to Christ. He causes people to believe what God declared as truth is no longer true.

Revelation 13:13, states: *"And he performs great signs, so that he even makes fire come down out of heaven to the earth in the presence of men."* Jesus warned His disciples of these two beasts in Matthew 24:24, saying, *"For false christs and false prophets will arise and will show great signs and wonders, so as to mislead, if possible, even the elect."* At the end of time, before final judgment comes, Satan will be allowed to impart his supernatural power upon the false prophet, or the false church, which will perform miraculous signs and wonders in an effort to make people worship the true beast—Satan. Satan still wants what he has always wanted, to be worshiped like God, and to elevate himself to a place above God. We hear in 2 Thessalonians 2:9 that these signs and wonders are the activity of Satan and are false, as it is written: ***"the one whose coming in accord with the activity of Satan, with all power and signs and false wonders."*** Just as Pharaoh's magicians attempted to duplicate the plagues God sent upon Egypt in an effort to discredit God, so will the false prophet duplicate signs and wonders identified with God, such as bringing fire down from the sky.

Revelation 13:14, states: ***"And he deceives those who dwell on the earth because of the signs which it was given him to perform in the presence of the beast, telling those who dwell on the earth to make an image to the beast who had the wound of the sword and has come to life."*** The entire intent of the signs and wonders is to deceive those who dwell on the earth. The power to deceive comes from the beast—Satan. The false prophet performs the signs and wonders "in the presence of the beast," or through the power of the beast. And again, to mock God and His commandments, the false prophet instructs the people of the earth to make an image to the first beast. This is a direct violation of the second commandment found in Exodus 20:4: ***"You shall not make for yourself an idol, or any likeness of what is in heaven above or on the earth beneath or in the water under the earth."*** The signs and wonders have prepared the people to commit idolatry—to worship what is false, what is not God or of God. Perhaps in this we see reflected the materialism of our time, where things and the possession of things rule our lives. Jesus said, ***"No one can serve two masters; for either he will hate the one and love the other, or he will hold to one and despise the other. You cannot serve God and mammon"*** (Matthew 6:24). The literal translation of mammon is riches and/or material possessions.

Revelation 13:15, states: ***"And there was given to him to give breath to the image of the beast, that the image of the beast might even speak and cause as many as do not worship the image of the beast to be killed."*** To give something breath is to give it life (Genesis 2:7). The reason for the image of the beast to be given life is so it can speak and cause those who do not worship it to be killed. Essentially, an image made by the people of the earth, and not by God, is given life to cause the people of the earth, who do not believe it is alive, to be killed. The image is man-made. The image is of the Antichrist. The image is to be worshiped by the people of the earth. The image will cause those who refuse to worship to be killed. Do you see the image and understand what it is? The image is that of <u>mankind elevating himself above God</u>. That's what Satan did, and thus the image reflects Satan. In the beginning, Genesis 1:27 says, *"And God created man in His own image, in the image of God He created him; male and female He created them."* And in Genesis 2:7 we are told: *"Then the Lord God formed man of dust from the ground, and breathed into his nostrils the breath of life; and man became a living being."* Satan seeks to recreate man into his own image. Satan mocks God by having man create an image of himself, which Satan breathes life into, and demands that all of mankind worship or die. Satan longs for our destruction. As he did in the Garden of Eden, he attempts to deceive us into thinking that we are more than dust, that we can be "like God." The serpent deceived Eve regarding the forbidden fruit of the tree that God had instructed them not eat or touch or they would die. That ancient serpent (Satan) told Eve: *"You surely shall not die! For God knows that in the day you eat from it your eyes will be opened, and you will be like God, knowing good and evil"* (Genesis 3:4-5). We now "know evil" and the sin it causes when we listen to Satan's lie. It leads to death!

Revelation 13:16, states: *"And he causes all, the small and the great, and the rich and the poor, and the free men and the slaves, to be given a mark on their right hand, or on their forehead."* We mark ourselves by our choices, by what we do and what we believe. In John's time, people were forced to make a choice. They could either bow to worship the Roman Emperor as a god or face death. Some biblical scholars believe that this is what this passage is about. But it is not a Roman Emperor that people have always been forced to choose to worship or not, but a false god—idolatry. That choice remains today. We show who is Lord over our lives by who we worship, who we serve, who we put first in our life. We worship what we are focused on, what dominates our thoughts and minds. This is the mark on the head. We show who we worship by our actions, what we do, where we spend our time, and how we spend our money. This is the mark on the hand, for our hands are symbolic of our actions. We use our hands for work, and our work produces fruit. We are recognized and "marked by our fruit. In Matthew 7:17-19 Jesus states: *"Every good tree bears good fruit; but the bad tree bears bad fruit. A good tree cannot produce bad fruit, nor can a bad tree produce good fruit. Every tree that does not bear good fruit is cut down and thrown into the fire."* In Luke 6:44 Jesus also says: *"Each tree is known by its own fruit."* We mark ourselves by the kind of fruit we bear. The fruit we bear indicates who our Lord truly is, Jesus the Christ, or oneself. These marks transcend all social, economic and political boundaries. It doesn't matter who you are, how great or small. Each of us declares who is Lord of our life through our worship, reflected in our beliefs and in our actions. Ultimately, we have two choices. You will either put the Lord Jesus Christ first in your life or you will put yourself first. If you put yourself first, you worship the image of the beast, you worship yourself.

Revelation 13:17, states: *"and he provides that no one should be able to buy or to sell, except the one who has the mark, either the name of the beast or the number of his name."* In early Christianity and in times of persecution, Christians were excluded from access to many public places, and often lost their jobs and homes because they refused to worship the Emperor, and refused to deny Christ as Lord. The implication here is that at the end of time, Christians again will be excluded from participating in public commerce unless they deny their Christianity and "conform to the world." The apostle Paul warns against this, saying, *"Do not be conformed to this world, but be transformed by the renewing of your mind, that you may prove what the will of God is, that which is good and acceptable and perfect"* (Romans 12:2). Did you hear him say the *"renewing of your mind, that you may prove what the will of God is"*? This again reinforces the understanding that the "mark" on the "head" and "hand" pertain to our thoughts or focus, and our works or actions. There has been great speculation and debate about the "mark of the beast" and the "number of his name." In John's time it was seen as the emperor's seal. In our time it has been speculated to be everything from credit cards to implanted microchips. I do not believe it will be something tangible or physical such as a device or visible mark. I believe the mark of God and the mark of the beast are seen only in how we live our lives, and in the fruit our lives bear. The closer we get to the end, the harder it will be to live as a Christian without being in conflict with the world. It will become harder and harder to choose God over self and survive in the world. As times get tougher, we will see greater and greater pressure to turn inward and preserve ourselves rather than reach outward and help others. This is Satan's plan, to make it increasingly more difficult to be and live as a Christian—to live one's life for others rather than for oneself. Already we have seen some family businesses sued and even put out of business because they refused to serve a gay couple because of their Christian principles. This is only the beginning of the attacks that will befall Christians for standing on their Christian beliefs in opposition to a degrading worldly majority view.

Revelation 13:18, states: ***"Here is wisdom. Let him who has understanding calculate the number of the beast, for the number is that of a man; and his number is six hundred and sixty-six."*** First of all it should be noted, that while the vast majority and the most reliable ancient manuscripts of the book of Revelation depict the number as "666," a few manuscripts depict it as "616." We are told that the number is that of a "man." Many interpret this to mean that the number depicts a man's name. Because both the Greek and Hebrew alphabets used letters to depict numbers, many believe that the name could be derived from the numerical equivalents of the letters of the beast's name. Many names throughout the centuries have been claimed to represent that of the beast, ranging from Roman emperors to Catholic Popes. The most famous of these names is the Emperor Nero, whose title was both "*Nero* Caesar" and "*Neron* Caesar." The name portion in some ancient manuscripts is sometimes spelled with or without the final "n." What is so interesting is that when you add the numerical values of the letters in the Hebrew spelling of the name, "*Neron* Caesar" adds up to 666, and "*Nero* Caesar" adds up to 616. No other human name or title has ever been found that fits both the 666 and 616 numbers. Does this mean that Nero Caesar is the Antichrist? Those who believe that Revelation is all about Rome in John's time probably do, but Revelation clearly points to a future time for Christ's return and the judgment of the world. Certainly, this has not yet occurred and therefore Nero Caesar, long dead and gone, could not be the final Antichrist.

Some view the number 666 in different ways. For example, some view the number symbolic for removing God from all that He created, i.e., taking the sacred number seven (6 days of creation, plus the Sabbath day when we honor God the Creator), less one (God's day), repeated three times. What is certain is that the number six is significant in Scripture. God created the world in six days. The world was destroyed by flood when Noah was six hundred years old. Six hundred thousand men, along with women and children fled Egypt led by Moses. Pharaoh came after them with six hundred chariots. God provided manna from heaven for six days of each week, and the people were instructed to labor for six days, but rest on the seventh. The seventh commandment given by God through Moses, states: *"Remember the Sabbath day, and keep it holy. Six days you shall labor and do all your work, but the seventh day is a Sabbath of the Lord your God; in it you shall not do any work, you or your son or your daughter, your male or your female servant or your cattle or your sojourner who stays with you. For in six days the Lord made the heavens and the earth, the sea and all that is in them, and rested on the seventh day; therefore the Lord blessed the Sabbath day and made it holy"* (Exodus 20:8-11). From all of this we might derive that "six" is associated with the created world, and seven, which is also symbolic for completeness, is set aside for rest and holiness, for it is the day God commanded us to honor Him, the Creator of all things. This sounds an alarm as we reflect on how we have seen a steady deterioration of the Sabbath, one day in seven, being set apart for rest and worship. The world has placed more and more pressure on the faithful to consider Sunday just one more day, and the secularization in our society has made it more and more difficult to attend worship. Is this a manifestation of the number of the beast?

I discovered an interesting coincidence with the chapter and verse numbers, and the content of Proverbs 6:16, which begins a passage of four verses, saying: *"There are __six__ things which the Lord hates, yes, __seven__ which are an abomination to Him: Haughty eyes, a lying tongue, and hands that shed innocent blood, a heart that devises wicked plans, feet that run rapidly to evil, a false witness who utters lies, and one who spreads strife among brothers."* It should be clear by now that the number "666" or "616" could be interpreted in a multitude of ways. People might find whatever they are looking for, and this has been the case as people throughout the ages have manipulated the numbers to label those they oppose as the Antichrist. The bottom line is that we will not know his identity, or if he is an actual person, until God chooses to reveal him. I have already shared my own personal insight into his identity. I believe the spirit of the antichrist lives nested in idolatry, in the worship of that which is false and not of God. I believe that Satan has and continues to manipulate mankind to worship himself, to turn inward and be selfish and self-serving, rather than reflect the image of Christ, which is selfless and servant to others. I believe the truth is revealed in the last portion of verse 13:18, where it states, ***"for the number is that of a man; and his number is six hundred and sixty-six."*** What I hear is that the beast is *"any* man" who is focused on the "creation" rather than the "Creator." I believe the three-fold number six represents the six days in which everything we know as the world was created, excluding the seventh day, the day set aside by God to keep holy. Satan wants us to "exclude" God from our lives, setting self (created) above God (Creator).

The question we must ask ourselves is what do we do with this information? We may not be able to know the exact identity of the beast and the code of his name, but we know through the example and words of Christ how we are to live. We are not to put ourselves first or turn inward either in self-preservation or self-glorification. We are not to be self-seeking or self-serving. We are too concerned today about our own self-image, self-esteem, and self-reliance. We are not the center of our world, and while the world might continue to proclaim that "we can make ourselves into anything we want," the truth is that we were made in the image of God, and God has revealed His image to be Jesus. Jesus has taught us that we must empty ourselves to be filled with Him. We must follow Jesus' words and example, being willing to sacrifice ourselves for the sake of others as He sacrificed Himself for us. Only through putting Christ in the center of our lives will we gain eternal life. Jesus Christ is our Lord and Savior, and upon Him and Him alone will we find salvation. Jesus said, ***"I am the way, and the truth, and the life; no one comes to the Father, but through Me"*** (John 14:6). And the apostle Peter proclaimed: ***"There is salvation in no one else; for there is no other name under heaven that has been given among men,***

by which we must be saved" (Acts 4:12). May all our thoughts and actions be in Christ!

PART 7

Seven Visions of Worshipers of the Lamb and Beast

In Part 6 we began to see God's plan and its ultimate completion through a wider lens and a broader context. We stepped back and began to see the big picture; what has been going on behind the scenes. On earth we can see only the physical manifestations of an even greater heavenly battle between good and evil. In chapters 12 and 13, we gained insight into a struggle that began in the Garden of Eden, but became fever pitched with the first coming of Christ. We have seen Satan cast out of heaven, and begin to pour out his wrath upon the people of the earth. We have seen how he mocks God, creating his own false and unholy trinity. We have seen how he attempts to destroy that which has been created in God's image by deceiving us into breaking God's law and creating a false image to worship. We have even become aware that Satan's master plan is to trick us into elevating ourselves above God just as he attempted to do, which resulted in his condemnation. We now know that we mark ourselves by our own actions and thoughts as to who we worship, God or Satan. We finally understand that Satan's great deception is to get us to worship ourselves, to put the created before the Creator. We know that the number of the beast is that of man, any man or woman who puts themselves above God, and places their faith in themselves rather than trusting in God.

In Part 7 we will witness an expanded view of the events immediately preceding the pouring out of the wrath of God. Part 7 will be limited to Revelation chapter 14 alone.

CHAPTER 14:

In this chapter, we begin with a stark contrast to the ending of chapter 13. We move quickly from the number of the beast and those who bear his mark, to the Lamb standing on Mount Zion with those who have been sealed with His name and His Father's name. We are shown seven visions, depicting worshipers of the Lamb and worshipers of the beast. Each is complete in itself, but they are not necessarily presented as a chronological sequence of events, but rather panoramically with details to be revealed in subsequent chapters. The visions will include: (1) the Lamb and the 144,000 on Mount Zion who have been found blameless; (2) the angel with the everlasting Gospel; (3) the fall of Babylon; (4) the judgment of the worshipers of the beast; (5) the blessing upon those who die in the Lord; (6) the harvest of the elect; and, (7) the gathering of the wicked for destruction, which many associate with the last great battle of Armageddon. We continue to see an expanded view of the events which followed the seventh trumpet that were compressed into Revelation 11:18. This chapter provides a final transition before God pours forth His wrath upon the wicked.

First Vision: The Martyrs and the Lamb on Mount Zion (14:1-5)

Revelation 14:1, states: *"And I looked, and behold, the Lamb was standing on Mount Zion, and with Him one hundred and forty-four thousand, having His name and name of His Father written on their foreheads."* The Lamb who stands on Mount Zion is clearly the Lord Jesus Christ, but the location of Mount Zion is not clear. You see there are two possibilities regarding its location. We might assume that Mount Zion is on earth at the place revealed in Scripture as the city of Jerusalem, the City of David, and even more specifically the Temple Mount. But in this passage it might also be a heavenly Mount Zion where Jesus stands with those who followed Him, and now prepares to return to the earth. Hebrews 12:22 seems to describe such a heavenly place, stating: *"But you have come to Mount Zion and to the city of the living God, the heavenly Jerusalem, and to myriads of angels..."* While ultimately, Mount Zion will be the place where Christ will reign in glory forever, in regard to the End Times, it will be a place of war and judgment.

Speaking of a great battle in the end, Zechariah depicts Jerusalem as the place, saying, *"For I will gather all the nations against Jerusalem to battle, and the city will be captured, the houses plundered, the women ravished, and half of the city exiled, but the rest of the people will not be cut off from the city. Then the Lord will go forth and fight against those nations, as when He fights on a day of battle. And in that day His feet will stand on the Mount of Olives, which is in front of Jerusalem on the east; and the Mount of Olives will be split in its middle from east to west by a very large valley, so that half of the mountain will move toward the north and the other half toward the south. And you will flee by the valley of My mountains, for the valley of the mountains will reach to Azel; yes, you will flee just as you fled before the earthquake in the days of Uzziah king of Judah. Then the Lord, my God, will come, and all the holy ones with Him!"* (Zechariah 14:2-5).

Speaking of the great and terrible Day of the Lord, the Prophet Joel references Mount Zion as the place God will come down and pass judgment upon the nations, saying, *"And it will come about that whoever calls on the name of the Lord will be delivered; for on Mount Zion and in Jerusalem there will be those who escape, as the Lord has said, even among the survivors whom the Lord calls. For behold, in those days and at that time, when I restore the fortunes of Judah and Jerusalem, I will gather all the nations, and bring them down to the valley of Jehoshaphat. Then I will enter into judgment with them there on behalf of My people and My inheritance, Israel, whom they have scattered among the nations; and they have divided up My land"* (Joel 2:32—3:2).

In the end, as we can see in the world today, Jerusalem will be at the center of conflict and the place where nations will gather in an attempt to destroy God's people. In the wide angle view we are being given in these final chapters of Revelation, and in consideration of the terrible wrath and battle that is to be fought at Jerusalem on earth, it seems more likely that John's vision of the Lord on Mount Zion is a heavenly one.

Regarding the one hundred and forty-four thousand who have the Lamb's name and the Father's name on their foreheads, many presume these are the same 144,000 from the tribes of Israel who were sealed in Revelation 7:4-8. The key may be in that they bear both names, that of the Lamb (Jesus Christ) and the Father (Jehovah). This could confirm that they are out of the tribes of Israel, but now follow the Lord Jesus Christ. Another insight comes from the letter to the church in

Philadelphia. This was the church praised because they "kept the word" and "did not deny Jesus' name" (3:8). Jesus said to them who overcome: *"I will write upon him the name of My God, and the name of the city of My God, the new Jerusalem, which comes down out of heaven from My God, and My new name"* (3:12). We are told that these people, who did not deny the Lord's name and remained faithful to His word, will receive the "name of My God" and "My new name." In other words, they receive the name of the Father and the Son. We will learn more about this 144,000 in the verses that follow.

Revelation 14:2, states: *"And I heard a voice from heaven, like the sound of many waters and like the sound of loud thunder, and the voice which I heard was like the sound of harpists playing on their harps."* The sound of the voice is given a three-fold description as being like many waters, thunder, and harps. In Ezekiel 43:2 the sound of many waters is associated with the Lord coming into His temple. In Revelation 1:15, the Lord's voice is said to be like the sound of many waters. In Revelation 19:6, the sound of many waters and the sound of thunder are used to describe the multitude, praising the Lord as He begins to reign. But verse 14:3 begins saying, "they sang a new song." This would imply that the song comes from the 144,000.

Revelation 14:3, states: *"And they sang a new song before the throne and before the four living creatures and the elders; and no one could learn the song except the one hundred and forty-four thousand who had been purchased from the earth."* The fact that no one can learn the song except the 144,000 reinforces that they are the source of the song. This could also imply that only those who have not denied the name of Jesus and have kept His word can learn this song. Also clear is that the 144,000 are in "heaven" because they sing *"before the throne and before the four living creatures and the elders."* This seems to verify that the Lamb and the 144,000 are standing at the heavenly Mount Zion rather than in the Jerusalem on earth. The ending phrase, *"purchased from the earth,"* could also imply that this group is not limited to converted Jews but people of all nations. We gain this insight from the new song sang by the four living creatures and twenty-four elders who had been given harps and sang: *"Worthy art Thou to take the book, and to break its seals; for Thou wast slain, and didst purchase for God* with Thy blood *men from every tribe and tongue and people and nation"* (5:9).

Revelation 14:4-5, states: *"These are the ones who have not been defiled with women, for they have kept themselves chaste. These are the ones who follow the Lamb wherever He goes. These have been purchased from among men as first fruits to God and to the Lamb. And no lie was found in their mouth; they are blameless."* Clearly the 144,000 have been purchased for God through the blood of the Lamb and are followers of Christ. But are the 144,000 limited to virgin men, who *"have not been defiled with women"* and *"kept themselves chaste"*? This interpretation would not be consistent with God's word. From the beginning God has sanctioned marriage, saying in Genesis 2:24: *"For this cause a man shall leave his father and his mother, and shall cleave to his wife; and they shall become one flesh."* Proverbs 18:22 states: *"He who finds a wife finds a good thing, and obtains favor from the Lord."* God has made a distinction between the sexual relations that occur in the marriage bed from those outside of marriage, as expressed in Hebrews 13:4, which states: *"Let marriage be held in honor among all, and let the marriage bed be undefiled; for fornicators and adulterers God will judge."* While it is possible that the Lord literally means virgin men, it seems more likely and consistent with the context that the 144,000 are sinless regarding "idolatry." In the Old Testament, often the word "adultery" is used to describe "idolatry" as in Ezekiel 23:37, where it is said: *"Thus they have committed adultery with their idols and even caused their sons, whom they bore to Me, to pass through the fire to them* (idols) *as food."* Also, and consistent with an understanding that the beast wants us to put ourselves and the things of this world before God, James 4:4 calls this adultery saying, *"You adulteresses, do you not know that friendship with the world is hostility toward God? Therefore whoever wishes to be a friend to the world makes himself an enemy of God."* We need to remember as well that the Church, made up of many people and many nations, is to follow one Lord, and is to be the virgin bride of Christ. Paul writes in 2 Corinthians 11:2, saying, *"For I am jealous for you with a godly jealousy; for I betrothed you to one husband, that to Christ I might present you as a pure virgin."* Therefore, the 144,000 may be considered "virgin" and "chaste" because they have been completely faithful to Christ and have not fornicated with the idols of the world.

Regarding the 144,000 being called first fruits, this term is generally used to describe the best of fruits. Consistently in Scripture we are told to offer up to God our first and best as first fruits. Exodus 23:19 says: ***"You are to bring the choice first fruits of your soil into the house of the Lord your God."*** The apostle James refers to the early followers of Christ as first fruits, saying, ***"In the exercise of His will He brought us forth by the word of truth, so that we might be, as it were, the first fruits among His creatures"*** (James 1:18). Even if we have been washed clean by the blood of Christ, most of us have fallen short of the glory of God, and have likely committed the sin of adultery or idolatry with the world at some point in our lives. But perhaps the 144,000 comprise those who have never failed to remain faithful to the Lord.

Finally in verse 5, we are told that "no lie was found in their mouth" and that the 144,000 are "blameless." Satan is the author of lies and the accuser of the saints. To say that these followers of Christ have not lied and are blameless is to say that they have never fallen under Satan's deception, listened to his lies, or strayed from Christ's example. Peter instructs us to follow the example of Christ, which is to never lie and to remain blameless. In 1 Peter 2:21-22, he says, ***"For you have been called for this purpose, since Christ also suffered for you, leaving you an example for you to follow in His steps, <u>who committed no sin</u>, <u>nor was any deceit found in His mouth</u>."***

Second Vision: Angelic Admonition to Worship God (14:6-7)

<u>Revelation 14:6-7</u>, states: ***"And I saw another angel flying in midheaven, having an eternal gospel to preach to those who live on the earth, and to every nation and tribe and tongue and people; and he said with a loud voice, "Fear God, and give Him glory, because the hour of His judgment has come; and worship Him who made the heaven and the earth and sea and springs of water."*** This passage may remind us of Revelation 8:13, when an eagle flying in midheaven spoke of three woes about to come upon the earth just prior to the fifth, sixth and seventh trumpets. In this case the angel brings both good news and

a stern warning of impending judgment. The word gospel literally means good news and we know the good news of the gospel is that Jesus Christ has died for the sins of the world, and through His blood we may be forgiven our sins and reconciled with God. But in order to be washed clean through Christ's blood, we must accept Him as our Lord and Savior, and through genuine repentance, change our lives to follow His teachings and example. Jesus told Peter when he first refused to allow Him to wash his feet, *"If I do not wash you, you have no part with Me"* (John 13:8). Likewise, if we fail to submit to Christ as our Lord, allowing Him to be Lord over our lives, we cannot be washed clean of our sins. The message of the angel is universal in that it is intended for all people. He warns the people of earth that they must worship the one true God, who is Creator of all things, or they will soon perish. This is God's final warning to the earth. It is apparent that God has kept the door for repentance open, but it is about to be closed, and quickly followed by judgment. This event is likely what Jesus was speaking of when in Matthew 24:14 He said: *"And this gospel of the kingdom shall be preached in the whole world for a witness to all the nations, and then the end shall come."*

Third Vision: Angel Pronounces Doom of Babylon (14:8)

Revelation 14:8, states: *"And another angel, a second one, followed, saying, "Fallen, fallen is Babylon the great, she who has made all the nations drink of wine of the passion of her immorality."* This is the first mention of Babylon in Revelation, but it will be a prominent subject in Revelation chapters 17 and 18. We know that Babylon was the empire that conquered Judah in 586 B.C., destroying the Jewish Temple, and carrying away God's people into exile. There they would remain for 70 years until after the fall of the Babylonian Empire. A Jewish remnant would return about 536 B.C. but many would continue to live around Babylon, having become established there. Is it the city of Babylon and the Babylonian Empire that is being addressed in Revelation? Perhaps our best clue is the phrase "Babylon the great." While the name Babylon is used 294 times in the Bible, the phrase "Babylon the great" is used only six times, all of which are found in

Revelation with the exception of Daniel 4:30. The context of its use in Daniel provides us great insight. After standing on the roof of his royal palace and looking out over the great city of Babylon, the king proclaims: *"Is this not **Babylon the great**, which I myself have built as a royal residence by the might of my power and for the glory of my majesty?"* Daniel 4:31 then states: *"While the word was in the king's mouth, a voice came from heaven, saying, 'King Nebuchadnezzar, to you it is declared: sovereignty has been removed from you..."* The king's declaration that the greatness around him is of his own creation and for his own glory results in God immediately stripping him of his kingdom. This lesson is consistent with what we learned in Revelation 13. Satan wants us to elevate ourselves above God, proclaiming ourselves as the creators of our world, and to worship ourselves as creators. King Nebuchadnezzar also had created a statue of himself and declared that everyone must worship it or die, similar to the beast instructing man to create an image of the beast that God's faithful must worship or be killed. The parallels are too similar to ignore. The Babylonian Empire is long gone and the city of Babylon long destroyed. Babylon the great is likely not a place or a nation, but a system of belief that elevates man above God, where man believes that he is his own creator and master of his own world, and fails to honor God as Creator. The angel declares that "Babylon the great" is fallen, and the nations will no longer drink of this deception that leads to immoral behavior and death. Before moving forward it should be noted that in the phrase, *"wine of the passion of her immorality,"* the word translated as passion literally means anger, wrath or violent emotion. Drinking of the wine of Babylon the great will result in God's anger and wrath being poured from His cup.

Fourth Vision: Condemnation of Worshipers of the Beast (14:9-11)

Revelation 14:9-10, states: *"And another angel, a third one, followed them, saying with a loud voice, "If anyone worships the beast and his image, and receives a mark on his forehead or upon his hand, he also will drink of the wine of the wrath of God, which is mixed in full strength in the cup of His anger; and he will be tormented with fire and brimstone in the presence of the holy angels and in the presence of the Lamb."* This is a clear and unmistakable warning that those who worship the beast, his image and receive his mark will face God's wrath. This simply means that those who elevate themselves above God, worship themselves, and mark themselves as belonging to the beast through their actions (hands), and focus of their mind (forehead) will be subject to God's wrath and punishment. Their punishment will be the fire and brimstone of hell. The fact that their torment will be in the presence of the holy angels and the Lamb may bother some people, who think this means that the Lord and His angels will gain some pleasure or satisfaction out of their torment, but I do not think this is the intent of what is being expressed. Rather, they will face eternal shame in that their evil actions and choices will be forever exposed in the presence of what is good and holy.

Revelation 14:11, states: *"And the smoke of their torment goes up forever and ever; and they have no rest day and night, those who worship the beast and his image, and whoever receives the mark of his name."* Many find the concept of eternal punishment unsettling. How could a loving God ever cause anyone to suffer punishment forever? This strikes us as unfair or too harsh, but it is not God who destines people to a place of eternal punishment, but the actions of those who have rejected God and His gift of eternal life through Christ. The Bible is consistent in its teaching. The place of punishment will be eternal, forever, and everlasting. Speaking of the eternal punishment at the end of time, the Lord proclaims through His prophet Isaiah, *"Then they shall go forth and look on the corpses of the men who have transgressed against Me. For their worm shall not die, and their fire shall not be quenched; and they shall be an abhorrence to all mankind"* (Isaiah 66:24). In Matthew 25:46, Jesus distinguishing between those who fail to serve Him and those who do, saying, *"And these will go away into eternal punishment, but the righteous into eternal life."* Later in Revelation 20:10, we will be told that this place is the "lake of fire" which is a place of torment, *"day and night forever and ever."* Choose Christ! Choose life! And escape the eternal fire!

<u>Fifth Vision</u>: Heavenly Benediction of the Martyrs (14:12-13)

<u>Revelation 14:12</u>, states: *"Here is the perseverance of the saints who keep the commandments of God and their faith in Jesus."* Most scholars link this verse with the condemnation found in the preceding verses 9-11, as an assurance to the saints that punishment will not be their fate if they keep the commandments of God and faith in Jesus. We were given a similar assurance in 13:10, when we learned that many saints would face captivity and death in the end. I am again reminded of Jesus' words to the church at Thyatira, saying, *"I know your deeds, and your love and faith and service and perseverance, and that your deeds of late are greater than at first"* (2:19). I believe there is a link between our perseverance and our continuing to do the deeds that Christ has called us to do. Therefore, I believe these two verses are linked. We witness best our perseverance of faith when we continue to openly serve the Lord even when it is most difficult, and from a worldly perspective, may cost us our very lives.

<u>Revelation 14:13</u>, states: *"And I heard a voice from heaven, saying, "Write, 'Blessed are the dead who die in the Lord from now on!'" "Yes," says the Spirit, "that they may rest from their labors, for their deeds follow with them.'"* There is some debate regarding the true meaning of this passage. I feel the key to understanding it is found in the words *"who die in the Lord from now on."* We know that the final warning has just been given and punishment is about to rain down on the earth. Christians who are still alive on the earth have presumably endured great hardship in living their faith. But perhaps also, this passage speaks hope to those who will genuinely repent and turn to the Lord in their final moments. Paul in Romans 10:13, quotes the words of the prophet Joel, speaking of the end times, saying, *"Whoever will call upon the name of the Lord will be saved."* Jesus reinforces this understanding in His story of the "Laborers in the Vineyard" found in Matthew 20. Here he gives those who enter the field to work in the last hour the same reward as those who worked all day. It should be our prayer that people will turn to Christ and be saved even at the last minute.

Regarding the phrase, *"their deeds follow with them,"* in 2:23 Jesus said, *"I will give to each one of you according to your deeds."* We are told that at the final judgment and the books are opened, that everyone will be judged *"according to their deeds"* (20:12-13). Even as Revelation closes, Jesus will remind us, saying, *"Behold, I am coming quickly, and My reward is with Me, to render to every man according to what he has done"* (22:12). Paul tells us in Romans 12:28 that *"man is justified by faith apart from works,"* but James reminds us that *"faith without works is dead"* (James 2:26). The bottom line is that how we live our faith and what we do with our faith will be remembered by God, and our deeds will follow us even after death.

Sixth Vision: The Son of Man and the Harvest of the Elect (14:17-20)

Revelation 14:14, states: *"And I looked, and behold, a white cloud, and sitting on the cloud was one like a son of man, having a golden crown on His head, and a sharp sickle in His hand."* Some Bibles translate the above as "son of man" and others as the "Son of Man." The distinction makes all the difference in how we understand the verses that follow. The Greek phrase is identical to that found in Revelation 1:13, *"one like a son of man."* In 1:13 the description which follows is clearly that of Jesus Christ. The cloud is an important clue. God has frequently appeared or been associated with a cloud. When Jesus was baptized, God spoke and a dove descended from a cloud. When Jesus was transfigured, God spoke from a cloud. Jesus was raised and disappeared into a cloud. And we are told Jesus will return on the clouds of heaven. Another clue may be that He has a golden crown on His head. Again, this may be intended to depict Him as Lord and King. On the other hand, the one who sits upon the cloud may be an "angel of the Lord" sent by Christ to gather the harvest, because in Matthew 24:31 Jesus, speaking of the time of His return, says: *"And He will send forth His angels with a great trumpet and they will gather together His elect from the four winds, from one end of the sky to the other."* Also, in the parable of the "Tares and the Wheat" Jesus says, *"and the harvest is the end of the age; and the reapers are angels"* (Matthew 13:39). In either case, whether this is Christ Himself or His angel, because He alone has been given authority to harvest the elect and punish the wicked, these actions are by Christ's authority.

Revelation 14:15, states: *"And another angel came out of the temple, crying out with a loud voice to Him who sat on the cloud, "Put in your sickle and reap, because the hour to reap has come, because the harvest of the earth is ripe."* It may trouble us to think that an angel could be directing Christ or Christ's agent, but Matthew 24:36 says: *"But of that day and hour no one knows, not even the angels of heaven, nor the Son, but the Father alone."* The angel comes "out of the temple" to inform the one on the cloud that the *"hour to reap has come."* Something else I found interesting in this particular verse is that the literal meaning of the Greek word translated as "ripe" is "has become dry." We harvest crops when they have reached their peak. With grain crops this is when they become dry, meaning the stalk will provide no additional nourishment and growth. A time is coming when God will determine the Church has grown dry and lacks the potential of further growth. Then the harvest will come swiftly.

Revelation 14:16, states: *"And He who sat on the cloud swung His sickle over the earth; and the earth was reaped."* The verb translated as "swung" in Greek literally means "to cast, throw, or bring," and in some cases can mean "to thrust or strike." In all cases it happens as an impulse or suddenly. Many see this moment as the moment that the elect are harvested from the earth. Scripture gives us numerous accounts of this sudden event. In 1 Corinthians 15:51-53, Paul speaks of the mystery of the moment we are all changed from perishable to imperishable. He says: *"Behold, I tell you a mystery; we shall not all sleep, but we shall all be changed, in a moment, in the twinkling of an eye, at the last trumpet; for the trumpet will sound, and the dead will be raised imperishable, and we shall be changed. For this perishable must put on the imperishable and this mortal must put on immortality."* Perhaps the best description of this scene from Revelation is described by Paul in 1 Thessalonians 4:16-17, saying, *"For the Lord Himself will descend from heaven with a shout, with the voice of the archangel, and with the trumpet of God; and the dead in Christ shall rise first. Then we who are alive and remain shall be caught up together with them in the clouds to meet the Lord in the air, and thus we shall always be with the Lord."* And of course, Jesus

Himself spoke of this moment in the Apocalyptic Discourse found in Matthew 24. Jesus says: *"And then the sign of the Son of Man will appear in the sky, and then all the tribes of the earth will mourn, and they will see the Son of Man coming on the clouds of the sky with power and great glory. And He will send forth His angels with a great trumpet and they will gather together His elect from the four winds, from one end of the sky to the other"* (Matthew 24:30-31). All of these descriptions may be of the same event, the gathering of the elect, and the reaping of the harvest.

But why does there appear to be two harvests back to back in Revelation 14:14-16 and then 14:17-20, which follows? Perhaps the explanation can be found in the parable of the "Tares and the Wheat" found in Matthew 13:24-30, and explained in verses 36-43. God plants a harvest with good seed, but the devil comes in the night and sowed tares among the wheat. Tares have the same appearance as wheat when they are growing, but when they yield their fruit it is different and poisonous. When it is apparent that tares are growing with the wheat the slaves want to pull them up, but the landowner tells them: *"Allow both to grow together until the harvest; and in the time of the harvest I will say to the reapers, "First gather up the tares and bind them in bundles to burn them up; but gather the wheat into my barn""* (Matthew 13:30). At the end of Revelation 14 we see a harvest followed by a second cutting. The first, which we have just depicted in 14:14-16 is clearly designated as a harvest, which by very definition is a crop that has been planted and is of value. The second cutting, as we will see in the following verses will be placed in the *"wine press of the wrath of God"* (14:19). This does not sound like a harvest but punishment and destruction.

<u>Seventh Vision</u>: The Destruction of the Wicked (14:17-20)

<u>Revelation 14:17</u>, states: *"And another angel came out of the temple which is in heaven, and he also had a sharp sickle."* A second angel comes from the temple in heaven, which we can interpret as being sent by God the Father. He comes after the harvest has been conducted by the one who is like the "Son of Man." If what is good has been harvested, then what will be the fate of that which remains?

Revelation 14:18, states: *"And another angel, the one who has power over fire, came out from the altar; and he called with a loud voice to him who had the sharp sickle, saying, "Put in your sharp sickle, and gather the clusters from the vine of the earth, because her grapes are ripe."* We are told this angel has power over fire, and comes from the altar. In Revelation 8:5, an angel took fire from the altar and threw it down upon the earth, which was clearly an act of punishment. It would seem immediately apparent that this event will be associated with punishment. Note that the sickle is to gather clusters of grapes from the *"vine of the <u>earth</u>."* In John 15:5, Jesus says: *"I am the vine, you are the branches; he who abides in Me, and I in him, he bears much fruit; for apart from Me you can do nothing."* This vine is not connected to Christ but to the earth. The beast has deceived people to worship the creation rather than the Creator, to depend on themselves rather than on God. This crop has grown out of the deception of Satan rather than the grace of the Lord. This crop is full of all that is evil and is ripe for judgment and destruction.

Revelation 14:19, states: *"And the angel swung his sickle to the earth, and gathered the clusters from the vine of the earth, and threw them into the great wine press of the wrath of God."* If there was any doubt about the nature of the grapes being gathered, it is dispelled when we learn they are to be placed in the *"great wine press of the wrath of God."* This is not a place you want to end up. The prophet Joel, speaking of the "Day of the Lord" and when the nations are judged, says: *"Let the nations be aroused and come up to the valley of Jehoshaphat, for there I will sit to judge all the surrounding nations. Put in the sickle, for the harvest is ripe. Come, tread, for the wine press is full; the vats overflow, for their wickedness is great"* (Joel 3:12-13). Those gathered into the wine press are doomed to destruction.

Revelation 14:20, states: *"And the wine press was trodden outside the city, and blood came out from the wine press, up to the horses' bridles, for a distance of two hundred miles."* According to Revelation 19:15, the one who treads the wine press is the coming Christ, for it is written: *"And from His mouth comes a sharp sword, so that with it He may smite the nations; and He will rule them with a rod of iron; and He treads the wine press of the fierce wrath of God, the Almighty."* It may be no coincidence that the river of blood that flows from the wine press is two hundred miles in length. This is the approximate length of the nation of Israel from its northern to southern borders. The numbers that are slaughtered will be great. According to Ezekiel 9:12-13, ***"For seven months the houses of Israel will be burying them in order to cleanse the land. Even all the people of the land will bury them; and it will be to their renown on the day that I glorify Myself, declares the Lord God."*** The battle of Armageddon will be revealed in more detail in Revelation 16 and 17. Many scholars associate this great slaughter with the battle of Armageddon. They make this association because, as we will learn in the chapters which follow, the great battle of Armageddon will occur in this same general area, and will be the ultimate culmination of the struggle between good and evil on earth, between God's people and those who oppose God and His people.

PART 8

Seven Visions of the Bowls of God's Wrath

Part 7 consisted of seven visions or scenes depicting a series of events or declarations associated with the end, and in preparation for the punishment which is about to be completed. We were shown a glimpse of the Lamb, and 144,000 who follow Him gathered at Mount Zion in heaven. We heard an angel proclaim the gospel to all nations and warn of impending judgment. We heard proclaimed the fall of Babylon, the proclamation that those who follow the beast will suffer God's wrath, and a blessing for those who die in Christ. And finally, we witnessed the harvest of the elect and gathering of the wicked for punishment. Part 7 covered only one chapter, Revelation 14.

Part 8 will comprise chapters 15 and 16. Chapter 15 sets the stage and introduces us to the final set of plagues—the six bowels of wrath. The first expressions of God's punishment began with the seven seals (6:1-17). Out of the seventh seal came the seven trumpets (8:1-13; 9:1-21; and 11:15-19). Out of the seventh trumpet follows the seven bowls of God's wrath (15:1; 16:1-21). Bowls are used because the contents can be poured out quickly. We should be reminded of Revelation 1:1 where we learned that coming soon did not mean a short time from now, but quickly as in when the end begins it will happen over a very short length of time. The tribulation of seven years is finished when the pouring of the seven bowls of wrath is completed, but this will not mark the end of Revelation. The pouring of the seven bowls of wrath will be the fiercest expression of God's anger. These seven judgments will include: (1) the bowl of loathsome and malignant sores covering the bodies of those who received the mark of the beast; (2) the sea of blood, which causes everything in the sea to die; (3) the rivers of blood, which will render rivers and springs undrinkable; (4) the scorching heat of the sun; (5) the darkness that causes pain; (6) the drying up of the river

Euphrates allowing an army to march on Israel; and, (7) the air being affected in such a way that the face of the earth is changed, and huge hailstones fall from the sky. Again we will witness a brief pause between the sixth and seventh bowl. This will be the gathering for the final great battle of Armageddon. Many of these final plagues seem to have parallels in the previous seals, especially in the trumpets. Some scholars believe the seals, trumpets and bowls are a three-fold expression of the same punishments, but there are differences. Perhaps they better represent God's deepening warning to repent or face eternal judgment.

CHAPTER 15:

In this chapter, we are provided an introduction to the seven last plagues of God's wrath. But this is more than an introduction because it also provides assurance that those who have remained faithful will not suffer God's wrath. We even hear a celebration of praise and thanksgiving for God's righteousness and justice.

 Revelation 15:1, states: *"And I saw another sign in heaven, great and marvelous, seven angels who had seven plagues, which are the last, because in them the wrath of God is finished."* Again we are shown a scene in heaven, a view of things happening that we cannot see on earth. The scene is "great and marvelous" for it depicts the greatest and fiercest of all the punishments, but it is also reassuring that this will be the finish of God's wrath. If God's wrath is finished then it must be satisfied, and therefore, justice for the wicked complete. Regarding the seven angels, we do not know if they are the same seven that were mentioned in 8:1 and 6, who blew the seven trumpets. Again, seven is a number of completeness. While we heard seven angels blow seven trumpets, in many places in Scripture we are told only that the end will come with the blowing of the "great" or "last" trumpet. We are now about to have seven angels pour out seven bowls of wrath, which can be seen as the great and final punishments.

 Revelation 15:2, states: *"And I saw, as it were, a sea of glass mixed with fire, and those who had come off victorious from the beast and from his image and from the number of his name, standing on the sea of glass, holding harps of God."* Revelation 4:6 described a sea of glass which was part of the first scene in heaven we were shown. This was the first time we were shown God on His throne surrounded by four living creatures and twenty-four elders. This time the sea of glass is mixed with fire. Any sea that looks like glass can be said to be calm, without turbulence, and peaceful. The "mixed with fire" may be a reference to the refining fire that those who have come off victorious from the beast and from his image and from the number of his name have endured. They have passed through fire to a place of peace. Isaiah 43:2-3a, describes those redeemed by God as having endured passing through flood and fire, saying, *"When you pass through the waters, I will be with you; and through the rivers, they will not overflow you. When you walk through the fire, you will not be scorched, nor will the flame burn you. For I am the Lord your God, the Holy One of Israel, your Savior."* These who are victorious now stand on the sea of glass, which indicates that they are above and present in heaven. In 5:8 we were told that each of the twenty-four elders around the throne of God was given a harp. Now we are told that all those who stand on the sea are holding harps of God. They have glorified God through remaining faithful, and thus becoming victorious over the beast. Now they will glorify God as instruments singing His praise.

Revelation 15:3-4, states: *"And they sang the song of Moses the bond-servant of God and the song of the Lamb, saying, "Great and marvelous are Thy works, O Lord God, the Almighty; righteous and true are Thy ways, Thou King of the nations. Who will not fear O Lord, and glorify Thy name? For Thou alone art holy; for all the nations will come and worship before Thee, for Thy righteous acts have been revealed."* The song of Moses is in Exodus 15 and was sang by Moses and the Hebrew people after God rescued them by allowing them to safely cross the Red Sea on dry land, and then causing the sea to return and drown Pharaoh and the Egyptian soldiers. When the people saw that God had delivered them through His mighty power they sang Him praise. The same applies here. The words are not the same as in the original song of Moses, but the meaning and intent are the same. They express glory to God for the victory He has provided. It is perhaps important to note that the term "righteous acts" at the end of verse 4 above can also be translated as "judgments." Therefore what is being revealed is that God is now about to pass judgment upon the wicked, which is considered a righteous act because those to be judged deserve the punishment they are about to receive.

Revelation 15:5-6, states: ***"After these things I looked, and the temple of the tabernacle of testimony in heaven was opened, and the seven angels who had the seven plagues came out of the temple, clothed in linen, clean and bright, and girded around their breasts with golden girdles."*** Previously, when the seventh trumpet was blown, heralding the beginning of the reign of Christ, we were told that ***"the temple of God which is in heaven was opened; and the ark of His covenant appeared in His temple"*** (Revelation 11:19). Now we are told again that the temple in heaven is opened. We are also given a new description, saying, ***"the tabernacle of testimony in heaven was opened."*** The tabernacle of testimony is mentioned several times in the Old Testament as part of the tent tabernacle that housed the Ark of the Covenant, and items used for the worship of God. Essentially, the tabernacle functioned as God's house or dwelling place. The Ark of the Covenant was viewed as God's seat, and was placed in the "holy of holies" inside the tabernacle. Within the Ark were placed the Ten Commandments and a jar of manna as a testimony. In Exodus 40:21 the Ark is referred to as the "Ark of Testimony." The Ark of Testimony resided in the tabernacle of testimony. The Ark of the Testimony was always kept concealed in the holy of holies, and it was only accessed once a year on the Day of Atonement by the high priest. The Greek word translated as "testimony" literally means "witness, evidence or proof." Therefore, what is happening in this scene is that God's tabernacle (dwelling place) is being opened so that the testimony (evidence and proof) can be witnessed.

The seven angels have an appearance similar to that described of Christ in Revelation 1:13, which described Him as "girded across His breast with a golden girdle." The angels are also said to be "clothed in linen, clean and bright," which is a description normally associated with purity and righteousness. We can glean from this entire description that the angels act for Christ, and the punishment about to be poured out is righteous and just.

Revelation 15:7, states: ***"And one of the four living creatures gave to the seven angels seven bowls full of the wrath of God, who lives forever and ever."*** We already know that the four living creatures constantly serve and worship God. Previous descriptions seem to place them closest to God's throne. It may seem an oversimplification, but perhaps from this we can surmise that the bowls of wrath given to the angels come directly from God by means of one of the four living creatures.

Revelation 15:8, states: *"And the temple was filled with smoke from the glory of God and from His power; and no one was able to enter the temple until the seven plagues of the seven angels were finished."* In Exodus 40:34-35 we are told that when the cloud of God rested on the tabernacle, it was filled with smoke and power and glory of God. During that time, Moses could not enter the tabernacle. Above the tabernacle God would appear as a column of smoke by day and a column of fire by night. Only when God lifted up and no longer rested and filled the tabernacle could it be entered. This earthly event seems a foreshadowing of this heavenly scene. The tabernacle in heaven cannot be entered by man or angel until the seven angels have finished pouring out God's wrath upon the wicked.

CHAPTER 16:

In this chapter we will hear described the final seven punishments of God through the pouring out of the seven bowls of wrath. We will discover the descriptions to have similarities to both some of the plagues that fell upon Egypt when God delivered His people, and the punishments described in the breaking of the seven seals, and especially the sounding of the seven trumpets. Again, some scholars believe the seals, trumpets and bowls of wrath depict the same events, while others see them as a series of escalating punishments. Because of the distinct differences and obvious partial nature of the punishments found in the seals and trumpets, it seems more likely that these events reflect separate, escalating punishments. One thing is certain, the punishments depicted in the bowls of wrath are extremely severe and the most complete. Let us now examine in detail the final punishments in the seven bowls of the wrath of God.

Revelation 16:1, states: *"And I heard a loud voice from the temple, saying to the seven angels, "Go and pour out the seven bowls of the wrath of God into the earth."* In 15:8 we were told that the temple was *"filled with the smoke from the glory of God and from His power and no one was able to enter the temple until the seven plagues of the seven angels were finished."* This means no one but God Himself is in the temple, therefore the voice coming from the temple is the voice of God. The seven bowls of wrath have come from God and it is God who commands they be poured into the earth. The NASB translates the Greek preposition as "into" but based on context it could equally be translated as "in, on, upon, or onto." There is no hidden meaning implied here. The NASB likely uses into because the bowls' contents will be poured out, and the earth will receive them. There is a sense that they will not be spilled beyond those who are destined to receive them, therefore, they are poured into the wicked on earth. They are for the wicked alone.

First Bowl: Plague of Ulcers (16:2)

Revelation 16:2, states: *"And the first angel went and poured out his bowl into the earth; and it became a loathsome and malignant sore upon the men who had the mark of the beast and who worshiped his image."* This plague seems partial fulfillment of the angel's warning in 14:9-10, that those with the mark of the beast will drink of the wine of the wrath of God. The description of the affliction closely resembles that described in Exodus 9:8-12, which depicts the fifth plague that God brought upon the Egyptians through Moses in order to force them to release His people. This was the plague of "boils breaking out as sores" (Exodus 9:9). This first plague is intended to cause misery but not death. This is also reminiscent to the "sore boils" that Satan inflicted Job with in an attempt to induce him to curse God, but Job remained faithful even in his suffering. This will not be the case for the wicked of the earth.

Second Bowl: Sea Turned to Blood (16:3)

Revelation 16:3, states: *"And the second angel poured out his bowl into the sea, and it became blood like that of a dead man; and every living thing in the sea died."* The second bowl plague, like the second trumpet (8:8-9), causes the sea to turn to blood. The second trumpet only affected a third of the sea, but this time all the sea will die. The water is turned into blood "like that of a dead man," which would be foul and coagulated. The trumpet sounded a warning and only a partial punishment, allowing room and opportunity for repentance. This time death in the sea is total and complete. The sea will no longer yield its fruit for man.

<u>Third Bowl</u>: Rivers and Springs Turned to Blood (16:4-7)

<u>Revelation 16:4</u>, states: *"And the third angel poured out his bowl into the rivers and the springs of water; and they became blood."* All life in the sea, the salt waters of the world, died with the pouring out of the second bowl. The third bowl makes all the drinking water in rivers and springs undrinkable. Through the blood of Jesus Christ the righteous have been saved. Jesus called the wine at the Last Supper, His blood of the new covenant. It is the cup of salvation, and the blood that washes away sin. The first plague upon Egypt was when the Nile River was turned to blood along with all the springs of the land (Exodus 7:14:25). Likewise, as the second trumpet killed a third of the sea, the third trumpet rendered a third of the rivers and springs bitter and undrinkable (8:10-11). Again, unlike the partial warning of the trumpet, the wicked of the earth are deprived all fresh water and forced to drink the blood of God's wrath.

<u>Revelation 16:5-6</u>, states: *"And I heard the angel of the waters saying, "Righteous art Thou, who art and who wast, O Holy One, because Thou didst judge these things; for they poured out the blood of saints and prophets, and Thou hast given them blood to drink. They deserve it.""* We have seen that there were four angels of the wind (7:1), and an angel over fire (14:18), so there apparently is an angel over the waters. Though the waters are turned from fresh to blood, the angel declares this to be righteous. Seemingly echoing the song of Moses sung by the bond-servants of God in 15:3-4, the angel proclaims the judgment of God to be righteous and the wicked to be deserving of the punishments they now receive.

<u>Revelation 16:7</u>, states: *"And I heard the altar saying, "Yes, O Lord God, the Almighty, true and righteous are Thy judgments.""* With the breaking of the fifth seal the martyrs under the altar cried out with a loud

voice asking God to judge the wicked, to avenge their blood. It seems fitting that the altar now cry out as God's judgment is poured out, and the blood of the martyrs is avenged. This voice confirms the words of the angel, that God's judgments are righteous and just.

Fourth Bowl: Scorching Heat of the Sun (16:8-9)

Revelation 16:8-9, states: *"And the fourth angel poured out his bowl upon the sun; and it was given to it to scorch men with fire. And men were scorched with fierce heat; and they blasphemed the name of God who has the power over these plagues; and they did not repent, so as to give Him glory."* We continue to see somewhat of a parallel between the trumpets and the bowls. Just as the second and third trumpets affected a third of the sea and rivers, the second and third bowls affected all of the sea and rivers. Likewise, the fourth trumpet and fourth bowl affect the sun. The fourth trumpet brought darkness to the sun as a warning (8:12). The fourth bowl affects the sun by increasing its heat and scorching the earth. Peter warns of an "intense heat" coming with the Day of the Lord, saying, *"But the day of the Lord will come like a thief, in which the heavens will pass away with a roar and the elements will be destroyed with intense heat, and the earth and its works will be burned up"* (2 Peter 3:10). It is not certain that this is the same heat that Peter speaks of because this heat inflicts great misery but does not kill. Instead, it causes the wicked to blaspheme the name of God who has power over the plagues. We are told *"they did not repent, so as to give Him Glory."* Even to the end, the wicked would rather suffer than change their ways and acknowledge God as Lord. What is interesting is scientists claim that the sun is getting hotter, especially over the past 70 years, which would roughly correlate to begin about the time that Israel was reborn as a nation. Global warming is the product of greenhouse gasses and increasing heat from the sun. We should take note that things are getting warmer on the earth. It is changing our seasons and causing damage. Is this a warning of an even greater heat to come?

Fifth Bowl: Darkening of the Beast's Kingdom (16:10-11)

Revelation 16:10-11, states: *"And the fifth angel poured out his bowl upon the throne of the beast; and his kingdom became darkened; and they gnawed their tongues because of pain, and they blasphemed the God of heaven because of their pains and their sores; and they did not repent of their deeds."* Again there is a strong correlation between the fifth seal and the fifth bowl of wrath. The fifth seal caused an opening in the bottomless pit, resulting in smoke coming out and darkening the earth (9:1-2). Also out of the pit came forth demon locust hidden in the darkness and afflicting pain on the wicked, but they were not allowed to touch those sealed by God (9:3-6). There is also a strong parallel in the second to the last plague upon Egypt. God commanded Moses, saying *"Stretch out your hand toward the sky, that there may be darkness over the land of Egypt, even a darkness which may be felt"* (Exodus 10:21). The darkness was a terror to the Egyptians, but God allowed light in the dwellings of the sons of Israel. The darkness that fell upon Egypt "could be felt," and it seems the darkness of the fifth bowl may cause "pain." There are a number of modern visionaries who claim that God has shown them visions of the end. They consistently describe a period of three days of darkness when demons roam the earth tormenting and perhaps killing the wicked, while the faithful take refuge in their homes in prayer, using candles that do not burn out to provide them with light during the three days of darkness. Also, the prophet Joel speaks of the darkness that will come on the Day of the Lord, describing it as: *"A day of darkness and gloom, a day of clouds and thick darkness"* (Joel 2:2a). With the fifth bowl we are told darkness will be poured out on the *"throne of the beast; and his kingdom became darkened."* In the letter to the church at Pergamum (2:12-17) we are told they dwell where "Satan's throne is" (2:13). I don't think this refers to just a specific location but a specific condition. This church suffered because it dwelled in a place of self-indulgence and idolatry, which is consistent with what we have learned to be the influence of the beast, or Satan. We can surmise that the content of the fifth bowl will be a darkness that can be felt, which will cause those who hold to self-indulgence and idolatry to suffer greatly. They will suffer to the point of blaspheming the God of heaven for the pain they suffer, but they will not acknowledge that their pain is the result of their own sin, and therefore they continue unrepentant.

Sixth Bowl: Kings of East Assemble for Armageddon (16:12-16)

Revelation 16:12, states: *"And the sixth angel poured out his bowl upon the great river, the Euphrates; and its water was dried up, that the way might be prepared for the kings from the east."* A strong correlation with the trumpets continues. The sixth trumpet *"released the four angels who were bound at the great river Euphrates"* (9:14). The release of the angels will result in an army of two hundred million killing a third of mankind with fire, brimstone and smoke (9:15-18). Many scholars identify this event with a great and terrible final battle or war. The verses which follow (16:13-14 & 16) make reference to the great and final battle known as Armageddon. The Euphrates River runs from near the Black Sea to the Gulf of Arabia, separating Israel from the eastern and Communist bloc countries of Russia and China. According to Ezekiel, the great forces which will come against Israel at the end could be led by Russia and a number of Middle Eastern nation allies, which include those currently in conflict with Israel. What is extremely interesting is that the great Euphrates River is "drying up." Turkey is primarily being blamed for hording waters and not allowing water to flow on to Iraq, causing crop failures. The problem according to scientists and conservationists is much larger. It seems that all of the nations along the Euphrates are overusing the waters, and combined with years of draught in the region, the river is literally drying up. Many see this as a sign of the end times.

Revelation 16:13-14, states: *"And I saw coming out of the mouth of the dragon and out of the mouth of the beast and out of the mouth of the false prophet, three unclean spirits like frogs; for they are spirits of demons, performing signs, which go out to the kings of the whole world, to gather them together for the war of the great day of God, the almighty."* The second plague upon the land of Egypt was the plague of frogs (Exodus 8:1-15). Pharaoh's magicians did the same with their secret arts, also making frogs come upon the land in an attempt to duplicate and negate God's power. Here we find "unclean spirits like frogs" which are "demons" coming out of the mouths of Satan's unholy trinity, consisting of the dragon, beast and false prophet. Their coming out of the mouth may indicate they will take the form of deceptive "words" to persuade the kings or leaders of the earth to gather to make war. This will be the great battle of Armageddon, which will take place near Jerusalem in Israel.

Revelation 16:15, states: *("Behold, I am coming like a thief. Blessed is the one who stays awake and keeps his garments, lest he walk about naked and men see his shame.")* This insertion seems out of place and a sudden intrusion, or perhaps a declaration to remind us that the signs of the end will not be so clear that we easily identify the Lord's return. Jesus warns us in Matthew 24:43-44 that we need to always be on the alert and ready for His return, saying, *"But be sure of this, that if the head of the house had known at what time of the night the thief was coming, he would have been on the alert and would not have allowed his house to be broken into. For this reason you be ready too; for the Son of Man is coming at an hour when you do not think He will"* (Matthew 24:43-44). A thief can only break in and steal if we are unaware of his presence, and unprepared for his coming. <u>Jesus is not a thief</u> for it is the devil that would have you distracted and unprepared so that he may steal your soul. Christians know that they must always be doing what is right, and ready for the Lord's return so that He does not overtake them like a thief. Paul essentially warns of this in 1 Thessalonians 5:4-6, saying, *"But you, brethren, are not in darkness, that the day should overtake you like a thief; for you are all sons of light and sons of day. We are not of night nor of darkness; so then let us not sleep as others do, but let us be alert and sober."* In the letter to the church of Sardis, Jesus also warns that if we are asleep we need to wake up, saying, *"Remember therefore what you have received and heard; and keep it, and repent. If therefore you will not wake up, I will come like a thief, and you will not know at what hour I will come upon you"* (Revelation 3:3). Regarding the reference to being naked, it refers to being unprepared, as in not being clothed in Christ but clothed in shame. In the letter to the church in Laodicea, Jesus said: *"Because you say, "I am rich, and have become wealthy, and have need of nothing," and you do not know that you are wretched and miserable and poor and blind and <u>naked</u>, I advise you to buy from Me gold* *refined by fire, that you may become rich, and white garments, that you may clothe yourself, and that the shame of your <u>nakedness</u> may not be revealed; and eye salve to anoint your eyes, that you may see"* (Revelation 3:17-18). Just as we saw between the sixth and seventh seals, and between the sixth and seventh trumpets, this verse provides a brief interlude before the final punishment.

<u>Revelation 16:16</u>, states: *And they gathered them together to the place which in Hebrew is called Har-Magedon."* Armageddon is the Greek transliteration of the Hebrew "Har-Magedon." It has come to be seen as the final battle, the last great confrontation between good and evil. The Hebrew prefix *har* means mountain or city, and many scholars believe that Har-Magedon refers to "the mountain of Megiddo," or the "city of Megiddo." Megiddo was a fortress city located in central Palestine, northwest of Jerusalem. Throughout history this area had been a primary thoroughfare into Jerusalem for invading armies. The hills that stood overlooking the plains protected the city and had often been a "last stand" battle position for the Hebrew armies. If there were any kind of final, cataclysmic battle that involved Palestine and Jerusalem, Armageddon would be seen, especially by the Jews, as the classic, timeless battleground. Mountains running north and south along the Jordan River valley would make a direct assault from the east impossible. The Jezreel Valley lies in front of Megiddo, and one must wonder if this will be the valley of judgment spoken of by the prophet Joel. Joel speaks of judgment coming after the nation of Israel is restored, saying: *"For behold, in those days and at that time, when I restore the fortunes of Judah and Jerusalem, I will gather all the nations, and bring them down to the valley of Jehoshaphat. Then I will enter into judgment with them there on behalf of My people and My inheritance, Israel, whom they have scattered among the nations; and they have divided up My land"* (Joel 3:1-2).

Regarding when the nations will gather and the battle of Armageddon will take place, according the Joel 3:1-2, it will take place sometime after the "fortunes of Judah and Jerusalem" are restored. Judah was the son of Israel and the nation of Israel was reborn in one day on May 14, 1948. This fulfilled the prophecy found in Isaiah 66:8, which declared: *"Who has heard such a thing? Who has seen such things? Can a land be born in one day? Can a nation be brought forth all at once?*

As soon as Zion travailed, she also brought forth her sons." Then, in 1967 during the Six-Day war, eastern Jerusalem and the temple mount were captured by Israel. Thus, Israel became a nation in one day and became complete in "seven."

Regarding why the nations will gather around and against Israel, Psalm 83 provides insight. Here we read that at some point the nations of the world will conspire against God and His people Israel, and gather in an attempt to destroy Israel. We must remember Revelation 12:17, when after being cast out of heaven, the dragon (Satan) *"went off to make war with the rest of her offspring, who keep the commandments of God and hold to the testimony of Jesus."* We know that the offspring of the woman is first the Jews, and also includes all Christians. Regarding God's chosen people, Israel, Psalm 83:1-4 states: *"O God, do not remain quiet; do not be silent and, O God, do not be still. For, behold, Thine enemies make an uproar; and those who hate Thee have exalted themselves. They make shrewd plans against Thy people, and conspire together against Thy treasured ones. They have said, "Come, and let us wipe them out as a nation, that the name of Israel be remembered no more.""* Certainly we see the Islamic nations surrounding Israel conspiring against Israel, and some have openly expressed their desire and pledge to wipe out the nation of Israel.

Regarding which nations will conspire against Israel, we need but continue forward reading Psalm 83:5-8, which states: *"For they have conspired together with one mind; against Thee do they make a covenant: The tents of Edom and the Ishmaelites; Moab, and the Hagrites; Gebal, and Ammon, and Amalek; Philistia with the inhabitants of Tyre; Assyria also has joined with them; they have become a help to the children of Lot."* Most of these names are of ancient peoples that settled in specific places. The descendants of these peoples still exist and continue to live in the places of their ancestors, but many of the place names have changed. Today, Gebal and Tyre would be in Lebanan (north of Israel), Assyria would be in Syria (northeast of Israel), Ammon, Moab and Edom would be in Jordan (East of Israel), Philistia would be the area of the Gaza Strip (southwest of Israel), Amalek would be in the southwest tip of Israel which borders Egypt, and the Hagrites would be to southeast of Israel in Arabia. You will recognize that all are enemies of Israel.

Regarding the power behind the invasion of Israel, God speaks to this through the prophet Ezekiel, saying: *"Son of man, set your face toward Gog of the land of Magog, the prince of Rosh, Mesheck, and Tubal, and prophesy against him, and say, 'Thus says the Lord God, "Behold, I am against you, O Gog, prince of Rosh, Meschech, and Tubal… Persia, Ethiopia, and Put with them, all of them with shield and helment; Gomer with all its troops; Beth-togarmah from the remote parts of the north with all its troops—many peoples with you."'"* (Ezekiel 38:2-3, 5-6). As previously mentioned, what is very interesting is that "Rosh" is the ancient name for "Russia." Historians have also tracked the migration of the sons of Japheth: Gomer, Magog, Mesheck, Tubal and Togarmah to the region today known as Russia. And finally, the Hebrew name "Mesheck" is the source of the city name "Moscow." The nations that are listed to be with them (with Russia) are also interesting. Persia is today modern Iran. Ethiopia in Hebrew is Kush or Cush, and is continually mentioned in the Old Testament in connection with Egypt. And Put is known today as Libya. All of these nations have received arms from Russia, and all have a history of being in opposition to Israel. It would seem the stage if very much set today for the fulfillment of Armageddon.

Seventh Bowl: Impending Destruction of Babylon (16:17-21)

Revelation 16:17, states: *"And the seventh angel poured out his bowl upon the air; and a loud voice came out of the temple from the throne, saying, "It is done."'"* Again, from 15:8 we know that God alone is currently in the temple, so the voice from the throne is that of God. With the pouring out of the seventh bowl God's punishments are complete, finished—"It is done." The punishment will now be described in the verses to follow as catastrophic and swift.

Revelation 16:18, states: *"And there were flashes of lightning and sounds and peals of thunder; and there was a great earthquake, such as there had not been since man came to be upon the earth, so great an earthquake was it, and so mighty."* The description of this verse is the same as that found in 8:5 when the seventh seal was broken, and in 11:19 when the seventh trumpet was blown. Each time there was lightning, thunder and a great earthquake. This leads many scholars to think that the seals, trumpets and bowls are three descriptions of the same thing. But while there are great similarities between the seals, trumpets and bowls, there are also very specific differences and an obvious escalation in their intensity as they progress. With the seals and trumpets, destruction was measured and served as both punishment and warning. With the pouring out of the bowls, destruction is complete and final.

Revelation 16:19, states: ***"And the great city was split into three parts, and the cities of the nations fell. And Babylon the great was remembered before God, to give her the cup of the wine of His fierce wrath."*** The "great city" we are told is split into three parts, but what is the great city? In the Old Testament only Nineveh is referred to as "the great city" built by Nimrod in Assyria (Genesis 10:8-12). This great city is best known as the city the prophet Jonah is sent to and repents when Jonah proclaims God's judgment against it. But Nineveh today is little more than a mound of ruins having fallen long ago. The city's ancient site is located about 250 miles north of Bagdad in Iraq. Revelation 11:8 is probably our best clue to the identity of the city, referring to it as ***"the great city which mystically is called Sodom and Egypt, where also their Lord was crucified."*** We may identify this place as Jerusalem where the "Lord was crucified," but it is also mystically called Sodom and Egypt, which may mean it is not simply a place but also a condition. Sodom was a place of great sin, and Egypt a place of great persecution. Sodom and Egypt probably here represent the characteristics of the evil great city which is actually the world which crucified Christ and continues to persecute and kill His followers. This is reinforced by our understanding that "Babylon the great" is also not simply a reference to the ancient city or empire that bears the name, but a symbol for all that causes people to place themselves above God as lord of their lives. In Revelation 14:8, Babylon the great is described as one who ***"made all the nations drink of the wine of the passion of her immorality."*** Now she will be given to drink of ***"the cup of the wine of His fierce wrath."***

Regarding the great city being split into three parts, this could simply mean that Jerusalem will be split into three parts, or in the case of the mystical interpretation of the great city as a condition rather than a physical place, it could mean that the evil influence will be divided into three parts. We know that Satan has been revealed as an unholy trinity, consisting of the dragon, beast and false prophet. Their evil influence has been joined to separate people from God by causing them to worship themselves, the image of the beast. Perhaps that evil and unholy trinity is what will be divided, broken apart, with the pouring of the seventh bowl prior to their destruction in the lake of fire.

Regarding the scale of destruction that will come with the pouring of the seventh bowl, we are told that the cities of all the nations will fall. Cities are often seen as symbolic for the power and strength of nations. Perhaps this is a physical destruction of all cities, or perhaps this represents the fall of all national and/or financial power.

Revelation 16:20, states: *"And every island fled away, and the mountains were not found."* When the sixth seal was broken we were told that *"every mountain and island were moved out of their places"* (6:14). This may be further evidence that the seals, trumpets and bowls are parallel depictions of God's punishments, or 6:14 could be a smaller scale foreshadowing of a final ultimate destruction. In 6:14 the mountains and islands were *"moved out of their place,"* while in 16:20 *"every island fled away"* and the *"mountains were not found."* Similarly, between the sixth and seventh trumpets we are told that there was a *"great earthquake"* and a *"tenth of the city fell"* (11:13). Is this still more evidence that the seals, trumpets and bowls are parallel, or is the fact that the destruction of the city was only partial before, distinguish it as different from the destruction caused by the pouring out of the seventh bowl? Again, both the apparent differences and escalating intensity of the destruction seems to indicate that the seals, trumpets and bowls are similar but different events.

Revelation 16:21, states: *"And huge hailstones, about one hundred pounds each, came down from heaven upon men; and men blasphemed God because of the plague of the hail, because its plague was extremely severe."* With the sounding of the last and seventh trumpet we were told that *"hail and fire, mixed with blood, and they were thrown to the earth"* (8:7). That hail storm burned up a third of the earth, including a third of the trees and all the green grass. Fire is not mentioned with the hail storm that follows the pouring of the seventh bowl, but instead, this hail is said to be very large and very severe. Exodus 9:18-35 describes a hail storm with *"heavy hail mixed with fire"* as one of the ten plagues that God cast upon Egypt to force Pharaoh to release His people. Similarly, God rained fire and brimstone on Sodom and Gomorrah in Genesis 19:24, destroying these cities for their wickedness. Again, we cannot know for certain if the hail storm described with the seventh trumpet is the same as the one experienced when the seventh bowl of wrath is poured out. What is consistent is that God punishes the wicked for their sin. When and in what form it comes may be debated, but God will ultimately punish the wicked. We must note again that the hail storm does not destroy mankind, for men continue to blaspheme God because of the plague of hail. Life on earth seems to continue although for the wicked it has become a living hell. Yet the wicked do not repent.

One final note regarding the seventh bowl of wrath should be explored. Revelation 16:17 said that the bowl was poured out upon the "air." The description of lightning, thunder and giant hail stones could easily be identified with the air, but also associated with the seventh bowl are a great earthquake that levels cities, causes islands to flee and mountains not to be found. These seem clearly earthly destructions. Perhaps a clue can be derived from Ephesians 2:2, which speaks of those who walk in sin as being *"according to the course of this world, according to the prince of the power of the air, of the spirit that is now working in the sons of disobedience."* Satan is the "prince of the power of the air" and it is his "spirit that works in the sons of disobedience." The prior bowls of wrath were poured out on the earth, sea, rivers, sun, throne of the beast, and great river Euphrates. All that remained was the "air," perhaps symbolic for the very "spirit" of all that is evil and wicked. There will be no place that God's punishment will not reach. There is no hiding or escaping the judgment God will administer at the end.

PART 9

Seven Visions of the Fall of Babylon

Part 8 consisted of seven visions depicting the pouring out of the bowls of God's wrath. Chapter 15 provided the introduction to the bowls, and chapter 16 described the pouring out of each of the seven bowls. We learned that the bowls of wrath are the final and ultimate punishment to befall the wicked while on the earth. The bowls were poured on the earth and the air. But we hear of none repenting and worshiping God. Rather, we are told repeatedly that those upon which God's wrath is poured deserve their fate.

Part 9 will comprise chapters 17, 18, and the first ten verses of chapter 19. Again, it will include a series of seven visions. These visions will elaborate on Babylon the great, the "Mother of Harlots and Abominations." She is revealed as both a religious and a political system. She is revealed as a persecutor of the saints and all who witness for Christ. She is contrasted as a "Harlot" because of her idolatry, as compared to the true Church, which is the pure and undefiled "Bride" of Christ. This portion of Revelation serves to inform the believer as to what will happen to those who commit idolatry under the influence of the beast, rather than remaining faithful to the Lord Jesus Christ. We are told that the world will mourn the destruction of Babylon, the Harlot, because the world profited from her. The world profits from the glorification of worldly things, but those who remain faithful to the Lord will profit from heavenly things. Worldly things are finite, temporal and temporary, but heavenly things are infinite and eternal. All that is done to glorify oneself will soon pass away, but all that is done to glorify God will last forever.

CHAPTER 17:

In this chapter, we will witness the doom of Babylon and the ultimate victory of the Lamb of God. This chapter seems to provide explanation of Revelation 14:8, where we heard the second angel proclaim Babylon the great has fallen. This second angel immediately followed the one who proclaimed the gospel to the entire world, warning all to repent and give glory to God because judgment was about to come. The message of these two angels clearly seems fulfillment of Jesus' words in Matthew 24:14, where He said: *"And this gospel of the kingdom shall be preached in the whole world for a witness to all the nations, and then the end shall come."* The end for the wicked!

<u>First Vision</u>: The Harlot, Babylon the Great (17:1-6a)

<u>Revelation 17:1-2</u>, states: *"And one of the seven angels [who]* **had the seven bowls came and spoke with me, saying, "Come here, I shall show you the judgment of the great harlot who sits on many waters, with whom the kings of the earth committed acts of immorality and those who dwell on the earth were made drunk with the wine of her immorality."** It is one of the seven angels who poured God's bowls of wrath upon the earth that now instructs John. The angel calls John to come and see the judgment of the great harlot, who will be revealed in 17:5 as Babylon the Great. She sits on "many waters," which will be revealed in 17:15 as "peoples and multitudes and nations and tongues." We are told that the kings of the earth "committed acts of immorality" with her, which literally means they "practiced fornication" or "idolatry" with her. And finally, we are told that the peoples of the earth "were made drunk with the wine of her immorality," which again literally means they became drunk on her "idolatry." She is, after all, a "harlot," therefore, to be in a relationship with her is to be unfaithful to Christ. The Church is the true "bride" of Christ, and must keep pure and faithful to the Lord.

<u>Revelation 17:3</u>, states: *"And he carried me away in the Spirit into a wilderness; and I saw a woman sitting on a scarlet beast, full of blasphemous names, having seven heads and ten horns."* You will remember that immediately after the letters to the seven churches, John was told to "come here" and he was taken "in the Spirit" to heaven to be shown things which were to take place in the future (Revelation 4:1-2). This time, John is taken away to a wilderness and shown a woman sitting on a scarlet beast with seven heads and ten horns. This

description is consistent with the description of the red dragon found in 12:3. It is also similar to that of the beast out of the sea, which is described further to have "blasphemous name(s)" on his heads (13:1). Clearly, the harlot sits on the dragon, the beast, all of which are depictions of Satan.

Revelation 17:4-5, states: ***"And the woman was clothed in purple and scarlet, and adorned with gold and precious stones and pearls, having in her hand a gold cup full of abominations and of the unclean things of her immorality, and upon her forehead a name was written, a mystery, 'Babylon the Great, the Mother of Harlots and of the Abominations of the Earth.'"*** Regarding the colors purple and scarlet, these colors are mentioned together twenty-six times in Exodus, chapters 25-28, 35-36, and 38-39. In all these cases they are connected to items used in the Tabernacle and for the worship of God. But in every single case, they are used with the color blue, which is perhaps symbolic for heaven, being the color of the sky. The Greek word translated as scarlet can also be translated simply as red. In the Old Testament, the Hebrew root word for red is the same as for the words "blood, earth, man, mankind and Adam." One could say that red represents the earth and/or man, and blue represents heaven. When blue and red are combined they make purple which is the color often associated with royalty and kings. It is likely deliberate that the color blue is absent here. This would be consistent with our understanding of Babylon the great and number of the beast in that purple and scarlet represent royalty with the earth or man, and the omission of heaven and God.

The adornment with gold, precious stones and pearls, may be a reference to worldly wealth and riches. The harlot holds a gold cup filled with abominations and unclean things of her immorality, which we know to mean idolatry. She drinks from the cup of Satan's influence, a drink of deceptions that causes one to elevate oneself above God and worship oneself and the things of this world. The name on her forehead is a mystery to those who dwell upon the earth, but not to those who are wise in the Lord. She is the "Mother of Harlots and of the Abominations of the Earth." She gives birth to the notion that the created are greater than the Creator, causing people to worship created things and themselves rather than God, the Creator of all things. All of the abominations are of this world, they are of the earth. Consistent with this view, some scholars believe that the harlot is associated with false religion that maligns the truth. Peter speaks to this in 2 Peter 2:1-3, saying: ***"But false prophets also arose among the people, just as there will also be false teachers among you, who will secretly introduce destructive heresies, even denying the Master who bought them, bringing swift destruction upon themselves. And many will follow their sensuality, and because of them the way of the truth will be maligned; and in their greed they will exploit you with false words; their judgment from long ago is not idle, and their destruction is not asleep."*** Certainly, all who malign the truth in God's Word will face judgment.

Revelation 17:6, states: ***"And I saw the woman drunk with the blood of the saints, and with the blood of the witnesses of Jesus. And when I saw her, I wondered greatly."*** The woman is drunk with the blood of the saints and the witnesses of Jesus means that she has participated in persecuting the Church and followers of Christ. The fact that she is drunk on their blood indicates that her persecution has been overindulgent. She has drank so much that she is drunk. As John gazes upon this sight he is filled with great wonder, perhaps to her and the beast's identity, or how God could allow such persecution. Some English Bibles translate the Greek to say "wonders with great admiration," but the literal translation would be "wonders with great wonder" or with great "amazement." I believe we are being told that John is mystified with what he is being shown. In other words, it is a mystery to him. Again, the testimony is that John is writing what he sees, as he has been instructed, but he perhaps doesn't fully understand what he sees.

Second Vision: Interpretation of Harlot and Beast (17:6b-18)

Revelation 17:7, states: ***"And the angel said to me, "Why do you wonder? I shall tell you the mystery of the woman and of the beast that carries her, which has the seven heads and the ten horns."*** The angel's question, asking John ***"Why do you wonder?"*** could imply that John should already know the answer to the mystery. Indeed, the answer has already been revealed, beginning in chapter 12. For God has revealed that Satan is behind everything, and has been revealed in the red dragon, the beast out of the sea, and in the false prophet. Now the angel will provide more details and insight to satisfy John's wonderings.

<u>Revelation 17:8</u>, states: ***"The beast that you saw was and is not, and is about to come up out of the abyss and to go to destruction. And those who dwell on the earth will wonder, whose name has not been written in the book of life from the foundation of the world, when they see the beast, that he was and is not and will come."*** First we must address the meaning of ***"was and is not, and is about to come."*** With the sounding of the seventh trumpet we were told that the reign of Christ began. We also know that between the sixth and seventh bowls of wrath there was a gathering for the great and final battle of Armageddon, when God will do battle and judgment will come. In Revelation 19:19, we will hear that the beast and the kings of the earth, and their armies, will assemble to make war against Christ and His army. Back in chapter 12:7-9 we heard of a war in heaven when the dragon (Satan) and his angels fought against Michael and his angels. Satan was defeated and thrown to the earth, along with his angels (now demons), who then waged war against God's people. Revelation 20:1-3 will reveal that when the final great battle of Armageddon occurs, Satan will be bound up and cast into the abyss where he will remain for a thousand years. Viewed through the wider lens of Revelation, it is Satan who "was" (past tense) and "is not" (present tense), and is about to come up out of the abyss and to go to destruction (future tense). Revelation 20:7-10 further states that when Satan is released it will be for a short time, and then he will be thrown into the lake of fire (destruction). Therefore the beast that the harlot sits upon seems certain to be Satan. Some scholars believe that it is actually the apostate church, or the church influenced and maligned by the antichrist. In either case, whether it is Satan or those under Satan's influence, Satan is the source of the problem.

Regarding the people who dwell on the earth wondering about whose name has <u>not</u> been written in the book of life, perhaps these are the people who dwell upon the earth during the thousand years that Satan is bound. According to Revelation 20:4-6, the faithful who suffered and died for Christ and did not worship the beast will be raised up and reign with Christ during the thousand years, but the rest of the dead will not come to life until the end of the thousand years. It would seem that those who live during the thousand years will wonder about those who have not been raised to life.

Revelation 17:9-10, states: *"Here is the mind which has wisdom. The seven heads are seven mountains on which the woman sits, and they are seven kings; five have fallen, one is, the other has not yet come; and when he comes, he must remain a little while."* This passage has been interpreted in many ways. Many have identified the seven mountains with the seven hills on which the city of Rome sits, identifying the harlot with everything from the Roman Empire to the Roman Catholic Church. But clearly the mountains are identified with a series of kings or kingdoms that begin in the past and continue until the end. Identified as mountains these are not just any kings or kingdoms but great kingdoms which should rise as mountains in history. We are told that five have fallen, presumably at the time Revelation was written, but perhaps this is in reference to when the time of the end begins. Another currently exists, which may mean existed at the time Revelation was written, or will exist when the time of the end begins. The final and seventh is to come in the future. The future and final king or kingdom will last only a short time, but the current or sixth kingdom must be one that stays in place for a long time, from the time Revelation was written all the way up to the final end time events. Previously, in our study of Revelation 13:1-2 we discussed the significance of the seven heads. We found that Daniel, chapter 2, identified a series of kingdoms which must come, leading up to the end. We identified the first five as: (1) Babylon; (2) Medo-Persia; (3) Greece; (4) the Roman Empire in its strength; and (5) as the corrupt and deteriorating Roman Empire. Although not mentioned in Daniel, some scholars add Egypt as the first great kingdom with the Roman Empire as the fifth, not separating the Roman Empire into two kingdoms. This makes a lot of sense but we don't really know. The rulers of all of these kingdoms considered themselves gods to be worshiped, clearly showing Satan's influence.

After the fall of Rome, no single power has dominated the world, but the world has continued to be influenced by the heavily Greek influenced western Roman culture. The real question seems to be what does the sixth head represent, or what is the sixth kingdom. At the time of Jesus' birth, death and resurrection, and still in place at the time Revelation was written, the Roman Empire was in place. More than any other reason this is why most of the symbolism in Revelation is so often identified with Rome. There is no great kingdom mentioned in Daniel beyond the Roman Empire, and it could be argued that there has been no single kingdom of equal greatness since the fall of the Roman Empire. Actually, many would say that our western civilization derives from the Roman Empire. Some associate this period with the ten toes of clay and iron on the statue described in Daniel's vision account, as indicating a period of many strong and weak worldly kingdoms. Some might even argue that the religion of Islam which began shortly after the fall of the Roman Empire could be the sixth kingdom. The fundamental beliefs of the Islamic religion call for a theocracy which is the belief that God is ruler rather than any government or institution. This is a similar religion as existed with the Hebrew people after the Exodus and before they had earthly kings to lead them, the first being King Saul, followed by King David. The difference is that radical Muslims believe the whole world should be Islamic, ruled as a Caliphate (many Islamic nations united under one rule), and ruled by a Caliph (a single spiritual and political leader selected by Allah). Also, as we have stated earlier in this study, the sixth kingdom or period may be a time when the spirit of the antichrist has entered the world and works against Christ. We have and continue to see this in the world manifested in many forms, including radical Islam.

John warns us to test the spirits because of the presence of false prophets and the presence of the spirit of the antichrist. John writes in 1 John 4:1-3, saying, ***"Beloved, do not believe every spirit, but test the spirits to see whether they are from God; because many false prophets have gone out into the world. By this you know the Spirit of God: every spirit that confesses that Jesus Christ has come in the flesh is from God; and every spirit that does not confess Jesus is not from God; and this is the spirit of the antichrist, of which you have heard that it is coming, and now it is already in the world."*** The spirit of the antichrist entices man to worship himself, and place himself above God. This period of struggle between the followers of Christ and those who oppose Him may be seen as the long period that began with Christ's first coming and leads up to the final end time events, and His second coming. Many believe the final king is the personified Antichrist, an individual and world leader that will not be revealed until the very end.

Others see this as something more universal but less obvious such as secularism that undermines the Church and Christian beliefs. Regarding Muslims, they believe Jesus was a prophet, but they do not believe He was the Son of God or God in the flesh. Because they do not confess Jesus as being of God, they meet John's definition of what is tested to be false. We could conclude that the rise of Islam is at least in part a manifestation of the spirit of the antichrist. What or who is yet to come may be highly debated, but one thing is clear, the stage is set for its arrival and its influence is already here.

Revelation 17:11, states: *"And the beast which was and is not, is himself also an eighth, and is one of the seven, and he goes to destruction."* Again looking forward to Revelation 19:20, it is revealed that the beasts and the false prophet will be cast into the lake of fire, while the dragon, Satan himself, will be bound and cast into the abyss for a thousand years (20:1-3), to be released later only to be cast into the lake of fire (destruction) (20:10). Satan, in his various forms and influences, is the only one who fits the description of the beast that "was" and "is not," and is also to come. Satan also fits as the seventh and eighth. First, because of his evil influence both before and after the thousand years, and second, because he ultimately goes to his destruction.

Revelation 17:12-13, states: *"And the ten horns which you saw are ten kings, who have not yet received a kingdom, but they receive authority as kings with the beast for one hour. These have one purpose and they give their power and authority to the beast."* Also as we have seen and discussed before, the ten horns represent ten kings which are earthly but of one mind. They are all controlled by the beast and give their power and authority to the beast. This means that they do Satan's bidding, working against Christ and His followers. God authorizes the beast and these kings to exert their power for only a short and limited time. Their purpose will be that of Satan, to deceive and destroy all that God has created in His image. Regarding which ten kingdoms they will be has been the subject of wide speculation. Some believe they will be a European union of ten nations. Others have looked to an Eastern threat and Communism. It may be coincidental, but Psalm 83:5-8 lists exactly <u>ten</u> peoples that will conspire against God and His people and attempt to destroy Israel. We know from Ezekiel 38 that the power and the prince who will lead them will come from the area we now know as Russia. Because the peoples listed in Psalm 83 currently surround and are hostile towards Israel, and are armed and supported by Russia, it is easy to picture how this could be taking place while the world watches; unaware that Scripture is being fulfilled before our eyes.

Revelation 17:14, states: *"These will wage war against the Lamb, and the Lamb will overcome them, because He is Lord of lords and King of kings, and those who are with Him are the called and chosen and faithful."* We know from 17:12-13 above that these represents the ten kings who "receive authority for one hour," have "one purpose," and "give their power and authority to the beast." Essentially, they are unified in their opposition to the Lamb, Jesus Christ. Therefore they wage war against Him, which means they wage war on those who are His, but the Lord will overcome them because He is the King of kings and the Lord of Lords. Just prior to giving Himself up for our sakes, Jesus told His disciples: *"In the world you have tribulation, but take courage; I have overcome the world"* (John 16:33b). We know this to be true. In this world we may suffer strife and great trials, but Christ has overcome the world, and through Him we have victory over even death. Paul advises us that when we face evil we should not counter it with evil but with good, saying, *"Do not be overcome by evil, but overcome evil with good"* (Romans 12:21). Just as John testified that every spirit that does not confess Jesus is not from God, he also reminds us that through Christ within us we overcome these spirits of opposition. John says: *"You are from God, little children, and have overcome them; because greater is He who is in you than he who is in the world"* (1 John 3:4). John goes on to remind us of the importance of our faith in Jesus as we struggle against those who oppose Him, saying: *"For whatever is born of God overcomes the world; and this is the victory that has overcome the world—our faith"* (1 John 5:4).

Regarding our being "called" and "chosen," in the parable of the wedding feast Jesus teaches us that many will be "called" to come to His feast, but many will be too busy or too distracted by the things of this world to respond. Those who respond to His call will be among the "chosen." As Jesus says to us: *"For many are called, but few are chosen"* (Matthew 22:14). But for those who are willing to be built into a spiritual house and make Jesus their foundation stone, Peter tells us that they will become a chosen people. Peter says: *"But you are a chosen race, a royal priesthood, a holy nation, a people for God's own possession, that you may proclaim the excellencies of Him who has called you out of darkness into His marvelous light; for you once were not a people, but now you are the people of God; you had not received mercy, but now you have received mercy"* (1 Peter 2:9-10). Truly, those who live their life with Christ on earth will be with Him forever.

Revelation 17:15, states: *"And he said to me, "The waters which you saw where the harlot sits, are peoples and multitudes and nations and tongues."* In verse 17:1 we were told that the harlot *"sits on many waters."* Here we are told that the many waters represent a multitude of different peoples from many nations, and speaking many languages. These are the people of the earth who are under the influence of the beast, for according to 17:2 they *"were made drunk with wine of her immorality."* We know that her immorality is actually the adultery of not remaining faithful to the Lord Jesus, and the idolatry of worshiping other gods, such as the beast, material possessions, and even themselves. Again, this is consistent with the pattern of Satan who attempted to elevate himself above God, and seeks mans' destruction by deceiving him to do the same.

Revelation 17:16, states: *"And the ten horns which you saw, and the beast, these will hate the harlot and will make her desolate and naked, and will eat her flesh and will burn her up with fire."* This verse seems a mystery but the clue to understanding it can be found in that the "ten horns" (ten kings) and the beast (Satan) will hate her and cause her to be "desolate" and "naked." Remember that the Lord warned the prideful church of Laodicea, saying, *"Because you say, 'I am rich, and have become wealthy, and have need of nothing,' and you do not know that you are wretched and miserable and poor and blind and naked, I advise you to buy gold refined by fire, that you may become rich, and white garments, that you may clothe yourself, and that the shame of your nakedness may not be revealed'"* (3:17-18). Satan was stripped of his beauty and cast to the earth because of his pride. Likewise, when we elevate ourselves and fill ourselves up with the pride of our accomplishments and possessions, we set ourselves up for a very great fall, not realizing that if not clothed in faith we are wretched and naked.

The beast (Satan) and the ten kings (worldly influence) that serve his purpose, show their hate for us and for God who created us in His image, by causing us to be filled with pride and self-glorification. We become consumed by our own pride and greed, which leads to death and the fires of hell. This is Satan's plan to destroy us by deceiving us to do what he did and thus doom ourselves for destruction. When we mark ourselves with the mark of the beast and fall prey to Satan's deception we become the harlot rather than the bride of Christ.

Revelation 17:17, states: *"For God has put it in their hearts to execute His purpose by having a common purpose, and by giving their kingdom to the beast, until the words of God should be fulfilled."* God often turns something bad into something good. He can serve His purpose through the errors of others. Understanding this verse requires a short history lesson in how when God's own people rejected Him, He used this to open the door for all people to become His people. God delivered His chosen people the Jews from Egypt, taught them that they could trust Him for their daily bread, and then gave them the land He had promised. He called the Jewish people His son, and commanded them to be faithful to Him or they would suffer consequences. They didn't listen, and rather than being a witness for God to the pagan nations around them, they entered into an adulterous relationship with these people and worshiped other gods. This resulted in the exile of God's people and the destruction of Israel. When God sent His own Son, Jesus Christ to reconcile the world to Himself, His own people again rejected Him and caused His death on the cross. This rejection opened the door for salvation to the gentiles, and peoples of all nations and languages. God speaks harshly against Jerusalem, His own people, calling them a "harlot" for their adultery and idolatry. Speaking through His prophet Ezekiel, God proclaims: *"Because your lewdness was poured out and your nakedness uncovered through your harlotries with your lovers and with all your detestable idols, and because of the blood of your sons which you gave to idols, therefore, behold, I shall gather all your lovers with whom you took pleasure, even all those whom you loved and all those whom you hated. So I shall gather them against you from every direction and expose your nakedness to them that they may see all your nakedness"* (Ezekiel 16:36-37). God's chosen people gave their kingdom to the beast, and have suffered continuously for their error for more than two thousand years. But, we are told this will continue only *"until the words of God should be fulfilled."* In other words, this will continue until all that has been revealed has happened and Christ's return comes to pass. Regarding things to come, Jesus declares in Luke 21:24, saying, *"and they will fall by the edge of the sword, and will be led captive into all the nations; and Jerusalem will be trampled underfoot by the Gentiles until the times of the Gentiles be fulfilled."* God will keep His promise to His chosen people, the Jews, preserving and delivering a remnant at the appointed time. In the meantime, the door remains open for the salvation of the gentiles until that door closes forever at the return of Christ.

Revelation 17:18, states: *"And the woman whom you saw is the great city, which reigns over the kings of the earth."* In 17:5 we were told that the harlot has the name "Babylon the Great" on her forehead, along with the title: "Mother of Harlots and of the Abominations of the Earth." We have previously identified "Babylon the great" as the "great city." We came to understand that relative to physical location, the "great city" was probably Jerusalem, because this is the place Christ was crucified. We also came to understand that "Babylon the great" and the "great city" also symbolized, along with the harlot, all that commits adultery against the Lamb, and idolatry against God. Ezekiel 16 speaks of Jerusalem as a harlot, but it is not the city that has committed idolatry against God but the people and nation that dwelled there. It is this adultery and idolatry that "reigns over the kings of the earth." Those nations that Jerusalem committed adultery with and who corrupted God's people with their idolatry are the ones who gather against Jerusalem, which also represents God's chosen people. Only the blood of Jesus Christ, the true Messiah, can wash them clean and reconcile them to God.

The victory of the Lamb, which we hear spoken of in verses 14 through 18 above, is the final victory of the Lamb over the adultery and idolatry of both God's original chosen people, the Jews represented by Jerusalem, and also all peoples who have sinned against God but washed themselves clean through the blood of the Lamb. Jesus Christ is Messiah to the Jews and Savior to all who will accept Him as their Lord. Now in chapter 18 we will hear more about the result of Babylon's fall.

CHAPTER 18:

While chapter 17 focused on Babylon the great as the "harlot," chapter 18 will focus on Babylon as the "great city." They are integrally connected as evidenced by 17:18, which stated: *"the woman you saw is the great city."* The "great city" was first mentioned in 11:8 as the place the bodies of the "two witnesses" lay dead for three and half days before God breathed life into them and they ascended into heaven. It was in this same verse we learned the great city was where "their Lord was crucified." But also the city was mystically identified with Sodom and Egypt, places of great sin and persecution. As has been previously discussed, the "great city" may both reference a place and a condition. The harlot also, as evidenced in Ezekiel 16, may be seen as both a place, Jerusalem, and a condition of immorality. This is reinforced by the other previous reference to the "great city" found in 16:19. Here we learned that with the pouring of the seventh and final bowl of wrath, the "great city" was split into three parts. Again as previously discussed, this could refer to the physical splitting of the city of Jerusalem, or the separation of the unholy trinity of dragon, beast and false prophet, or both. Some scholars view chapters 17 and 18 as depicting two separate aspects of Babylon the great. Chapter 17 is viewed to describe the doom of the religious aspect. It may depict the influence of Satan on religious and spiritual understandings, perhaps as it has manifested itself in secularism, relativism and pluralism. Chapter 18 is then seen as the political and commercial aspect. It depicts Satan's influence on our physical desires, perhaps as it has manifested itself in materialism and self-centeredness. Put simply, Satan has promoted pride and greed. With all of this in mind let us now reflect on chapter 18.

<u>Third Vision</u>: Angelic Proclamation of Babylon's Fall (18:1-3)

<u>Revelation 18:1</u>, states: *"After these things I saw another angel coming down from heaven, having great authority, and the earth was illumined with his glory."* One of the seven angels that poured out the bowls of wrath took John in the Spirit to the wilderness to show him the judgment of the harlot. By contrast, an angel with such great authority

and glory that it illuminates the earth comes down from heaven to show John the demise of the "great city." This may be another indicator that this second depiction of the demise of Babylon is associated with the physical and visible rather than the mystical and spiritual. Note that the angel comes down from heaven, indicating we are in the "wilderness" of the earth and not in heaven.

Revelation 18:2, states: *"And he cried out with a mighty voice, saying, "Fallen, fallen is Babylon the great! And she has become a dwelling place of demons and a prison of every unclean spirit, and a prison of every unclean and hateful bird."* We first heard the proclamation of Babylon the great's fall in 14:8, immediately after the angel preached the gospel to the whole world. What was warned has now come to pass. Babylon the great has fallen and is now a dwelling place only for demons, unclean spirits, and a prison, also translated as "haunt," of unclean and hated birds. Speaking of the desolation of the fall of Babylon, Jeremiah states: *"Therefore the desert creatures will live there along with the jackals; the ostriches also will live in it, and it will never again be inhabited or dwelt in from generation to generation"* (Jeremiah 50:39). The ancients always viewed the desert or wilderness as a place where demons, unclean spirits and wild animals roamed. Desert ostriches were particularly hated because of their loud screeches during the night which people found terrifying and devilish. If Babylon the great is here seen as symbolic for the lavish decadence of accumulated wealth and luxury derived from selfishness and greed, then the desert or wilderness provides a fitting contrast to the luxury that was, but is now no more. Babylon the great has truly fallen.

Revelation 18:3, states: *"For all the nations have drunk of the wine of the passion of her immorality, and the kings of the earth have committed acts of immorality with her, and the merchants of the earth have become rich by the wealth of her sensuality."* If materialism, greed and selfishness are seen as "the wine of the passion of her immorality," then we see this immorality all around us in the world today. We are bombarded by advertising, attempting to convince us that we need more and more possessions to be happy. Merchants become wealthy feeding our unjustified want and greed for material possessions. The word "sensuality" in this verse and following verses can be a little misleading. The Greek word translated as sensuality also means "luxuriousness," which seems more fitting. The kings or leaders of the earth have all become caught up in this wasteful and fruitless endeavor to obtain more and more wealth and luxuries. Again, this is part of Satan's deception and the fundamental nature of Babylon the great, that the creature should become obsessed with created things rather than the Creator.

Fourth Vision: Exultation and Mourning over Fall of Babylon (18:4-20)

Revelation 18:4-5, states: *"And I heard another voice from heaven, saying, "Come out of her, my people, that you may not participate in her sins and that you may not receive of her plagues: for her sins have piled up as high as heaven, and God has remembered her iniquities."* Just as Lot was called to come out of Sodom before God destroyed it for its sin (Genesis 19), and just like God called His people out of the original Babylon before He overthrew it for its sin (Jeremiah 51:45), God will call His people out of a world of sin before He rains judgment upon it. In the case of Sodom, the Lord told Abraham that, *"The outcry of Sodom and Gomorrah is indeed great, and their sin is exceedingly grave"* (Genesis 18:20). In the case of Babylon, the Lord states: *"For her judgment has reached to heaven and towers up to the very skies"* (Jeremiah 51:9b). In all cases God is aware of the great sin in the world, and calls His people to remove themselves from it so that they will not suffer in the punishment He will pour out upon it. At the time of the end, God calls His people to separate from "Babylon the great" and not to be caught up in its sin that they also suffer in its punishment. This doesn't mean we have to move off the planet or retreat to a deserted island. We can separate ourselves from the sin of the world even though we live in the world. The story of Sodom and Gomorrah provides an example of this in that Lot left the city but not the valley. The entire valley was destroyed along with the five sinful cities that were located there, but God protected Lot in the midst of the valley. I am reminded of Psalm 91 where God promises to protect His people who take refuge in Him even in the midst of the punishment of the wicked all around them.

Revelation 18:6, states: *"Pay her back even as she has paid, and give back to her double according to her deeds; in the cup which she has mixed, mix twice as much for her."* In Jeremiah 50:29 we find an example of what is called the law of revenge. Speaking of the punishment about to be sent against the original Babylon, the Lord says: *"Summon many against Babylon, all those who bend the bow; encamp against her on every side, let there be no escape. Repay her according to her work; according to all that she has done, so do to her; for she has become arrogant against the Lord, against the Holy One of Israel"* (Jeremiah 50:29). In the case of "Babylon the great" the arrogance against the Lord and His people is so great that God calls for double punishment. The sin she has poured out will be poured out double upon her.

Revelation 18:7, states: *"To the degree that she glorified herself and lived sensuously, to the same degree give her torment and mourning; for she says in her heart, 'I sit as a queen and I am not a widow, and will never see mourning.'"* In Exodus 21 God outlines a system of justice that is fair and balanced. It provides an alternative means of repayment for an injury or offense other than violence for violence. But for the repeat offender God prescribes a harsher rule that we often call "eye for eye." Exodus 21:23-24, states: *"But if there is <u>any further injury</u>, then you shall appoint as a penalty life for life, eye for eye, tooth for tooth, hand for hand, foot for foot."* This harsher judgment is merited because the offender has remained unrepentant and continued to offend. The same is true in regard to "Babylon the great." To the same degree that people have elevated themselves and glorified themselves with luxury and material possessions they will now be brought low. This is a fulfillment of the prophetic words of Mary's Song, the song the Virgin Mary sang glorifying God for the child Jesus within her. She proclaims what is to come through Jesus, saying, *"He has brought down rulers from their thrones, and has exalted those who were humble. He has filled the hungry with good things; and sent away the rich empty-handed"* (Luke 1:52-53). When king Nebuchadnezzar stood on the roof of his palace, and proclaimed the great city of Babylon as his creation and for his glory (Daniel 4:30), he immediately lost everything and was brought low like an animal. The great harlot and great city, Babylon the great, proclaims herself queen and sees no loss or mourning in her future. God declares that He will bring her as low as the heights she has elevated herself. Only God is to be glorified, and God will not tolerate mankind's self-glorification.

Revelation 18:8, states: *"For this reason in one day her plagues will come, pestilence and mourning and famine, and she will be burned up with fire; for the Lord God who judges her is strong."* God spoke through the prophet Isaiah an oracle against the original Babylon, saying: *"Now, then hear this, you sensual one, who dwells securely, who says in your heart, I am, and there is no one besides me. I shall not sit as a widow, nor shall I know loss of children. But these two things shall come on you suddenly in one day: loss of children and widowhood. They shall come on you in full measure in spite of your many sorceries, in spite of the great power of your spells"* (Isaiah 47:8-9). Like ancient Babylon, many in the world today have elevated themselves and see themselves as gods. They believe that mankind can do anything and they have no need of God. They believe that their science and technology and reason can solve any problem they may face. They believe that nothing can bring down the world they believe they have created for themselves. But they are wrong! God is the creator all of things, including the gifts, skills and intellect that has allowed mankind to excel. But God is in control and must be honored and acknowledged as the source of all that is good, and as the Creator of all life. Like king Nebuchadnezzar and every leader of every kingdom, and every person that has ever lived, all will die and face judgment before God. As God has proclaimed so many times throughout Scripture, He will bring down those who exalt themselves and He will exalt the humble. Also as foretold so many times in Scripture, one day the great "day of the Lord" will come. When it does, all who exalt themselves will be brought down quickly, in one day, because the Lord is truly Lord of lords and King of kings.

Revelation 18:9-10, states: *"And the kings of the earth, who committed acts of immorality and lived sensuously with her, will weep and lament over her when they see the smoke of her burning, standing at a distance because of the fear of her torment, saying, 'Woe, woe, the great city, Babylon, the strong city! For in one hour your judgment has come.'"* The kings or leaders of the earth "who committed acts of immorality and lived sensuously" with the "harlot" and "great city," both identified as Babylon the great, will mourn over her loss. We are not told everyone will mourn, but only those who indulged themselves in the greed and self-indulgence she represents. It is those who lavish and spoil themselves in the luxuries of wealth and decadence that will be filled with remorse when it is taken away. The poor do not miss the loss of luxury. These powerful leaders who once indulged themselves now keep their distance so they are not caught up in her demise. They were willing to partake of her sins but want none of her punishment. The great city, Babylon, receives judgment in "one hour." This means that judgment comes swiftly, beginning and completed in a very short time.

What if the wealth and luxuries of the world were taken away? What would it look like? How would it come about? Would it begin with a crisis within our financial institutions and world economies? Would we see nations and governments spending money they don't have for luxuries they can't afford? Would all this lead ultimately to a financial and economic collapse, resulting in the loss of wealth and luxuries? Many believe we are currently on the eve of such an event. Only time will tell, and only God knows what will happen next.

Revelation 18:11-13, states: ***"And the merchants of the earth weep and mourn over her, because no one buys their cargoes anymore; cargoes of gold and silver and precious stones and pearls and fine linen and purple and silk and scarlet, and every kind of citron wood and every article of ivory and every article made from very costly wood and bronze and iron and marble, and cinnamon and spice and incense and perfumes and frankincense and wine and olive oil and fine flour and wheat and cattle and sheep, and cargoes of horses and chariots and slaves and human lives."*** The kings, leaders and wealthy of the earth mourned because of the luxuries they have lost, and now the merchants of the earth weep for no longer will anyone buy their luxurious cargoes. Every luxury is listed, ranging from precious metals and jewels, to fine clothing, to expensive building materials, to exquisite spices and foods, and finally to livestock and even slaves. All the things that mankind hoarded and relished in, and collected in excess, will be stripped away. The merchants who profited through selling and transporting them mourn their loss.

Revelation 18:14, states: ***"And the fruit you long for has gone from you, and all things that were luxurious and splendid have passed away*** *from you and men will no longer find them."* The "fruit" spoken of here is the fruit of wealth and of greed. The "things" that men collect in excess, unnecessary for life, but symbolic of power and prestige, have been taken away. Men will not glutton themselves while others go hungry. Men will no longer hoarde in excess while others struggle to survive with nothing.

Revelation 18:15-18, states: *"The merchants of these things, who became rich from her, will stand at a distance because of the fear of her torment, weeping and mourning, saying, 'Woe, woe, the great city, she who was clothed in fine linen and purple and scarlet, and adorned with gold and precious stones and pearls; for in one hour such great wealth has been laid waste!' And every shipmaster and every passenger and sailor, and as many as make their living by the sea, stood at a distance, and were crying out as they saw the smoke of her burning, saying, 'What city is like the great city?'"* While the merchants were made rich in her sin, like the kings of the earth, they want nothing of her punishment. They mourn the loss of wealth, and prestige and the power that comes through wealth and an abundance of material possessions. It has all been taken away in a very short time. A loss that has come suddenly with surprising swiftness, and was not anticipated. The reference to "shipmasters" and "sailors" does not mean that the loss is confined to a single island or continent, a place that is only reached by sea travel. In John's day and even today, most exports are transported by sea, which is the most economical means of transport. The sea transport references may be intended to communicate that the great city of Babylon is not a single land, such as the Middle East, Europe, Asia or Africa, which are all connected by land, but will involve the entire world, every continent. Some identify the United States of America with the great city of Babylon as described in this passage because it is the wealthiest nation on earth where people enjoy luxuries unheard of in other parts of the world. It is also a place where the majority of all imports arrive by sea. While the U.S. may be a center for wealth, as we have seen in previous scriptural accounts, the great city and harlot Babylon is not limited to a single place but is a condition that permeates peoples of all nations.

Revelation 18:19, states: *"And they threw dust on their heads and were crying out, weeping and mourning, saying, 'Woe, woe, the great city, in which all who had ships at sea became rich by her wealth, for in one hour she has been laid waste!"* The people who profited by greed, who became rich transporting the wealth and material things that are the object of greed, now mourn the loss of their livelihood. When greed, self-indulgence, and self-centeredness are taken away, then what is left for those who profited from it? They have also lost, for what once fed them now leaves them hungry.

Revelation 18:20, states: *"Rejoice over her, O heaven, and you saints and apostles and prophets, because God has pronounced judgment for you against her."* While those who profited from the greedy and self-serving now mourn, the self-sacrificing servants of God who suffered persecution at the hands of the greedy and self-serving will now rejoice. God has pronounced judgment upon the wicked on behalf of the righteous. God has pronounced judgment upon those who have grown fat on behalf of those who they caused to hunger.

Fifth Vision: Millstone into Sea and Final Dirge over City (18:21-24)

Revelation 18:21, states: *"And a strong angel took up a stone like a great millstone and threw it into the sea, saying, "Thus will Babylon, the great city, be thrown down with violence, and will not be found any longer."* Some scholars identify the "stone" in this verse with Jesus, *"the stone rejected by you, the builders, but which became the cornerstone"* (Acts 4:11). They also see Daniel 2:34-35, which describes a stone that strikes the feet of the great statue, turning it all into chaff, and then the stone grows to become a mountain that fills the whole earth. While these are all clearly references to Christ, and His power to overcome the wicked and reign over all, this verse seems clearly to reference punishment. It seems clear that it is Babylon that will be thrown into the sea and destroyed. Babylon has caused the righteous to suffer and therefore has earned its fate. Jesus speaks of what happens to those who cause believers to stumble, saying in Mark 9:42: *"And whoever causes one of these little ones who believe to stumble, it would be better for him if, with a heavy millstone hung around his neck, he had been cast into the sea."* Satan was thrown down from heaven to the earth. All the evil and violence that Satan causes on earth will also be thrown down and destroyed.

Revelation 18:22-23, states: *"And the sound of harpists and musicians and flute-players and trumpeters will not be heard in you any longer; and no craftsman of any craft will be found in you any longer; and the sound of a mill will not be heard in you any longer; and the light of a lamp will not shine in you any longer; and the voice of a bridegroom and bride will not be heard in you any longer; for your merchants were the great men of the earth, because all the nations were deceived by your sorcery."* Note that everything that previously might have been associated with pleasure has been removed, and no longer heard. There is no more music, finely crafted things, fine foods, bright lights, or even weddings. All that brought joy is gone. Note also that the "merchants" were the "great men" of the earth. I am reminded of that cable television show entitled, "Mad Men" about powerful advertisers. This is the image I see of these merchants who have sold the world a bill of goods, making us think we need things we don't need, feeding our greed, and corrupting our souls. The reference to "sorcery" is similar, in that it speaks of the deception which causes people to desire what they don't need, confusing the boundaries between need and want.

Revelation 18:24, states: *"And in her was found the blood of prophets and of saints and of all who have been slain on the earth."* Those with power and possessions, want more, and take away from the powerless and those with little to lose. The greedy and self-centered have little regard for the righteous and self-sacrificing. They are but prey to be consumed and devoured. Satan uses greed and pride as weapons against God's chosen, having the powerful prey on the weak, and turning the wicked against the righteous. Everyone ultimately has two choices. They will make Satan their lord and will live their lives selfishly centered on themselves, or they will make Jesus their Lord and will live their lives selflessly centered on the needs of others. Following Satan will lead to darkness and death. Following Jesus will lead to light and eternal life.

CHAPTER 19:

Part 9 of our study will only include the first ten verses of chapter 19. These verses are connected with chapters 17 and 18 in that they focus on the celebration by the righteous following the demise of the harlot and Babylon the great. The harlot and the great city, respectively, discussed in chapters 17 and 18 above, depicted the spiritual (religious) and physical-political (worldly) adultery and idolatry of people putting themselves before God, and worshiping the creation rather than the Creator. This wrong relationship is represented as a harlot. The right relationship is one that is Christ centered, and follows Christ's teachings. Those who follow Christ comprise of the Body of Christ, which is depicted as the Bride of Christ. We all have two simple choices. We can chose to be a harlot or the bride of Christ.

Sixth Vision: Hymn of Praise to God (19:1-5)

Revelation 19:1-2, states: *"After these things I heard, as it were, a loud voice of a great multitude in heaven, saying, "Hallelujah! Salvation and glory and power belong to our God; because His judgments are true and righteous; for He has judged the great harlot who was corrupting the earth with her immorality, and He has avenged the blood of His bond-servants on her.""* The beginning reference to "after these things" seems to obviously refer to the demise of the religious and material-political Babylon the great, which is the demise of everything that corrupts and causes people to worship themselves and the luxuries of this world rather than Christ their Creator. The "great multitude" could be the heavenly hosts of angels and/or the "multitude" dressed in white robes who have washed themselves clean through the blood of Christ (7:9-14). Their words echo the words of Psalm 19:9b, which says, *"The judgments of the Lord are true; they are righteous altogether."* This has been proclaimed several times in Revelation, including by the Altar before God in 16:7, saying, *"Yes, O Lord God, the Almighty, true and righteous are Thy judgments."* This is important because in 6:10, with the breaking of the fifth seal, we heard the voice of those slain because of the word of God speaking from beneath the altar, saying, *"How long, O Lord, holy and true, wilt Thou* refrain from judging and avenging our blood on those who dwell on the earth?"* Voices of a multitude in heaven now proclaim it is done. God has righteously judged the harlot and avenged the blood of God's servants. We hear the first "Hallelujah!"

Revelation 19:3, states: *"And a second time they said, "Hallelujah! Her smoke rises up forever and ever.""* We often say, "Where there is smoke there is fire." The smoke that rises up forever and ever, affirms that the punishment of Babylon the great is forever, and assures us that never again will God's people suffer due to its evil influence. We know that ultimately all that is evil, both Satan and his angels (demons) and people who followed him, will burn in the lake of fire forever. This place is most commonly called hell from which there is no return. We hear repeated the second "Hallelujah!"

Revelation 19:4, states: *"And the twenty-four elders and the four living creatures fell down and worshiped God who sits on the throne saying, "Amen. Hallelujah!"* The last time we heard the "twenty-four elders" and the "four living creatures" fall down and worshiped God was in 5:8 when the Lamb (Jesus Christ) received the scroll (book) bearing the seven seals from the hand of God. The scroll contained the judgments and punishments that only Christ was found worthy to administer. The first time they all bowed down was the beginning of the last judgment. They now bow again at the end as judgment is completed. This is the third of four great "Hallelujahs."

Revelation 19:5, states: *"And a voice came from the throne, saying, "Give praise to our God, all you His bond-servants, you who fear Him, the small and the great.""* Those closest to the throne, and perhaps even the twenty-four elders and the four living creatures call for all who fear and serve the Lord, small and great, to give Him praise. We are all called to praise God regardless of our rank, or gifts or status. We are His.

Revelation 19:6, states: *"And I heard, as it were, the voice of a great multitude and as the sound of many waters and as the sound of mighty peals of thunder, saying, "Hallelujah! For the Lord our God, the Almighty reigns.""* In response to the call for praise in the previous verse, the voice of the multitude responds, declaring that the Lord God Almighty reigns. In 14:2, the voice of the 144,000 who stand with Christ were said to sound like "many waters" and "loud thunder." The voice that responds is the voice of all those who fear and serve the Lord God Almighty. It is the voice of an uncountable multitude, louder than the mightiest river or thunder. It is the voice of the faithful. This is the fourth and greatest "Hallelujah!" of all.

Seventh Vision: Marriage Hymn to the Lamb and His Bride (19:6-10)

Verses 7-10 proclaim the marriage of Christ's Church, the Bride, to the Lamb (Jesus Christ). The marriage could not happen until the Church was complete, and all who would chose Christ had the opportunity to do so. Now it is time for the promised wedding feast, for the banquet promised by Christ for His bride.

Revelation 19:7, states: *"Let us rejoice and be glad and give the glory to Him, for the marriage of the Lamb has come and His bride has made herself ready."* Just as a bride groom and his bride become one in marriage, so after the judgment of the wicked and at the return of Christ, will Christ's Church be joined with Christ in marriage. This is a time for rejoicing and gladness, and giving glory to God.

Revelation 19:8, states: *"And it was given to her to clothe herself in fine linen, bright and clean; for the fine linen is the righteous acts of the saints."* Fine linen is worn by the wealthy and by the pure. God's faithful are rich in the Lord, and here, the fine linens, bright and clean, are similar to a bride's white wedding dress. They are an adornment, symbolizing both purity and preparation for marriage.

Revelation 19:9, states: *"And he said to me, "Write, 'Blessed are those who are invited to the marriage supper of the Lamb.'" And he said to me, "These are true words of God.""* The Greek word here translated as "blessed" literally means "being in the state of Christ" or "blessed because filled with the joy of Christ." All who belong to Christ are invited, including both those who believed in God's Promise of a Deliverer, and those who believed in God's fulfillment of the Promise—Jesus Christ, the Lamb. But Jesus provided two parables regarding the wedding feast that we should hear and take heed. First, in the "Parable of the Wedding Feast" found in Matthew 22:1-14, Jesus teaches us that even the poor and sinful will be invited. In this parable, those initially invited decline to come because they are distracted with the things of this world, so the king sends his servants to gather the poor and even sinners to partake of the feast. At the feast, the king notices that one guest lacks wedding clothing, and has him cast out into the outer darkness. The lesson teaches that all are invited, even the poor and sinful, but those who chose to attend must be properly clothed—clothed in Christ who washes our garments clean.

The second parable is the "Parable of the Ten Virgins" found in Matthew 25:1-13. In this parable ten virgins await the coming of the bride groom and the wedding feast, but only five have come prepared, having both their lamps and extra oil to last them through the night. Those who are not prepared because they failed to bring enough oil are not ready when the groom arrives, and are locked out of the wedding feast. The lesson teaches that we must be prepared, and we will not be able to acquire preparedness at the last minute from someone else, but must be prepared for ourselves.

Regarding these being the "true words of God," the Greek word translated as "words" is the exact same as used in John 1:1, referencing "Christ." We know from John 14:6 that Jesus is the "way" and the "truth" and the "life." Perhaps we are being given assurance that this truly is the word of Christ and we can trust in it. God's purpose and promise have finally been fulfilled.

Revelation 19:10, states: *"And I fell at his feet to worship him. And he said to me, "Do not do that; I am a fellow servant of yours and your brethren who hold the testimony of Jesus; worship God. For the testimony of Jesus is the spirit of prophecy.""* In the relationship between John and the angel who speaks to him, we see both affirmation and warning concerning a right relationship with God. John naturally falls down to worship the one who shows him these glorious events in heaven, but the angel corrects him, and reminds him that we are to worship God alone. Never are we to worship that which is created, but only our Creator. The angel testifies that he is a fellow servant and John's brethren, bearing witness with John concerning the one true God. We are also again reminded that all we are being told and shown is the Revelation of Jesus Christ, for the "testimony of Jesus is the spirit of prophecy." Like the angel and John, we too are called to bear witness to the testimony of Jesus. We are to serve with our brothers and sisters in faith the one true God, our Lord and Savior, Jesus Christ.

PART 10

Seven Visions of End of Evil and Beginning of God's Righteous Age

Part 9 provided vivid insight into the fall of Babylon the great, which we have come to understand as representing both the religious and secular aspects of our society which put self above God. In chapter 17 we saw the demise of the "harlot," representing the religious idolatry as people worship themselves and things rather than God. These people chose to be the "harlot," putting themselves before God, rather than the "bride" of Christ, who keep themselves pure and right with God. In chapter 18 we saw the visible and worldly manifestation of this same orientation represented in the "great city." This is the aspect that is focused on worldly self-indulgence and luxury, even at the expense of the poor and needy. The rich become richer and are indifferent to the demise of those who suffer at their expense. Merchants and leaders profit from the greed and wealth of the powerful. But the Lord reveals to us that all of this will come falling down quickly and violently at the time of judgment. Those who exalted themselves will be brought low, and the humble will be exalted. In the first verses of chapter 19 we first heard the fourfold "hallelujah" of the righteous as God brought down the wicked who shed the blood of the righteous. We then heard the marriage of the Lamb to His bride proclaimed for it was finally time for all that God has planned to come to pass. Christ will now rule, the righteous will be rewarded, and the wicked will do no more harm. This entire section seems to be provided so that we gain greater insight into the importance of our decision to be faithful to Christ as His bride, rather than to enter into an unfaithful, adulterous relationship with the harlot. We must remain true to Christ until the end, and resist Satan's self-serving temptations. Our choice will be eternal.

Part 10 will be the last major section of our study followed only by the description of the New Jerusalem (Part 11) and the closing epilogue

(Part 12). Part 10 will comprise the seventh and final set of seven visions. These visions will include: (1) the conquering Christ (19:11-16); (2) victory of Christ over the beast and Antichrist (19:17-21); (3) Satan being bound and his rule suspended for 1,000 years (20:1-3); (4) the reign of Christ—the millennium (20:4-6); (5) the defeat of Gog and Magog, and Satan being cast into the lake of fire (20:7-10); (6) the disappearance of heaven and earth, the second resurrection, and final judgment (20:11-15); and, (7) the new creation and beginning of God's eternal age (21:1-8). Part 10 is very important and reassuring because it reveals to us how things will ultimately turn out, with the righteous being rewarded and the wicked being destroyed. God will make all things new and there will be eternal peace. Many of the things described were first introduced in 11:18, but here they will be revealed in greater detail.

First Vision: The Conquering Christ (19:11-16)

When the seventh trumpet sounded we heard proclaimed: ***"The kingdom of the world has become the kingdom of our Lord, and of His Christ; and He will reign forever and ever"*** (11:15b). But a few verses later we learned that Christ's reign would begin with violence and judgment for we are told in verse 18: ***"And the nations were enraged, and Thy wrath came, and the time came for the dead to be judged, and the time to give their reward to Thy bond-servants the prophets and to the saints and to those who fear Thy name, the small and the great, and to destroy those who destroy the earth."*** Chapters 12 through 15 followed, providing us with a broad view and context for the end, depicting the rise and source of evil's influence leading up to and through the harvest of the elect. Chapter 16 illustrated the rapid destruction of the wicked as God poured out His wrath upon the world in seven bowls. What was proclaimed upon the sounding of the seventh trumpet we now witness, the second and final coming of Jesus Christ.

Revelation 19:11, states: ***"And I saw heaven opened; and behold, a white horse, and He who sat upon it is called Faithful and True; and in righteousness He judges and wages war."*** We know from John 10:7-9 that Jesus is the door through which we gain access to heaven. In Revelation 4:1, John was shown a "door standing open in heaven" through which he was summoned to "come up" so he could be shown "what must take place." Now heaven is opened so that Christ can return to the earth.

Next we hear mentioned a "white horse" upon which a rider sits who is called "Faithful and True." We are further told this rider "in righteousness He judges and wages war." It might seem we are seeing the same scene as the riders of the first two horses of the apocalypse from Revelation 6:2-4. In 6:2 a rider on a "white horse" went out "conquering, and to conquer." In 6:4 he was followed by the rider of a "red horse" who "was granted to take peace" so that men "should slay one another." We came to understand that the rider of the "white horse" in 6:2 to be the Antichrist (or spirit or movement of the Antichrist) who comes striving to conquer mankind by separating us from God. The "red horse" then represented the war that comes as we struggle and compete against each other when God is removed from our lives. The antichrist is the wolf in sheep's clothing that mimics Christ in appearance but not in purpose. The antichrist desires to divide and destroy us while Christ desires to make us whole and give us eternal life. In Revelation 3:14, Jesus is described as "Faithful and True." And it is Jesus who wages war "in righteousness."

Revelation 19:12, states: *"And His eyes are a flame of fire, and upon His head are many diadems; and He has a name written upon Him which no one knows except Himself."* In the first vision found in Revelation 1:14, the risen and glorified Christ is described as having eyes "like a flame of fire." Revelation 2:18 further clarifies the One with this description to be the "Son of God." The emphasis is on the fact that His eyes see everything, every deed of every person, and nothing escapes His sight. Regarding the "many diadems," these are crowns of authority. Christ, we are told has many, but we are not given a quantity, or perhaps better said, they are not limited to a specific number. The red dragon of Revelation 12:3 had seven diadems, a sign of complete authority, and the beast out of the sea in 13:1 had ten, symbolic for worldly authority. Jesus Christ returns with "many diadems" and ultimate authority, for Jesus tells us in Matthew 28:18, *"All authority has been given to Me in heaven and on earth."* Regarding the name written upon Him that no one knows except Himself, there is only one other mentioning of such a hidden name which is found in Revelation 2:17. In the letter to the church in Pergamum, and speaking to the faithful, those who persevere and overcome, we are told they will be given a "white stone, and a new name written on the stone which no one knows but he who receives it." This is a mystery and clearly "no one knows" either the name or names written upon the stones or the name written on the returning Christ. But we may find comfort in knowing that both Christ and those who remain faithful and overcome will share in an unknown, and perhaps the same name.

Revelation 19:13, states: *"And He is clothed with a robe dipped in blood; and His name is called The Word of God."* Jesus returns wearing a "robe dipped in blood" as a sign that He comes to judge the world, which means to punish and wage war on the wicked. He is called "The Word of God," which takes us back to John 1:1, where John describes Jesus, saying, *"In the beginning was the Word, and the Word was with God, and the Word was God."* We may also be reminded of John's first vision in 1:16, which described Him, saying, *"out of His mouth came a sharp two-edged sword."* The sword is also representative of the Word. There is power in God's Word. God speaks and things are created. God speaks and the wicked are judged and the evil are destroyed. John 3:17 provides evidence that Jesus' first coming was not to judge but to save, saying, *"For God did not send the Son into the world to judge the world, but that the world should be saved through Him."* But regarding the Lord's return, the Apostle Paul proclaims in Acts 17:31, saying, *"He has fixed a day in which He will judge the world in righteousness through a Man whom He has appointed, having furnished proof to all men by raising Him from the dead."* Jesus now returns in judgment.

Revelation 19:14, states: *"And the armies which are in heaven, clothed in fine linen, white and clean, were following Him on white horses."* The "armies" in "heaven" that accompany Christ at His return are widely debated. To those who believe in the rapture, these armies are comprised of all who were removed from the earth prior or during the tribulation. Other scholars see them as angels. When Jesus spoke of His return in the Gospels of Matthew and Luke, He states that He will be accompanied by angels. For example, Matthew 24:30b-31 states: *"…and they will see the Son of Man coming on the clouds of the sky with power and great glory. And He will send forth His angels with a great trumpet and they will gather together His elect from the four winds, from one end of the sky to the other."* Luke's account provides evidence that God's elect will be gathered and will join Christ in the air, being gathered from both "heaven" and "earth." Jesus in Luke 13:27 states, *"And then He will send forth the angels, and will gather together His elect from the four winds, from the farthest end of earth, to the farthest end of heaven."* Further evidence that the "armies" are angels is inferred from Revelation 12:7, used in conjunction with Daniel 12:1. Remember that in 12:7 we learned that the archangel, Michael, *"and his angels waging war with the dragon"* drove the dragon and his angels out of heaven and to the earth. Speaking of the end times, Michael is again referenced in Daniel 12:1 as the protector of God's people. Daniel 12:1 states: *"Now at that time Michael, the great prince who stands guard over the sons of your people, will arise. And there will be a time of distress such as never occurred since there was a nation until that time; and at that time your people, everyone who is found written in the book, will be rescued."* The "rescued" here may be tied to the gathering of the elect at Christ's return. But the elect may also be with Christ upon His return, because in 17:14 we were told that *"those who are with Him are the called and chosen and faithful"* and because they are clothed in white linen is a sign they have been washed clean by His blood (7:14).

<u>Revelation 19:15</u>, states: *"And from His mouth comes a sharp sword, so that with it He may smite the nations; and He will rule them with a rod of iron; and He treads the wine press of the fierce wrath of God, the Almighty."* Here we have three important statements contained in one verse. First, we have the reference to the "sword" that comes from His "mouth." Hebrews 4:10 states, *"For the word of God is living and active and sharper than any two-edged sword, and piercing as far as the division of soul and spirit, of both joints and marrow, and able to judge the thoughts and intentions of the heart."* In both Revelation 1:16 and 2:16 we also see references to a sword coming out of the mouth of Christ that will wage war. Revelation 2:16 states: *"Repent therefore; or else I am coming to you quickly, and will make war against them with the sword of My mouth."* The Word of

God, which is the sword that comes out of His mouth, will "smite the nations" of the earth, and will strike those who are unrepentant.

Second, we hear that Christ will rule with "a rod of iron." The first reference in Scripture is found in Psalm 2:9, which when speaking of the Reign of the Lord's Anointed, says, *"Thou shalt break them with a rod of iron, Thou shalt shatter them like earthenware."* Speaking of Jesus as the Son of the woman clothed with the sun in Revelation 12:5 we are told: *"And she gave birth to a son, a male child, who is to rule all the nations with a rod of iron; and her child was caught up to God and to His throne."* Christ is the One who rules with an iron rod, which He uses to shatter the clay vessels of the wicked.

Third, here we are told that it is the returning Jesus who will tread the fierce winepress of God's wrath previously mentioned in Revelation 14:19-20. Jesus' return will not be the peaceful and loving event of His first coming when He came to save the world. This will be a violent event in which He will deliver judgment upon the wicked.

Revelation 19:16, states: *"And on His robe and on His thigh He has a name written, "King of Kings, and Lord of Lords.""* The title declares Christ's absolute authority over everyone and everything. He is truly the King above all kings and the Lord over all lords. In Revelation 17:14 we heard how the Lamb will be victorious over all who oppose Him, saying, *"These will wage war against the Lamb, and the Lamb will overcome them, because He is Lord of lords and King of kings, and those who are with Him are the called and chosen and faithful."* The Lamb, our Lord and Savior Jesus Christ, will return with great power and authority, greater power and authority than those who oppose Him. The Lord will be victorious over Satan and his followers.

Second Vision: Victory of Christ over Beast and Antichrist (19:17-21)

In this second of seven visions or scenes in Part 10, we see Christ's victory over the beast and the false prophet, often also referred to as the Antichrist. Whether these entities are personifications of the religious (spiritual) and worldly (physical) influences of Satan, which caused many to elevate the creation above the Creator and worship themselves, or they are real people, they will be destroyed when Christ returns.

Along with them, all who followed them will be destroyed, all those who worshiped the false image and marked themselves through their thoughts and actions as belonging to the beast. They will become bird food.

Revelation 19:17-18, states: *"And I saw an angel standing in the sun; and he cried out with a loud voice, saying to all the birds which fly in midheaven, "Come, assemble for the great supper of God; in order that you may eat the flesh of kings and the flesh of commanders and the flesh of mighty men and the flesh of horses and of those who sit on them and the flesh of all men, both free men and slaves, and small and great.""* While in heaven there will be a great and wonderful wedding feast as Christ and His bride the Church will celebrate their joining, on earth there will be a terrible supper as birds feast on the remains of the slaughtered who opposed Christ. In both the Gospels of Matthew and Luke we hear of birds gathering where there are corpses upon the return of Christ. Matthew 24:28 says: *"Wherever the corpse is, there the vultures will gather."* Luke provides even greater insight through the context of the disciples' question. After Jesus speaks of several situations upon His return when one is taken and one is left behind, the disciples ask the question, "Where, Lord?" Answering where they will be taken, Jesus says, *"Where the body is, there also will the vultures be gathered"* (Luke 17:37). Those who believe that these references to being taken refer to God's people being raptured from the earth, could be mistaken. Jesus said to His disciples in Matthew 24:37-39: *"For the coming of the Son of Man will be just like the days of Noah. For as in those days which were before the flood they were eating and drinking, they were marrying and giving in marriage, until the day that Noah entered the ark, and they did not understand until the flood came and <u>took them all away</u>; so shall the coming of the Son of Man be."* It is possible that this reference means that Noah and his family were taken away in the ark, lifted above the waves and destruction on the flood waters. But more likely, it means that the people left behind are taken away by the flood to destruction. Upon Christ's return, we know He will gather and protect His elect and punish the lives of the wicked, those who are not His own. The corpses of the wicked will become food for the birds. It will not matter if they were great or small, free or slave, in the end they will all be the same—dead.

Revelation 19:19, states: *"And I saw the beast and the kings of the earth and their armies, assembled to make war against Him who sat upon the horse, and against His army."* With the pouring out of the sixth bowl of wrath we heard that the Euphrates River was dried up, clearing the way for the kings of the east to come (16:12). And then in 16:13-14 we were told that demons came out of the mouth of the dragon and the beast and the false prophet, which went out *"to the kings of the whole world, to gather them together for the war of the great day of God, the Almighty."* And finally, in 16:16 we were told of the place where they were to be gathered for the great battle, a place called in Hebrew "Har-Magedon," which we know more commonly as Armageddon. This place is believed to be situated north of Jerusalem between Mount Megiddo and Mount Tabor in the Jezreel Valley where the Kishon River flows. According to an account in Judges, chapters 4 and 5, the Canaanites came against the people of Israel with a vast army led by 900 iron chariots. God called His prophetess, Deborah, to advise His people to confront their enemy in this same location. And then God did battle for them, causing a heavy rain to fall, which flowed down from the mountains, causing the iron chariots and heavily armored Canaanite army to become stuck in the mud and easy to defeat. As part of Deborah's song, she sings, *"The stars fought from heaven, from their courses they fought against Sisera* [Canaanite leader]. *The torrent of Kishon swept them away, the ancient torrent, the torrent of Kishon. O my soul, march on with strength"* (Judges 5:20-21). She says "the stars fought from heaven." To the ancients, stars were often equated with angels, implying that God's angels did battle for them.

The prophet Joel seems to speak clearly of the final battle of Armageddon in Joel, chapter 3. Joel says this great battle will come about *"in those days and at that time, when I restore the fortunes of Judah and Jerusalem"* (Joel 3:1). Many believe this means when God has restored Israel as a nation and Jerusalem as its capital. The nation of Israel was restored in 1948 and Jerusalem was captured by Israel in 1967. Israel declared Jerusalem its capital in July of 1980, which had formerly been Tel Aviv. Regarding the nations opposing Israel, God speaks to Joel specifically against *"Tyre, Sidon and the regions of Philistia"* (Joel 3:4), which today would be Lebanon and the Gaza Strip. We know these to be places where the terrorist group, Hezbollah, constantly launches attacks against Israel. Then Joel provides us with a series of signs, which are consistent with the symbolism we have seen in both Revelation, and the Gospel accounts describing Jesus' return. Joel reveals to us that all of this will happen near Jerusalem and in Israel. Joel 3:12-16 states: *"Let the nations be aroused and come up to the valley of Jehoshaphat, for there I will sit to judge all the surrounding nations. Put in the sickle, for the harvest is ripe. Come, tread, for the wine press is full; the vats overflow, for their wickedness is great. Multitudes, multitudes in the valley of decision! For the day of the Lord is near in the valley of decision. The sun and moon grow dark, and the stars lose their brightness. And the Lord roars from Zion and utters His voice from Jerusalem, and the heavens and the earth tremble. But the Lord is a refuge for His people and a stronghold to the sons of Israel."* The sun and the moon grow dark. The sickle is ready for the harvest. The wine press is full. It seems the place and conditions are ready for the return of Christ. But take heart, "the Lord is a refuge for His people."

Revelation 19:20, states: *"And the beast was seized, and with him the false prophet who performed the signs in his presence, by which he deceived those who had received the mark of the beast and those who worshiped his image; these two were thrown alive into the lake of fire which burns with brimstone."* We were introduced to the "beast" and the "false prophet" in chapter 13. This is also where the "image of the beast" and the "mark of the beast" were introduced and described. The beast came up out of the sea, and as we have previously discussed, was seen as a world leader, and/or influence. A second beast coming up out of the earth was identified as the "false prophet" and a religious leader, and/or influence. The "false prophet" caused the people of the earth to create an "image of the beast" and worship it. And the "mark of the beast" on the hand and forehead was understood to be a mark of ownership. As we have discussed, the beast and false prophet cause us to worship ourselves and the creation rather than the Creator. The image of the beast could be seen as the image of man worshipping himself. The mark of the beast on the head and hand could be seen as our marking ourselves through our thoughts and actions as focused either on God or self. The verse above would strongly suggest that the beast and false prophet are actual persons or entities. This may be, but they may also be personifications of worldly and religious influences, corrupted by Satan, that cause us to worship ourselves and elevate created things above our Creator. In this case, what is immediately removed and thrown into the lake of fire are the false worldly and spiritual beliefs that the creation is greater than the Creator. Let's face it. When God shows up in all of His power and glory, the first thing to fall will be the belief that He doesn't exist. The second belief to fall will be that He is powerless, and our faith in Him is irrelevant. These notions will be proven false forever.

Revelation 19:21, states: *"And the rest were killed with the sword which came from the mouth of Him who sat upon the horse, and all the birds were filled with their flesh."* Remove the deceiver's deception and the truth shines for all to see. In one respect, the Word of God kills all that is false, exposing lies and illuminating the truth. That is a spiritual understanding and truth. But in another respect, this also applies to the physical world. Sin and evil have always brought about death and destruction. Ultimately, that which is corrupt and unrepentant will die because the *"wages of sin is death"* (Romans 6:23). As in the days of Noah, the wicked were killed. The same will apply when Christ returns. The wicked will be killed by the Word of God, and the birds of the earth will be filled with their flesh. But we are about to read about a 1,000 year period of peace, which will be followed by Satan again deceiving the nations and gathering a vast number of followers to come against God's people. Therefore, we must question if all who are wicked and all evil are destroyed at this time. Could it be that only the armies that gathered and came against God and His people are destroyed when Christ returns, and are eaten by the birds? This is supported by the fact that Christ will rule with "an iron rod." Would such a stern rule be necessary if all evil and wickedness had been completely eliminated from the earth?

Third Vision: Satan Bound and Rule Suspended 1,000 Years (20:1-3)

In this third of the seven visions or scenes in Part 10, we see Satan being bound and his rule suspended for a thousand years. We might ask why Satan was not also destroyed with the beast and false prophet? Why is

Satan's demise delayed? What is the purpose of the 1,000 years of peace? These are good questions and we will seek answers to these questions as we continue through Part 10.

Revelation 20:1, states: *"And I saw an angel coming down from heaven, having the key of the abyss and a great chain in his hand."* While we are told only that an angel coming down from heaven bears the key and the chair that will lock Satan in the abyss for a thousand years it is likely this is the archangel Michael. What is clear is that he comes from heaven, from God, with the power an authority to do God's will.

Revelation 20:2-3, states: *"And he laid hold of the dragon, the serpent of old, who is the devil and Satan, and bound him for a thousand years, and threw him into the abyss, and shut it and sealed it over him, so that he should not deceive the nations any longer, until the thousand years were completed; after these things he must be released for a short time."* While made clear other places in Scripture, here it is made abundantly clear that the "dragon, serpent of old, devil and Satan" are all one of the same. From the Garden of Eden to the present, though he has appeared in many forms with many names, the one who was cast down from heaven for attempting to elevate himself above God and for rebelling against God is the same entity that has always worked to deceive mankind into doing the same. God creates and gives life. Satan destroys and takes life. Satan is now not only locked away in the abyss but "sealed" in so he can no longer deceive or influence mankind. We must ask the question why? Why the delay in Satan's destruction? Why must we wait another 1,000 years before the books are opened and all are judged before the throne of God?

Fourth Vision: The Reign of Christ and the Millennium (20:4-6)

In this fourth of the seven visions or scenes in Part 10, we see a partial resurrection which consists of only those who have died in Christ, who were faithful and did not worship the beast or his image, and did not receive the image of the beast on their forehead or hand. This is called the first resurrection. The remaining dead are required to wait until the end of the 1,000 years when the dead will face judgment before the throne of God.

While it might be impossible for us to understand the mystery of the 1,000 years, God invites us to seek answers to our questions as we seek a deeper relationship with Him. This is not to say we may question if God is right or wrong, for we must trust God that whatever He does and for whatever reason, He knows best and His judgment is perfect. We have previously wondered why God would not destroy Satan outright, and delay for 1,000 years His final judgment and ultimate destruction of all unbelievers. We can only speculate on why God choses to do what He will certainly do. We should find comfort in the fact that upon Christ's return, our life with God will begin anew, and no longer with temptations and interference from Satan. For a thousand years we will live with Christ in the "camp of the saints" and then in the New Jerusalem for the rest of eternity. Even when Satan is released to "tempt the nations" and bring them against God's people, God will destroy them with fire before they can harm us. Perhaps a clue to why we are given this 1,000 years before the final judgment can be found in Revelation 17:8b, which says, ***"And those who dwell on the earth will wonder, whose name has not been written in the book of life from the foundation of the world, when they see the beast, that he was and is not and will come."*** We are not told that "those who dwell on the earth" are limited to the saints of God, but it is evident that those who dwell on the earth will be aware that they live in a limited time period before Satan will be released. Perhaps the thousand years is given as a time for mankind to reflect on all that has happened and the judgment that awaits. Perhaps the thousand years is to provide us with a period of transition between life on earth as we remember it, and the eternity to come in the New Jerusalem. When God delivered His people out of Egypt they ultimately spent forty years in the wilderness learning how to depend on God for their daily bread, and to become God's people. This was a period of preparation before entering the Promise land. Perhaps the 1,000 years is a period of preparation, a time for both reflecting on all that God has done in delivering His people out of the bondage of slavery to sin and death, and to prepare them for God's Promise of eternal life with God.

Revelation 20:4, states: *"And I saw thrones, and they sat upon them, and judgment was given to them. And I saw the souls of those who had been beheaded because of the testimony of Jesus and because of the word of God, and those who had not worshiped the beast or his image, and had not received the mark upon their forehead and upon their hand; and they came to life and reigned with Christ for a thousand years."* This verse begins with John seeing thrones set up, and they who sat upon them who were given the right to judge. The first question that comes to mind is who they are who sit upon these thrones and are given the power to judge. The answer might be found in Matthew 19:28 and in Luke 22:28-30. Matthew 19:28 states: *"Truly I say to you, that you who have followed Me, in the regeneration when the Son of Man will sit on His glorious throne, you also shall sit upon twelve thrones, judging the twelve tribes of Israel."* While Revelation 4:4 and 11:16 reference twenty-four elders sitting on twenty-four thrones in heaven there is no evidence that these are the thrones being set up on the earth for Christ's 1,000 year reign. Some scholars interpret Matthew 19:28 to imply that all of the faithful, both those of the Old Testament before Christ's first coming, and those who have lived and died after Christ's coming are included in the first resurrection. They believe this based on the fact that Jesus said His disciples would judge the twelve tribes of Israel. This belief is also at least partially supported by the understanding that those who died believing in God's promise of a Messiah, actually believed in Him before He was revealed. This view is reinforced by Jesus' words to Thomas in John 20:29, when Jesus says, *"Because you have seen Me, have you believed? Blessed are they who did not see, and yet believed."* Here Jesus is saying those who believed in Him, even though they lived and died before His first coming, are blessed because of their belief in the Promise which Jesus' first coming fulfilled. While we may not know for certain the full extent of who is included in the first resurrection, it is certainly clear that those who have died for their belief in Christ and remained faithful through the tribulation will be raised and will reign with Him. While it is clear that those who remained faithful during the tribulation have been raised to live through the millennium, we do not know for certain that all the faithful whose names are written in the book of life have yet been raised. We will discuss this further later.

Revelation 20:5, states: *"The rest of the dead did not come to life until the thousand years were completed. This is the first resurrection."* This verse raises another important question, Is anyone still alive when Christ returns or is everyone dead? If those who died in Christ are raised at the first resurrection, and the remaining dead must wait until the end of the thousand years, then is anyone alive? The judgment before the throne of God in 20:11-15 mentions only "dead" being judged, but upon Satan's release we are told that a vast number will gather against the saints and be devoured (killed?) by fire that comes down from heaven. Scripture implies that all those who were faithful to Christ, whether dead or alive, will be lifted up and begin to reign when Christ returns. This is supported by both 1 Thessalonians 4:16-17, and 1 Corinthians 15:50-55. There appears to be faithful Christians still alive when Christ returns because 1 Thessalonians 4:16-17 says, *"For the Lord Himself will descend from heaven with a shout, with the voice of the archangel, and with the trumpet of God; and the dead in Christ shall rise first. Then we who are alive and remain shall be caught up together with them in the clouds to meet the Lord in the air, and thus we shall always be with the Lord."* Paul clearly assumes there will be faithful still alive when Christ returns because both the dead and the living are "caught up in the air." The faithful are removed from the earth, presumably to escape the wrath that will rain down upon the wicked. It also seems apparent that all faithful Christians will be changed upon the Lord's return, and this is when we will take on immortality even if we are still alive. Paul writes in 1 Corinthians 15:50-55, saying, *"Now I say this, brethren, that flesh and blood cannot inherit the kingdom of God; nor does the perishable inherit the imperishable. Behold, I tell you a mystery; we shall not all sleep, but we shall all be changed, in a moment, in the twinkling of an eye, at the last trumpet; for the trumpet will sound, and the dead will be raised imperishable, and we shall be changed. For this perishable must put on the imperishable, and this mortal must put on immortality. But when this perishable will have put on the imperishable, and this mortal will have put on immortality, then will come about the saying that is written, "Death is swallowed up in victory. O death, where is your victory? O death, where is your sting?""* Paul clearly states that we cannot inherit the kingdom of God in our perishable, mortal bodies, but must first put on our imperishable, immortal bodies. Those who are still alive will be changed instantly. It would appear then that all faithful Christians will begin their immortal lives upon Christ's return, and share in His 1,000 year reign on earth. But what about those who are still alive, but not part of the faithful when Christ returns? And, what about those who are long dead, but believed in the promise of God, living and dying before Christ first came? We will discuss this further after the next verse.

Revelation 20:6, states: *"Blessed and holy is the one who has a part in the first resurrection: over these the second death has no power, but they will be priests of God and of Christ and will reign with Him for a thousand years."* We know from Revelation 20:14 that the "second death" is the "lake of fire" where those whose name does not appear in the "book of life" will be cast for eternal punishment. We are now being told that the "second death" has "no power" over those who partake of the "first resurrection." Therefore, those who are included in the "first resurrection" must be among those whose names are written in the book of life. But does this mean that if you are not included in the "first resurrection" you will be included in the "second death"? Not necessarily, because it is possible that some whose names are written in the book of life may still sleep, not to be raised until the judgement. We only know for certain that those who remained faithful, whether they died or lived until the end of the tribulation, will be included in the "first resurrection" and reign with Christ for the 1,000 year millennium.

Fifth Vision: Satan Released and Cast into Lake of Fire (20:7-10)

In this fifth of the seven visions or scenes in Part 10, we see Satan released from the abyss for a short time and allowed to again deceive the nations. He again gathers them for war and surrounds God's saints and beloved city. This time there is no great battle, but God simply sends down fire from heaven and devours them all. Satan is then cast into the lake of fire where he will be punished for all eternity, and never deceive or cause trouble again.

Revelation 20:7-8, states: *"And when the thousand years are completed, Satan will be released from his prison, and will come out to deceive the nations which are in the four corners of the earth, Gog and Magog, to gather them for war; the number of them is like the sand of the seashore."* Here we have the key to a great mystery that is unlocked by the names, "Gog and Magog." We are told that when Satan is released he will deceive the nations and gather them from the "four corners of the earth," which are called "Gog and Magog." The following verse, 20:9, says they will surround the camp of the saints and the beloved city indicating that God's people are gathered in one location, and likely that location is Jerusalem, which has always been called God's beloved city. Zion is identified with Jerusalem and God proclaims in Psalm 87:2-3, saying through His servant David, *"The Lord loves the gates of Zion more than all the other dwelling places of Jacob. Glorious things are spoken of you, O city of God."* Therefore, "Gog and Magog" will come from four directions, which means from all directions to surround God's people who have lived for a 1,000 years in peace in Jerusalem. Now let us look at the only other place in all of Scripture where the names "Gog and Magog" are used, which is Ezekiel 38:2. The verses which immediately precede the mention of "Gog and Magog" describe God's restoration of Israel into a nation, and the beginning of an everlasting kingdom ruled by David, God's prince.

Ezekiel 37:21-28, says: *"And say to them, 'Thus says the Lord God, "Behold, I will take the sons of Israel from among the nations where they have gone, and I will gather them from every side and bring them into their own land; and I will make them one nation in the land, on the mountains of Israel; and one king will be king for all of them; and they will no longer be two nations, and they will no longer be divided into two kingdoms. And they will no longer defile themselves with their idols, or with their detestable things, or with any of their transgressions; but I will deliver them from all their dwelling places in which they have sinned, and will cleanse them. And they will be My people, and I will be their God. And My servant David will be king over them, and they will all have one shepherd; and they will walk in My ordinances, and keep My statutes, and observe them. And they shall live on the land that I gave to Jacob My servant, in which your fathers lived; and they will live on it, they, and their sons, and their sons' sons, forever; and David My servant shall be their prince forever. And I will make a covenant of peace with them; it will be an everlasting covenant with them. And I will place them and multiply them, and will set My sanctuary in their midst forever. My dwelling place also will be with them; and I will be their God, and they will be My people. And the nations will know that I am the Lord who sanctifies Israel, when My sanctuary is in their midst forever.""* The above speaks of there no longer being a divided kingdom, but one kingdom in Israel. While we know that God's people were once divided into two kingdoms, Israel and Judah, the joining of the two kingdoms here may imply not only Israel being restored into a single nation, but also Jews and Christians being restored into a single fellowship believing in the same Lord and Savior. Jesus is the descendant of David and we can clearly see how the above passage of Scripture could be a vivid description of Jesus' reign on earth, with both Jews and Christians living together and finally serving the same Lord, Jesus the Christ.

Now let us look closely at the passage which begins with the reference to "Gog and Magog." Ezekiel 38:2-10, says: *"Son of man, set your face toward Gog and Magog of the land of Rosh, Mechech, and Tubal, and prophesy against him, and say, 'Thus says the Lord God, "Behold, I am against you, O Gog, prince of Rosh, Mechech, and Tubal. And I will turn you about, and put hooks into your jaws, and I will bring you out, and all your army, horses and horsemen, all of them splendidly attired, a great company with buckler and shield, all of them wielding swords; Persia, Ethiopia, and Put with them, all of them with shield and helmet; Gomer with all its troops; Beth-togarmah from the remote parts of the north with all its troops—many peoples with you. Be prepared, and prepare yourself, you and all your companies that are assembled about you, and be a guard for them. After many days you will be summoned; in the latter years you will come into the land that is restored from the sword, whose inhabitants have been gathered from many nations to the mountains of Israel which had been a continual waste; but its people were brought out from the nations, and they are living securely, all of them. And you will go up, you will come like a storm; you will be like a cloud covering the land, you and all your troops, and many peoples with you."* Thus says the Lord God, *"It will come about on that day, that thoughts will come into your mind, and you will devise an evil plan, and you will say, 'I will go up against the land of unwalled villages, I will go against those who are at rest, that live securely, all of them living without walls, and having no bars or gates, to capture spoil and to seize plunder, to turn your hand against the waste places which are now inhabited, and against the people who are gathered from the nations, who have acquired cattle and goods, who live at the center of the world.''''* As previously discussed, the evil prince leading the nations that come against Israel and God's people originally comes from the region we know today as Russia, but the other nations listed comprise historic enemies that we located on all sides of Israel. We are told that a day will come in the later years when it "will come into your mind" to go against the "gathered" people who "live securely without walls." This could clearly represent God's people gathered in Israel and Jerusalem. Having lived there in peace for 1,000 years under Christ's reign, they would have no need for walls or bars to protect them. These two passages from Ezekiel also provide further evidence that those raised in the first resurrection will include both faithful Jews and Christians alike. We still do not know with certainty if those who do not believe in Christ are all dead or some remain alive. The following verses perhaps shed light on this question and provide an answer.

<u>Revelation 20:9</u>, states: *"And they came up on the broad plain of the earth and surrounded the camp of the saints and the beloved city, and fire came down from heaven and devoured them."* We have ample evidence that the "camp of the saints" is in Israel, and the location is Jerusalem, the "beloved city" of God. Here we are told that those who Satan now deceives "came up" on the "broad plain of the earth." The Greek word translated as "came up" literally means to "arise," to come up from a lower to a high place. They "came up" onto the "broad plain of the earth," which might be interpreted as rising to the surface of the earth from below it. Is this a second resurrection? You will note that we were told about the "first resurrection" but is there a second resurrection? In John 5:28-29 Jesus states: *"Do not marvel at this; for an hour is coming, in which all who are in the tombs shall hear His voice, and shall come forth; those who did the good deeds to a resurrection of life, those who committed the evil deeds to a resurrection of judgement."* Perhaps this is the raising of the dead who oppose Christ. Perhaps Satan's release for a "short time" before being thrown into the Lake of Fire will also correspond to the "release" of all

those who died separated from God and Christ because they opposed God and Christ. Perhaps this verse describes Satan's attempt to again lead all those who followed his evil influence to "rise" against God's people, only to be destroyed by fire along with Satan.

Regarding the fire from heaven, again speaking of "Gog and Magog" and those nations and peoples that surround and come against God's people in Israel, Ezekiel 38:22, says, *"And with pestilence and with blood I shall enter into judgment with him; and I shall rain on him, and on his troops, and on the many peoples who are with him, a torrential rain, with hailstones, fire, and brimstone."* As in our verse above, God will rain fire on those who come against His people. They will be "devoured by fire." Does this mean they have become mortal to be killed again? Or, does this fire refer to the "second death" they will receive in the "lake of fire." Because only the "dead" are mentioned regarding those who appear before the throne to be judged in Revelation 20:11-15, it seems clear that none of the wicked will be alive after the "devouring fire," but this does not inform us of their status before the fire. All whose names are not written in the "book of life" will end up in the "lake of fire."

Revelation 20:10, states: *"And the devil who deceived them was thrown into the lake of fire and brimstone, where the beast and the false prophet are also; and they will be tormented day and night forever and ever."* Finally, the one who deceived and tempted mankind to rebel against God has been permanently removed. The unholy trinity is gone and will suffer eternal punishment. Now it is time for all mankind to be judged based on who they made lord of their lives, and who they followed. If they followed Satan then they are destined to his fate, eternal punishment. If they were faithful to God and His Deliverer and Shepherd, then their life will continue in Him, and they will not face the "second death," which is the "lake of fire."

Sixth Vision: End of Heaven and Earth, and Judgment (20:11-15)

In this sixth of the seven visions or scenes in Part 10, we see the dead standing before the "great white throne" where they will receive judgment. We are told that the sea, death and Hades give up their dead so they can receive judgment. The dead are judged based on what is written in books, and are judged according to their deeds. Only those whose names are written in the "book of life" are spared the "second death" in the "lake of fire."

Revelation 20:11, states: *"And I saw a great white throne and Him who sat upon it, from whose presence earth and heaven fled away, and no place was found for them."* White is symbolic for purity and righteousness, therefore the "great white throne" can be seen as the seat of righteous and fair judgment. Jesus is the one who will sit upon the throne and pass judgment. There are many places in Scripture that speak of this, but John 5 may be the best. In John 5:22 Jesus says, *"For not even the Father judges anyone, but He has given all judgment to the Son."* More specific to the final judgment, Jesus says in John 5:25-29 that He will judge the dead according to His Father's will, saying, *"Truly, truly, I say to you, an hour is coming and now is, when the dead shall hear the voice of the Son of God; and those who hear shall live. For just as the Father has life in Himself, even so He gave to the Son also to have life in Himself; and He gave Him authority to execute judgment, because He is the Son of Man. Do not marvel at this; for an hour is coming, in which all who are in the tombs shall hear His voice, and shall come forth; those who did the good deeds to a resurrection of life, those who committed the evil deeds to a resurrection of judgment."* This simple passage provides us additional evidence that the "first resurrection" may include all those who were faithful to God, with the second resurrection including all those who were not faithful and therefore deserve judgment because of their evil deeds. The reference to earth and heaven having "fled away" from the Lord's presence, and there being no place "found for them," could mean there will be "no place" for anyone to hide. Everyone not clothed in Christ and still wearing their shame will stand naked before the Lord.

Revelation 20:12, states: *"And I saw the dead, the great and the small, standing before the throne, and books were opened; and another book was opened, which is the book of life; and the dead were judged from the things which were written in the books, according to their deeds."* Notice that "books" were opened that contain "deeds" and a separate "book of life" is opened that we will learn in 20:15 contains names. The dead are judged according to their "deeds." This is not simply a judgment between good and bad. It is a judgment that may rank people based on how much evil they did, or if they were repentant for the evil they did. Remember Jesus' words to the unrepentant cities where He preached and wasn't received. In Matthew 11:22, Jesus said, *"Nevertheless I say to you, it shall be more tolerable for Tyre and Sidon in the day of judgment, than for you."* And again in Matthew 11:24, He says, *"Nevertheless I say to you that it shall be more tolerable for the land of Sodom in the day of judgment, than for you."* Jesus is showing us in these examples that some people will be judged harsher than others based on their deeds, and repentance. Many visionaries who have been granted to see images of hell, or perhaps the lake of fire, have witnessed that there are levels of suffering, with the torment of those on the surface being less than those who are held deeper in the fire. Perhaps those whose names do not appear in the book of life, who had remorse for their evil deeds will suffer less than those without remorse.

Revelation 20:13, states: *"And the sea gave up the dead which were in it, and death and Hades gave up the dead which were in them; and they were judged, every one of them according to their deeds."* Here we see the "sea, death and Hades" give up their dead so that they may be judged. The word "death" literally means not physically or mortally alive. The word "Hades" literally means the "world of the dead" or "place of the dead," but most scholars see it as a sort of "prison for the dead not yet judged." It is important that we remember that Jesus said in John 11:25-26, *"I am the resurrection and the life; he who believes in Me shall live even if he dies, and everyone who lives and believes in Me shall never die."* This means that when we accept Christ as our Lord and Savior we obtain a life that does not die when our physical body dies. Our life continues. Therefore, the dead that are raised are not in Christ, and will all be judged based on their deeds, and then cast into the lake of fire. They are not being judged as worthy for heaven or condemnation to hell. They are judged to determine their level of suffering.

Revelation 20:14, states: *"And death and Hades were thrown into the lake of fire. This is the second death, the lake of fire."* Looking ahead, Revelation 21:4 says that after the judgment "there shall no longer be any death." We see above the end of death and Hades. No one else will ever die, and there is no longer need for a prison or place to hold the dead who have not been judged. All not found in the book of life are now judged and cast into the lake of fire, which is the second and final death.

Revelation 20:15, states: *"And if anyone's name was not found in the book of life, he was thrown into the lake of fire."* We have previously been told both in Revelation 13:8 and 17:8 that those whose names have been written in the "book of life" have been written there from "the foundation of the world." God has always known who would be saved, and which of us would ultimately chose Him over Satan as our lord. He has always allowed us our freedom of choice, but He knew us even before we were born and knew also the choices we would make. Only those who are His, as evidenced by their choosing Him, and remaining faithful to Him, will be saved from the lake of fire. All others, regardless of how good or bad their deeds, will face the second death. We who belong to Christ also sin, make mistakes, and fall short of the glory of God, but we are not saved by "our" merits, but by the "perfection and merits of Christ our Lord."

Seventh Vision: The New Heaven and Earth (21:1-8)

In this seventh of the seven visions or scenes in Part 10, we are told of the creation of a new heaven and earth, and that God is "making all things new." This means everything from the old order, including sin and death, has been abolished. There will be no more tears or crying, but only the joy of being in God's presence for all eternity. It is finished, everything is as God always planned and intended. That portion of mankind that has chosen to live in a relationship with God, their Creator, will now do so in peace and in paradise forever. Those who chose otherwise will burn forever in the lake of fire.

Revelation 21:1, states: *"And I saw a new heaven and a new earth; for the first heaven and the first earth passed away, and there is no longer any sea."* In Matthew 24:35, Mark 13:31 and Luke 21:33, Jesus tells us: *"Heaven and earth will pass away, but My words shall not pass away."* The apostle Peter also tells us in 2 Peter 3:10, saying, **"But the day of the Lord will come like a thief, in which the heavens will pass away with a roar and the elements will be destroyed with intense** *heat, and the earth and its works will be burned up."* As God did in the beginning, creating a heaven and earth for us to live in, He will do so again at the end. God will create a new heaven and earth, without a sea, and this shall be our new home forever.

Revelation 21:2, states: *"And I saw the holy city, new Jerusalem, coming down out of heaven from God, made ready as a bride adorned for her husband."* In addition to this newly created heaven and earth, God will replace also His beloved city, Jerusalem, with a "new Jerusalem." This new city will be described in great detail in 21:10-27. This new city comes down out of heaven, making it clear that it is created by God as a place of dwelling for His people to share and live with Him.

Revelation 21:3-4, states: *"And I heard a loud voice from the throne, saying, "Behold, the tabernacle of God is among men, and He shall dwell among them, and they shall be His people, and God Himself shall be among them, and He shall wipe away every tear from their eyes; and there shall no longer be any death; there shall no longer be any mourning, or crying, or pain; the first things have passed away.""* This is the final and complete fulfillment of God's Word. Now Emmanuel, which means "God with us," is not limited to the short time Christ dwelled in the flesh and walked among men, or the sending of God's Holy Spirit to be with us for guidance and comfort and strength. No, now God and man will both spiritually and physically dwell together as we did in the beginning in the Garden of Eden before we sinned and fell from grace. Knowing of good and evil, we have chosen God and He has adopted us as His children. The evil influence and temptation of Satan are no more. Never again will we suffer death, mourning, tears or pain. All these things have passed away and are no more.

Revelation 21:5, states: *"And He who sits on the throne said, "Behold, I am making all things new." And He said, "Write, for these words are faithful and true.""* This is the third time in Revelation that we have heard that God and His Word are "faithful and true." God is making all things new. This is a new beginning that will last for all eternity. Everything from before is gone. The slate is washed clean. A new adventure and an eternity of discovery await everyone who has remained faithful to God.

Revelation 21:6, states: *"And He said to Me, "It is done. I am the Alpha and the Omega, the beginning and the end. I will give to the one who thirsts from the spring of the water of life without cost."* All that God planned and intended is complete—it is done! What God began in the beginning has reached its end. God created the beginning and He has created the ending. God provides the thirsty with water from the spring of the water of life without cost. God provides! God will always provide for every need of those who dwell with Him. God is the source and sustainer of all life.

Revelation 21:7, states: *"He who overcomes shall inherit these things, and I will be his God and he will be My son."* Now God turns His attention to the readers of Revelation. He reminds us all, that if we overcome the temptations of Satan and trials of this world, remaining faithful to the Lord, that we too will inherit all these things. We too will become the children of God, and live with God for all eternity.

Revelation 21:8, states: *"But for the cowardly and unbelieving and abominable and murderers and immoral persons and sorcerers and idolaters and all liars, their part will be in the lake that burns with fire and brimstone, which is the second death."* Likewise, as in verse 21:7 above where the faithful are reminded of the promise of their reward, here the wicked are warned of their fate if they do not repent but chose to continue to live in sin and remain separated from Christ.

Part 10 is powerful, having revealed the ultimate fate of those who chose Christ, and those who do not. Clearly, all those who claim Christ as Lord and Savior, and live their life as best they can in accord to His will, will live with Christ forever. And equally clear, all who remain unrepentant and never accept the life that comes through a commitment to Christ as their Lord and Savior will die, separated from Christ and suffering forever. We see that even the end of the world as we know it, and even after a new heaven and earth are created, the consequences of our decisions and choice for or against Christ will live on. We have a choice, and have been given clear and adequate warning of the consequences of our choice. It is not God that forces us to live our eternity in paradise or hell, but our free choice of who we will serve and have as our Lord. May everyone choose Christ, and may everyone bear witness to those who do not realize the dire consequences of the choices they are making every day. Everyone will face their end of time and will be judged by God. May we be judged by the merits of Christ rather than our own inadequate deeds. We all fall short of God's glory.

PART 11

The New Jerusalem

Part 10 provided insight into the last set of seven visions in the seven sets of seven visions found in Revelation. The focus was on Jesus' return, the 1,000 years of His reign on earth between the first and second resurrections, and the judgment before the throne of God.

Part 11 will provide a very detailed description of the New Jerusalem where God's faithful will live forever and ever. This description will be introduced and described in Revelation 21:9 through 22:5. This description is the basis for people's understanding of heaven as a place with streets paved with gold. Indeed, we will hear described an enormous golden city where God resides with His people.

External Appearance of the City (21:9-14)

Revelation 21:9, states: *"And one of the seven angels who had the seven bowls full of the seven last plagues, came and spoke with me, saying, "Come here, I shall show you the bride, the wife of the Lamb.""* As we have previously discussed, the bride of the Lamb is the Body of Christ, those who have made themselves pure through the blood of Christ. Revelation 19:7-8 gave us this insight, saying, *""Let us rejoice and be glad and give the glory to Him, for the marriage of the Lamb has come and His bride has made herself ready." And it was given to her to clothe herself in fine linen, bright and clean; for the fine linen is the righteous acts of the saints."* The New Jerusalem is more than a city, but the place where God will reside for all eternity. Also note the use of the word "wife" of the Lamb. The use of the word "wife" indicates that the marriage is concluded and that the bride and the Lamb are now joined in marriage.

Revelation 21:10-11, states: *"And he carried me away in the Spirit to a great and high mountain, and showed me the holy city, Jerusalem, coming down out of heaven from God, having the glory of God. Her*

brilliance was like a very costly stone, as a stone of crystal-clear jasper." John was in the Spirit when he saw his first vision of the Lord (1:10). John was also in the Spirit when he was taken up to heaven to see the things that would take place in the future (4:2). And John was carried away in the Spirit to see the vision of the harlot sitting on the scarlet beast in the wilderness (17:3). In all these cases, John is being taken to be shown something he could not see in his physical life, but only in the Spirit or through the Spirit. John is being shown something that either does not yet exist, or exist only in a heavenly place beyond the boundaries of our physical world and time. The fact that it sits on a "great and high mountain" would indicate that it is a high and mighty place. The fact that it is described as "coming down out of heaven" indicates that it is a creation of God and comes from God.

Regarding the reference to the city "having the glory of God" and "brilliance like a very costly stone, as a stone of crystal-clear jasper," both of these references illustrate that the city will be extremely pure. Precious stones that are considered very clear are considered very pure. They shine with exceptional brilliance. In the ancient world, and still today, the greater the clarity (clearness) of a precious stone, the purer it is considered.

Revelation 21:12, states: ***"It had a great and high wall, with twelve gates, and at the gates twelve angels; and names were written on them, which are those of the twelve tribes of the sons of Israel."*** The "it" obviously refers to the New Jerusalem. The city is surrounded or enclosed in a "great and high wall" and has "twelve gates" with an angel stationed at each gate. We are told names were written on them, but it is not made clear if them is in reference to the gates or the angels. Most presume the "gates" are named with the names of the twelve tribes of the sons of Israel. In ancient Jerusalem the gates in the wall that surrounded the temple each had names, so it is logical that the gates are named. But the names could also apply to the angels with the understanding that each of the tribes of Israel may have been assigned an angel to look over them. Perhaps the angels that look over the gates are the same as those who looked over the sons of Israel. The names on the gates would therefore include: Reuben, Simeon, Levi, Judah, Issachar, Zebulun, Joseph, Benjamin, Dan, Naphtali, Gad and Asher (Genesis 35:23-26). The significance of the twelve gates bearing the names of the sons of Israel may be that we all enter into God's presence through the descendants of Israel. Ezekiel 48:30-35 also describes a city with three gates on each side bearing the names of the tribes of Israel. The vision of the city and division of the land in Ezekiel's vision may be of the earthly camp of the saints which exists for 1,000 years before the coming of the New Jerusalem.

Revelation 21:13, states: *"There were three gates on the east and three gates on the north and three gates on the south and three gates on the west."* The number "three" is symbolic for God's holy Trinity, and is therefore God's number. God's gates face east, north, south and west, or in all directions. Perhaps this is symbolic of the fact that God receives people from all directions or places. The gates are named beginning with the east gate and progressing to the west gate. This is similar to our understanding that Christ comes from the east moving to the west. God seems consistent in everything, even in the order in which He describes His city.

Revelation 21:14, states: *"And the wall of the city had twelve foundation stones, and on them were the twelve names of the twelve apostles of the Lamb."* As the gates bear the name of the twelve tribes of the sons of Israel through which we enter, the city's walls are built upon twelve foundations that bear the names of the twelve apostles. Jesus told Peter in Matthew 16:18, *"And I also say to you that you are Peter, and upon this rock I will build My church; and the gates of Hades shall not overpower it."* And Peter will declare to those who follow Christ, saying, *"You also, as living stones, are being built up as a spiritual house for a holy priesthood, to offer up spiritual sacrifices acceptable to God through Jesus Christ"* (1 Peter 2:5). Jesus came bearing witness of the good news and instructed His disciples to bear witness of His teachings, saying to them, *"...you shall be My witnesses both in Jerusalem, and in all Judea and Samaria, and even to the remotest part of the earth"* (Acts 1:8). Jesus is the foundation stone and cornerstone of our faith, and His apostles were the first layer of living stones upon which His mighty Church would be built.

Measurement of the City (21:15-17)

Revelation 21:15, states: *"And the one who spoke with me had a gold measuring rod to measure the city, and its gates and its wall."* The literal Greek translation of a "gold measuring rod to measure" would be a gold measure reed in order that he might measure. The word "reed" could also be translated as cane or stalk. It was a reed that was first placed in Jesus' hand and then used to beat Him by the guards who mocked Him prior to His crucifixion. The straight and stiff reed was used for many purposes in Jesus' time. In this case, a reed of gold will be used as a measuring device to measure the city and its gates and wall.

Revelation 21:16, states: *"And the city is laid out as a square, and its length is as great as the width; and he measured the city with the rod, fifteen hundred miles; its length and width and height are equal."* The city of New Jerusalem is enormous in size, 1,500 miles long and wide and high. This is calculated from the Greek twelve thousand stadia with one stadion equaling approximately 600 feet. The proportions of the city are that of a cube, the length and width and height are "equal." The only similar reference I could find in Scripture was of the square size of the city in the midst of the land God will give to His people. The size is stated to be 4,500 in length with the north, south, east and west sides being the same (Ezekiel 48:16). The unit of measure is not given, but is reflected in most Bibles as cubits or reeds. In either case, this city seems much smaller than the New Jerusalem described in Revelation. The scale of the city also would require a new creation because the current land of Israel is too small to contain such an enormous city.

Revelation 21:17, states: *"And he measured its wall, seventy-two yards, according to human measurements, which are also angelic measurements."* The actual Greek measure is "one hundred forty-four cubits." We should note that the number 144 is the sum of twelve times twelve, or twelve squared. Therefore, even the wall thickness reflects the symmetry of the city. It is interesting that we are told that the "human" measurements are also "angelic" measurements. It is uncertain what this might intend to imply, but it could simply mean that now humans and angels share the same standards.

Composition of the City (21:18-21)

Revelation 21:18, states: *"And the material of the wall was jasper; and the city was pure gold, like clear glass."* The city wall is made of jasper. In 21:11 we were told the city appeared as "a stone of crystal-clear jasper," which would imply a very pure jasper stone devoid of blemishes or imperfections. The jasper stone is first mentioned in Revelation 4:3 when we are told that God, sitting on His throne, was *"like a jasper stone and a sardius in appearance."* The jasper stone was also the last of the stones listed in Exodus 28:17-20 of the twelve stones placed on the breast plate of the high priest. In Exodus, the twelve stones are seen to represent the twelve sons who form the twelve tribes of Israel. The twelfth is seen to represent Benjamin who was born last as found in Genesis 35:18. The birth order of the first eleven sons of Jacob (Israel) can be found in Genesis 29:32—30:24. The significance of the jasper is that it is associated with the twelfth and final son and tribe of Israel, and it is the first stone listed in Revelation 21:19. Because Jesus told Peter (stone) that He was the rock (bed-rock) on which He would build His Church, and because 21:14 above states that the "foundation stones" bear the names of the "twelve apostles of the Lamb," many equate Peter with the first foundation stone of jasper. Therefore it is the jasper that connects the Old Testament foundation of the twelve tribes of Israel to the New Testament foundation of the twelve apostles. They are the bed-rock of the Church, the Bride of Christ, the New Jerusalem.

Revelation 21:19-20, states: *"The foundation stones of the city wall were adorned with every kind of precious stone. The first foundation stone was jasper; the second, sapphire; the third, chalcedony; the fourth, emerald; the fifth, sardonyx; the sixth, sardius; the seventh, chrysolite; the eighth, beryl; the ninth, topaz; the tenth, chrysoprase; the eleventh, jacinth; the twelfth, amethyst."* The list of precious stones is substantially the same as the list of stones decorating the breast plate of the high priest given in Exodus 28:17-21 and 39:10-14. Apparent differences are largely due to the fact Exodus is written in Hebrew and Revelation in Greek, and the Hebrew and Greek names for some stones are different. The order in which the stones are listed is definitely different. As discussed in 21:18 above, the jasper stone is listed last of the stones representing the twelve tribes of Israel, but is listed first in Revelation when representing the twelve apostles (21:14). The names of the twelve apostles of Christ are listed in Matthew 10:2-4 with Peter listed first and Judas Iscariot, who betrayed Christ, listed last. Judas would not be included in the final twelve and many scholars believe that Paul would be the most likely replacement, but according to Acts 1:26, the eleven apostles replaced Judas with Matthias, selecting him through the casting of lots. The twelve precious stones could also have an additional meaning because according to the ancient Jewish writers Philo and Josephus, the twelve stones on the high priest's breastplate were also equated with the twelve signs of the zodiac.

While the listing of the stones is significant, the meaning behind their listing is a mystery we may not be able to resolve. Some speculate that the shift from the stones being associated with the twelve tribes of Israel to the twelve apostles is intended to imply that the faithful Christians are now the true Israel. Considering the astrological reference provided by Philo and Josephus, then Daniel's words regarding the time of the end have new significance. Daniel 12:3 states: *"And those who have insight will shine brightly like the brightness of the expanse of heaven and those who lead the many to righteousness, like the stars forever and ever."* Daniel may be referencing the apostles as those who lead the many to righteousness and are now brightly shining stars. On the other hand, Isaiah 54:11-12, speaking of the future Zion provides a description filled with references to precious stones, saying, *"O afflicted one, storm-tossed, and not comforted, behold, I will set your stones in antimony, and your foundations I will lay in sapphires. Moreover, I will make your battlements of rubies, and your gates of crystal, and your entire wall of precious stones."* Perhaps our ultimate understanding should be that we enter the New Jerusalem through the gates of the twelve tribes of Israel, but it is built on the foundation of Christ's twelve apostles.

Revelation 21:21, states: *"And the twelve gates were twelve pearls; each one of the gates was a single pearl. And the street of the city was pure gold, like transparent glass."* While Isaiah 54:12 described the gates to be of "crystal" (literally "carbuncles" in original Hebrew), the Jewish Talmud, professedly based on the verse in Isaiah, states that the gates of the New Jerusalem would be composed of single precious stones and pearls each thirty cubits (45 feet) square. It is incredible to think of a gate, perhaps 45 feet square being formed of a single pearl. Only God could create such a magnificent city. Regarding the streets of pure gold like transparent glass, we do not know if the streets are truly transparent or this is a reference to their purity. In ancient times pure glass was very rare, and most glass was milky and filled with impurities. The term "transparent glass" could simply mean that the gold is absolutely pure, but it could also mean that the gold is transparent. We will have to wait until we get there to know for sure.

Temple of the City (21:22-27)

Revelation 21:22, states: *"And I saw no temple in it, for the Lord God, the Almighty, and the Lamb, are its temple."* Jesus said to those who asked for a sign, saying, *"Destroy this temple, and in three days I will raise it up"* (John 2:19). Of course Jesus was talking about His body and pending death and resurrection, but those listening believed He was talking about the temple that had taken forty-six years to build. Clearly, Jesus did not see God residing in buildings but the human heart. The Church is the Body of Christ, comprised of those who believe in Christ rather than one or many buildings. In Revelation 3:12, speaking to those who overcome in the church in Philadelphia, He said, *"I will make him a pillar in the temple of My God."* Again, this is an indication that God will no longer live in temples made from brick and mortar but will dwell in the midst of His people who will be His Church. It should be no surprise that there will be no temple structure and that the *"Lord God, the Almighty, and the Lamb,"* will be the temple.

Revelation 21:23, states: *"And the city has no need of the sun or of the moon to shine upon it, for the glory of God has illumined it, and its lamp is the Lamb."* We might remember that in the beginning there was no light. Genesis 1:2-3 states: *"And the earth was formless and void, and darkness was over the surface of the deep; and the Spirit of God was moving over the surface of the waters. Then God said, "Let there be light"; and there was light."* It is not until the fourth day of creation that God created the sun, moon and stars to separate the day from the night and to govern over the day and the night (Genesis 1:14-18). Jesus said, *"I am the light of the world; he who follows Me shall not walk in darkness, but shall have the light of life"* (John 8:12). Jesus would teach His disciples, saying, *"You are the light of the world… Let your light shine before men in such a way that they may see your good works, and glorify your Father who is in heaven"* (Matthew 5:14a, 16). The apostle John would testify regarding the light, saying, *"And this is the message we have heard from Him and announce to you, that God is light, and in Him there is no darkness at all"* (1 John 1:5). The truth is simple and extraordinary. God has always been the one and only light from the very beginning, but has shared and imparted that light with us. God illuminates our hearts and our lives, and in Him we have life. God's light outshines the sun and the moon and the stars, and in the presence of God no other light is necessary. In the New Jerusalem, God will be our light and will illumine our world and our lives.

Revelation 21:24, states: *"And the nations shall walk by its light, and the kings of the earth shall bring their glory into it."* This passage seems contradictory and confusing since we already know that the righteous have been saved and the wicked judged. The nations and kings as we have previously understood them no longer exist. Some scholars believe that John is referencing Isaiah 60:3 and 11, which read respectively, *"And nations will come to your light, and kings to the brightness of your rising… And your gates will be open continually; they will not be closed day or night, so that men may bring to you the wealth of the nations, with their kings led in procession."* Indeed, Isaiah may be referring to what we now see revealed in Revelation, but this may not be a contradiction. Let us remember that in the first vision of heaven we heard the four living creatures and the twenty-four elders give glory to God (4:5-11). The twenty-four elders *"cast their crowns before the throne,"* and said: *"Worthy art Thou, our Lord and our God, to receive glory and honor and power; for Thou didst create all things, and because of Thy will they existed, and were created"* (4:11). We have been told that the saved include a *"great multitude, which no one could count, from every nation and all tribes and peoples and tongues"* (7:9). We have been told that the saved include the *"small and the great"* (19:5). God has never required we lose our identity. Repeatedly, we are identified as peoples of many nations, tribes and tongues. We are a diverse group but we worship one God and are illuminated by one Light—the Light of God. And even the greatest among us, the kings among us, will give their glory to God, who created and saved us. We will forever give glory to God, for only God deserves all glory.

Revelation 21:25-27, states: *"And in the daytime (for there shall be no night there) its gates shall never be closed; and they shall bring the glory and the honor of the nations into it; and nothing unclean and no one who practices abominations and lying, shall ever come into it, but only those whose names are written in the Lamb's book of life."* Again we see references from Isaiah 60:11, speaking of the gates being "continually open." There is no longer any night or darkness but only continual day because God's light is continually present. The reference to "nothing unclean" or anyone "who practices abominations and lying" coming into the city does not mean they still exist. They cannot exist because everyone who's name was *"not found in the book of life, was thrown into the lake of fire"* (20:15). I believe what we are hearing is an assurance that never again will anything unclean or abominable or any lie ever contaminate what God has now made completely pure. Satan and his deceptions are gone forever. Only those whose names are written in the book of life remain and they are "free" to enter the New Jerusalem anytime to give honor and glory to God. We can possibly surmise that our world will not be exclusively the New Jerusalem. There will apparently be a world beyond where people will live in nations or groups of like kinds. If God has created us each unique, and allowed us to live as many peoples with different languages and traditions, why would He make us all the same in heaven? Perhaps God will forever allow us to live among our like kind, grouped together based on our backgrounds and traditions and even languages. But we will share in common our love for the Lord God, and we will all give Him glory for all He has done for each and all of us. Praise be to God!

The River and the Tree of Life (22:1-5)

Contained within the New Jerusalem we are given a glimpse of a few details. Although the city is massive (1,500 miles cube) there seems to be only one street, and one river, which flow from the throne of God, and one tree, which yields fruit and healing.

Revelation 22:1-2, states: *"And he showed me a river of the water of life, clear as crystal, coming from the throne of God and of the Lamb, in the middle of its street. And on either side of the river was the tree of life, bearing twelve kinds of fruit, yielding its fruit every month; and the leaves of the tree were for the healing of the nations."* We were told regarding the great multitude that come out of the tribulation and are clothed in white, having washed their robes in the blood of the Lamb, that *"They shall hunger no more, neither thirst anymore; neither shall the sun beat down on them, nor any heat"* (7:16). And then in 7:17 that the *"Lamb in the center of the throne shall be their shepherd, and shall guide them to springs of the water of life."*

Regarding the "tree of life," it is first mentioned in Genesis 2:9 as being in the Garden of Eden. We were told in Genesis 3:22 that those who eat from it will live forever. But when Adam and Eve sinned and ate of the forbidden fruit of the tree of knowledge, God removed them from the garden and from the tree of life by a *"flaming sword which turned in every direction"* (Genesis 3:24). And then in Revelation 2:7, the church of Ephesus was told that for those who overcome, God *"will grant to eat of the tree of life, which is in the Paradise of God."* Now the promises of God are fulfilled. Those who have put their faith in the Lord will never again thirst or be hungry for God will provide for them forever. I am reminded of Jesus' words in John 6:35, saying, *"I am the bread of life; he who comes to Me shall not hunger, and he who believes in Me shall never thirst."*

Regarding the single street, in the middle of which is the throne of God and of the Lamb, it seems impossible that there could be but one street in the New Jerusalem. But Jesus said to us: *"I am the way, and the truth, and the life; no one comes to the Father but through Me."* The word "way" in Greek literally means "way, path or road in which one travels." There is only one way to eternal life and that is through and to Jesus Christ. We must heed Jesus' warning found in Matthew 7:13-14, saying, *"Enter by the narrow gate; for the gate is wide, and the way is broad that leads to destruction, and many are those who enter by it. For the gate is small, and the way is narrow that leads to life, and few are those who find it."* Unfortunately, most will chose the way of the world rather than the way that leads to eternal life with

Christ. Let us chose the narrow gate and live, and let us lead others down this path.

Regarding "leaves" for "healing of the nations," Ezekiel 47:12 speaks of water flowing from the temple, which waters trees along its bank that bear fruit monthly and have leaves that heal. Ezekiel speaks of many trees and not just one. Leaves are normally for collection of sunlight and creation of oxygen from carbon dioxide. In the new creation they will be for healing.

Revelation 22:3-4, states: *"And there shall no longer be any curse; and the throne of God and of the Lamb shall be in it, and His bondservants shall serve Him; and they shall see His face, and His name shall be on their foreheads."* The "curse" spoken of here began in the Garden of Eden when Adam and Eve sinned against God (Genesis 3:14-19). Regarding Adam, the ground was cursed and man would have to work in order to eat (Genesis 3:17-19). Regarding Eve, pain would be greatly multiplied in childbirth and women would be ruled over by their husbands (Genesis 3:16). And of course, both would die and return to the earth as dust (Genesis 3:19). And finally, mankind was driven out of the Garden of Eden and from the tree of life. Mankind would now be separated from God by sin, and because of sin, no longer be able to look upon the face of God. But Christ has paid the price for all sin on the cross, and through His sacrifice for us we are reconciled with God. In the end the curse is removed and we shall serve God and gaze upon His face again. We will bear His name on our foreheads for we will be His and He will be our Lord forever.

Revelation 22:5, states: *"And there shall no longer be any night; and they shall not have need of the light of a lamp nor the light of the sun, because the Lord God shall illumine them; and they shall reign forever and ever."* This verse summarizes what has already been declared above in 21:23-25, that there shall be no need of sun or lamp for the day or the night because the Light of God will illuminate the New Jerusalem. The verse also seems to fulfill the promise made to the church at Laodicea to those who overcome, saying, *"He who overcomes, I will grant to him to sit down with Me on My throne, as I also overcame and sat down with My Father on His throne"* (3:21). Just as in the 1,000 years on earth, now for eternity in the New Jerusalem, believers will reign with Christ forever and ever. It is important to note that we do not reign over Him but reign with Him, serving the suffering servant who came to earth as both servant and sacrifice. Jesus is our example and teacher. He taught us to serve the Lord who gave us life and saved us through His sacrifice, so we can have life eternally.

Part 11 has revealed some details regarding the incredible and magnificent fulfillment of God's promise to provide a place for us. Jesus told His disciples before leaving them, saying, *"In My Father's house are many dwelling places; if it were not so, I would have told you; for I go to prepare a place for you. And if I go and prepare a place for you, I will come again, and receive you to Myself; that where I am, there you may be also"* (John 14:2-3). In the end, God will be our light and will provide for all our needs. God will restore things as they were in the beginning in the Garden of Eden. We will live in paradise with God never again to be separated from His presence. The New Jerusalem is the place God has prepared for us to dwell with God. It is beyond our imaginations and beyond our reach, accept through Christ. We cannot earn it through good deeds or right living, but can only receive it through faith in Christ, and by taking up our cross and following our Lord and Savior, Jesus Christ.

While we will someday see this magnificent city for ourselves, I believe most of us are more than curious of what it might look like. The image we have been given in Revelation provides the dimension of an enormous cube but no detail regarding its shape. We have also heard about twelve precious stones of dazzling color and translucent gold. What will the city look like? While through this study we have attempted to largely stay within the confines of the Bible and the Scriptures it contains, I would like to share a description and drawing from my late wife, Carolyn Rene' Dailey. She had a series of visions through which she was shown images for a purpose. In one of her visions, which she entitled, "City in the Clouds," she describes an enormous city partially obscured by clouds and high in the heavens nestled in a valley of clouds. Her drawing of the city is found below, and her brief description of the city is as follows: *"It seemed cradled... gently held... like the clouds were loving arms supporting it. I stood admiring its magnificence, desperately trying to make out any kind of detail, but I couldn't... it was too far away. What I could see were* colors, so brightly emanating from the city that they were almost blinding to look at. A rainbow of colors... and gold... translucent gold mixed with all the other colors... The city shone so brilliantly, it was as if it contained the source of all light. Jesus stretched out His left hand towards the city and said, **"This is your home."**"

PART 12

Closing Message

Part 11 provided a relatively detailed view of the New Jerusalem, which will come down from heaven and replace the original Jerusalem. The original Jerusalem was the center of the Jewish faith located in Israel but subject to the corruption and limitations of this world. The New Jerusalem has been described as a magnificent city 1,500 miles square and high made of gold and precious jewels. It will be the place where God and His people reside together forever. God and the Lamb will provide light for the city which will know no night but only day. Its gates will be always open and ready to receive those whose names are written in the book of life. Nothing unclean or impure will ever enter it. Within it are the tree of life, and the water of life, providing food, drink and healing for the nations.

Part 12 will be the final part and provide the closing message of Revelation. It will comprise chapter 22, verses 6 through 21. It is bracketed with Jesus' reminder that He is coming quickly, which is also its central theme. It also contains warnings to anyone who would add or take away from His message. It is the closing word and final revelation of Jesus Christ found in the Bible.

Revelation 22:6, states: ***"And he said to me, "These words are faithful and true"; and the Lord, the God of the spirits of the prophets, sent His angel to show to His bond-servants the things which must shortly take place."*** This is the fourth time in Revelation we have heard the words "faithful and true." In 3:1, the words coming from the Lord are preceded with "I am." In 19:11, we are told the rider of the white horse "is called" faithful and true. In 21:5, when we were told God will create "all things new," we were also told "these words are" faithful and true. Now in the closing of the book, we are being assured one final time that everything that has been written, in its entirety, is "faithful and true." The same God, who sent His prophets to speak His words throughout history, has now sent His angel to show His bond-servants what "must shortly take place." Notice that the message is not to a singular bond-servant but to the plural "bond-servants." The message is not simply for the apostle John, but for all the servants of God. Regarding the phrase "must shortly take place," as we discussed in the beginning of the book, the term does not necessarily mean will take place in the near future, but that it could take place at any time, and when it takes place, it will happen quickly so we must always be prepared.

Revelation 22:7, states: *"And behold, I am coming quickly. Blessed is he who heeds the words of the prophecy of this book."* This verse is attributed to Christ Himself, interrupting the words of His angel to express the urgency of His message. This is the first of three times Christ will declare to us in this final section of Revelation that He is coming quickly. In verse 1:3, John informed us that the time is near for Christ's return. In the letter to the church at Pergamun, Christ warns: *"Repent therefore; or else I am coming to you quickly, and I will make war against them with the sword of My mouth"* (2:16). In the letter to the church at Philadelphia, Christ provided assurance to those who are holding on to their faith, saying, *"I am coming quickly; hold fast what you have, in order that no one take your crown"* (3:11). The entire book of Revelation is intended to both assure the faithful that Christ will come quickly to save them, and to warn the wicked to repent and change their ways because He is coming quickly.

Revelation 22:8-9, states: *"And I, John, am the one who heard and saw these things. And when I heard and saw, I fell down to worship at the feet of the angel who showed me these things. And he said to me, "Do not do that; I am a fellow servant of yours and of your brethren the prophets and of those who heed the words of this book; worship God.""* Here, John reminds us of his own response in 19:10, when he beheld the images and message of Jesus' revelation. John fell down at the feet of the angel that showed him the visions, but was corrected by the angel. The angel told him not to worship him because he was a fellow servant of God, and to worship God alone. It is important to note that the angel, the apostle John, the prophets who have shared God's word, and all "those who heed the words of this book" will be considered brethren. None of us should see ourselves as greater or less than another because we all serve the same Lord, and we should worship and honor only the Lord.

Revelation 22:10, states: *"And he said to me, "Do not seal up the words of the prophecy of this book, for the time is near.""* As we were told in the opening verses of the book of Revelation (1:3) we are now told again, *"the time is near."* The word translated as "near" does not necessarily mean within a short time from the present, but that these events could happen at any time so we need to be ready. This interpretation is consistent with Jesus' words in Matthew 24:42, where He states: *"Therefore be on the alert, for you do not know which day your Lord is coming."* We must live our lives heeding the warning that the future events depicted in Revelation could be very near. And Jesus doesn't want us to keep this message to ourselves but to share it. Daniel was told to *"conceal these words and seal up the book until the end of time"* (Daniel 12:4), but Jesus is saying that the "end of time" has arrived. Therefore He declares: *"Do not seal up the words of the prophecy of this book."* Sadly, the book of Revelation is today seldom preached, poorly understood, and its message widely debated. Jesus is saying that it is time for His Revelation to be both heard and heeded.

Revelation 22:11, states: *"Let the one who does wrong, still do wrong; and let the one who is filthy, still be filthy; and let the one who is righteous, still practice righteousness; and let the one who is holy, still keep himself holy."* Many times throughout the book of Revelation we have heard that some will refuse to repent. We are told they will continue in their evil ways, blaming God for the consequences they have brought upon themselves. In 2:21, to the "woman Jezebel" who led people astray in the church at Thyatira, Jesus said, *"I gave her time to repent; and she does not want to repent of her immorality."* Upon the sounding of the sixth trumpet and after three plagues of fire, smoke and brimstone had killed a third of mankind, we were told that *"the rest of mankind, who were not killed by these plagues, did not repent of the works of their hands, so as not to worship demons, and the idols of gold and of silver and of brass and of stone and of wood, which can neither see nor hear nor walk; and they did not repent of their murders nor of their sorceries nor of their immorality nor of their thefts"* (9:20-21). Even when the final bowls of wrath were poured out, the wicked refused to repent and continued to curse God. Revelation

16:9 and 11 say, respectively, *"And men were scorched with fierce heat; and they blasphemed the name of God who has the power over these plagues; and they did not repent, so as to give Him glory,"* and *"they blasphemed the God of heaven because of their pains and their sores; and they did not repent of their deeds."* What Jesus is trying to help us understand is that many of the wicked will never repent. In their pride and stubborn foolishness they will remain defiant against God to the very end. This does not mean we should not offer the good news of the gospel and attempt to lead people into repentance; it just means that some will never change. On the other hand, those who practice righteousness and holiness are encouraged to continue to do so. God will help those who struggle to keep the faith.

But some see this verse in another way. They see Jesus telling us that a time will come when it will be too late for repentance. We all have a bad habit of putting off to tomorrow what we can do today. Many put off doing the right thing while they continue to do the wrong, assuming they will have time later to get right with God. Perhaps Jesus is warning us to not delay in our repentance, and start living right before it's too late.

Revelation 22:12, states: *"Behold, I am coming quickly, and My reward is with Me, to render to every man according to what he has done."* This is the second time in the closing verses of Revelation that Jesus has reminded us that He is *"coming quickly."* As in 22:7 above and 22:20 to follow, the three-fold emphasis cries out as both warning to those who haven't repented, and as an assurance to those who are repentant but continue to be persecuted and suffer for their faith.

Regarding the "reward" that Jesus will bring with Him, while Scripture testifies that in this life our reward will be children (Psalm 127:3), and riches and honor (Proverbs 10:4), upon Christ's return our reward will be salvation and eternal life. Christ was lifted up from death and exalted because of His dedication to His Father and willingness to sacrifice Himself for the sake of us all. He received the inheritance of His Father, the Lord God Almighty. Our reward is closely tied to this example. When we remain obedient to the Lord's teachings, loving our neighbors as ourselves, and being willing to live our lives as a "living sacrifice" for others out of love for Christ, then we too will inherit divine salvation. In the story of the divine judgment found in Matthew 25:31-

46, in which the righteous (sheep) are separated from the wicked (goats) based on their willingness to help others, Jesus says: *"Truly I say to you, to the extent that you did it to one of these brothers of Mine, even the least of them, you did it to Me."* Therefore, what we do to help those in need we do for Christ. Paul states in Colossians 3:23-24: *"Whatever you do, do your work heartily, as for the Lord rather than for men; knowing that from the Lord you will receive the reward of the inheritance. It is the Lord Christ whom you serve."* Paul is saying we should not work to make people happy with us, or to impress them with our good works, but to serve and honor our Lord. Jesus makes this clear in Matthew 6:1, saying, *"Beware of practicing your righteousness before men to be noticed by them; otherwise you have no reward with your Father who is in heaven."* Our reward is tied to what we do for God and for others out of love for God, and not what we do for ourselves or our own self-glorification. Actually, even when we make sacrifices and suffer persecution for the sake of our faith in Christ, we gain reward because we are following Christ's example. In Matthew 5:11-12, Jesus declares to us, saying, *"Blessed are you when men cast insults at you, and persecute you, and say all kinds of evil against you falsely, on account of Me. Rejoice, and be glad, for your reward in heaven is great, for so they persecuted the prophets who were before you."* If we are to receive the reward that Christ brings with His return, then let us be about His business, making disciples and serving our neighbor to His glory.

Revelation 22:13, states: *"I am the Alpha, and the Omega, the first and the last, the beginning and the end."* This is the third time in Revelation that we have heard God declare that He is the *"Alpha and Omega."* The previous occurrences were 1:8 and 21:6. The words apparently come from Christ, but there is no distinction now between the Father and the Son and the Holy Spirit for they are One with one another. This verse is a declaration that God is eternal, and that He has been present from our creation through to our judgment and reward. He was there at our beginning and now we can be confident that He will be there for us in the end. These words are an assurance to those who place their faith in the Lord. They are a terror for the wicked that reject and despise Him.

Revelation 22:14, states: *"**Blessed are those who wash their robes, that they may have the right to the tree of life, and may enter by the gates into the city.**"* Immediately our thoughts should go back to the "great multitude" in heaven "standing before the throne and before the Lamb," and "clothed in white robes" (7:9). The angel of the Lord told John: *"**These are the ones who come out of the great tribulation, and they have washed their robes and made them white in the blood of the Lamb**"* (7:14). When we accept Jesus Christ as our Lord and live our lives according to His commands, then our sins are washed away through His blood sacrifice, and we are allowed to enter the place He has prepared for us. That place is the New Jerusalem. There, we will be allowed to partake of the tree of life and live with the Lord forever and ever in paradise.

Revelation 22:15, states: *"**Outside are the dogs and the sorcerers and the immoral persons and the murderers and the idolaters, and everyone who loves and practices lying.**"* This verse may seem confusing because at this point in the book of Revelation the judgment has come and all whose names were not written in the book of life have been cast into the lake of fire which is the second death. The reality is that the moment we accept Jesus as our Lord and Savior and begin to follow Him down the path that leads to salvation, the New Jerusalem becomes destined as our permanent home. We are like those who have come before us who believed in the promises of God, *"**having seen them and having welcomed them from a distance, and having confessed that they were strangers and exiles on the earth**"* (Hebrews 11:13). But for those who refuse to repent and accept the gift of salvation, continuing to love evil and put themselves first rather than putting God first in their lives, they are destined to be excluded from salvation and the place God has prepared for the faithful. These closing words in Revelation are a warning to those who have not repented, and an assurance to those who have. Ultimately, the wicked will be excluded so that the righteous may live in peace.

Revelation 22:16, states: *"**I, Jesus, have sent My angel to testify to you these things for the churches. I am the root and the offspring of David, the bright morning star.**"* Jesus now clearly affirms that the message of Revelation comes directly from Him and is intended for the churches. As we have previously discussed, this means His message is for the Church Universal. Jesus claims to be "the offspring of David," which was proclaimed by one of the twenty-four elders in 5:5. Indeed, Jesus as the Messiah is a descendant of King David, but He existed before David and is the One David called Lord. This historic reference to David is matched with His identification as the "bright morning star." In Revelation 2:28, those in the church at Thyatira who would "hold fast," "overcome," and "keep My [Christ's] deeds until the end," were told they would receive the "morning star." Peter also spoke of the "morning star" arising in the hearts of faithful believers, saying, ***"And so we have the prophetic word made more sure, to which you do well to pay attention as to a lamp shining in a dark place, until the day dawns and the morning star arises in your hearts"*** (2 Peter 1:19). Christ is declaring that He is both our past and our future.

Revelation 22:17, states: ***"And the Spirit and the bride say, "Come." And let the one who hears say, "Come." And let the one who is thirsty come; let the one who wishes take the water of life without cost."*** Here is the Christian invitation to "come" to Christ and receive life. First the invitation is extended through the Holy Spirit and the Church, where the Spirit of God resides and bears witness that Jesus is Lord. Remember from Revelation 1:20, that we were told that the ***"seven lampstands are the seven churches,"*** and that the ***"seven lamps burning before the throne of God"*** are the ***"seven Spirits of God"*** (4:5). The light of Christ shines in the Church by the power of the Holy Spirit. The invitation continues through those who hear and heed the word of God, for if we are of one mind with Christ, we also will extend the invitation to others, saying, "Come."

And finally, we hear a call to all who are thirsty for the only One who can quench our thirst is the Lord Jesus Christ. He has already paid the price for our salvation and offers life to anyone who is willing to accept His precious gift of life. In Matthew 11:28, Jesus says, ***"Come to Me, all who are weary and heavy-laden and I will give your rest."*** In John 7:37, Jesus declares, ***"If any man is thirsty, let him come to Me and drink."*** Jesus desires for all to come to Him in repentance and receive the life that only He can provide. A life that will last forever.

Revelation 22:18-19, states: ***"I testify to everyone who hears the words of the prophecy of this book; if anyone adds to them, God shall add to him the plagues which are written in this book; and if anyone*** *takes away from the words of the book of this prophecy, God shall take away his part from the tree of life and from the holy city, which are written in this book."* Here is the warning and the reason so few pastors preach or teach the book of Revelation. To distort the meaning of the book by adding something it doesn't say, or by subtracting something that you disagree with, will result in one receiving both the curse of the plagues it describes, and the loss of eternal life. Using Scripture for one's own personal gain or out of context to support one's own personal viewpoint will have tragic consequences. We must be careful to allow Scripture to speak to us as God intends without adding or subtracting from its meaning. This applies not only to the book of Revelation but to all Scripture contained in the Bible.

Revelation 22:20-21, states: *"He who testifies to these things says, "Yes, I am coming quickly." Amen. The grace of the Lord Jesus be with all. Amen."* For the third and final time in the closing verses of Revelation Jesus declares He is "coming quickly." Another way of looking at verse 20 is that he who witnesses what is testified to in Revelation will be compelled to tell others that the Lord is coming quickly. In either case the intent is to share the news that Christ is returning, and that everyone should be prepared for His return. The final verse and words in the book extend a blessing, saying, *"The grace of the Lord Jesus"* be with those who hear and read the prophecies of the book. The final word is *"Amen,"* the word we use to close a prayer, and to affirm belief in what has been said and shared. Therefore, let us raise a resounding "Amen!"

The final verses of the book of Revelation are intended to affirm the truth contained within the entire book. This is the Revelation of Jesus Christ, the revealing of what is to come. It is a warning to those who are not right with God, and it provides assurance and comfort to those who walk by faith in spite of persecution and tribulation. While the message of Revelation may seem complex and mysterious, it is actually very simple: Christ will return and we better be ready when He does. The letters to the churches provide insight into the many ways we error and what we can do to correct our errors. The insights regarding how Satan operates provide us new understanding and will help us to recognize and stay clear of His deceptions and traps. And clearly, these visions of the end make it clear that God will keep His word and there will be consequences regarding how we live our lives, and who we follow as our Lord. Let us all prepare ourselves and help others to prepare for the Lord's return. And let us say, "Come, Lord Jesus," knowing we are ready and we have done all we can to help others be ready. Amen!

About the Author

I can still remember being mesmerized as a young child sitting in a Sunday school class as my teacher talked about the time of Christ's return. She said it would be proceeded by a great battle in which the Lord would stand on the Mount of Olives and the mountain would be split from east to west, forming a valley in which God's people would escape as the Lord did battle for His people (Zechariah 14:2-5). She said she had stood herself on the Mount of Olives and had seen with her own eyes a crack in the mountain that ran east to west, and how she felt the time of Christ's return was near. From that moment forward I have always been intrigued by End Times prophecy.

I was raised in the United Methodist Church and we always attended church and Sunday school. My Christian education was typical, defined by church doctrines and traditional teachings. While I had a very personal relationship with the Lord in prayer, my understandings of God were very limited by my upbringing; God was in a box. It wasn't until I had been married and had two children, that I discovered that God was still communicating with His children through visions and apparitions all over the world. As my mind opened to this, my wife informed me that she herself had experienced a vision when she invited Christ to come live in her heart at age 12, and had heard Jesus' voice ever since. She had never before been able to share this with me because she knew I wouldn't be open to God doing such things today. As my heart and mind opened to the miraculous things God was continuing to do in the world, God came out of the traditional box in which I had kept Him. Suddenly, her visions started again with intensity, and I too experienced some eye-opening encounters through the Lord.

God separated us from the business we had founded together, and after a six month period of unemployment, which we viewed as a time of testing in the wilderness, God called us both into the ministry. We both became United Methodist Church pastors, but on the same day we were ordained, my wife was forced to take disability leave because the cancer she had been fighting had become terminal. Through her and her incredible relationship with the Lord, my eyes had been opened to all that God is doing, to a better understanding of His Word, and to the time in which we live. My calling in His church has always been to "comfort the afflicted and afflict the comfortable." By that I mean to help churches wake up and shift their focus from maintenance to mission. Too many churches and too many Christians today are only going through the motions in living their faith. We have forgotten that the purpose of the church is to reach new people for Christ.

My deep study of the book of Revelation began in 2009, five years after my wife's death. It took me two years to finish my original Bible study that was comprised of twelve parts. I taught the study at two consecutive churches where I was appointed and people always seemed very blessed by it. It has become one more way of expressing the urgency I feel for awakening people that they must chose Christ over self. The world continues to turn inward, but Christ directs our attention outward, to care and love others who don't know of His great love and His gift of salvation.

I retired from my full-time role in ministry in 2020 after serving the Lord as a pastor for 21 years. Even though I know that God has a specific plan for me that will be fulfilled in His own good time, I have come to believe that part of that plan is to share this Revelation Bible study. He has guided and empowered me to complete this book so that it could be shared with a larger audience. May God bless you in your reading as He has blessed me in its preparation. All glory, honor and praise be to our Lord Jesus Christ.

Made in the USA
Middletown, DE
14 October 2021